American Indians and the Mass Media

American Indians and the Mass Media

Edited by

META G. CARSTARPHEN and JOHN P. SANCHEZ

UNIVERSITY OF OKLAHOMA PRESS : NORMAN

Library of Congress Cataloging-in-Publication Data

American Indians and the mass media / edited by Meta G. Carstarphen and
John P. Sanchez. — 1st ed.
     p. cm.
   Includes bibliographical references and index.
   ISBN 978-0-8061-4234-0 (pbk. : alk. paper) 1. Indians in mass media.
2. Indians in popular culture. 3. Indians—Public opinion. 4. Indians—Press
coverage. I. Carstarphen, Meta G. II. Sanchez, John P.
   P94.5.I53A64 2012
   305.897'073—dc23

                           2011044197

The paper in this book meets the guidelines for permanence and durability of
the Committee on Production Guidelines for Book Longevity of the Council
on Library Resources, Inc. ∞

To our families

Contents

Illustrations

Preface

The Call

META G. CARSTARPHEN

At one time in their combined history, American Indians represented five hundred nations and "perhaps as many as 40 million people" in North America, with a diversity of cultures and languages to rival any other known civilizations of our imagination or understanding.[1] What we now know of our cultural forebears exists in tenuous and often inscrutable places. If we rely on our media to tell us the truth about past custom and lost histories, we will be left wanting.

In the broadest sense, the mass media offer ways of communicating to audiences beyond physical boundaries of time and space. Media are the conduits through which ideas are transported from their originators to their intended recipients. Often, they reflect the interplay between the polarities of message and meaning. And these differences often create tensions between producers and audiences, between shared stories and lost histories.

American Indians and the Mass Media is a book with a broad scope that aims to present a multi-lens view of the impact of media upon American Indian histories, cultures, and communities. Poised at a critical juncture for examining American Indians and the media, this book offers timely insights and new interpretations of media practices and American Indian sensibilities.

American Indian media have provided key sources of information about nation-tribes, and *American Indians and the Mass Media* offers an incisive look at American Indians and the media through the exploration of both Native experience and the mainstream media's relationship to Indigenous people. The debate ranges not just over how the media historically have so gravely mistreated Indigenous American peoples, but also over whether the media today can enhance assimilation or independence, or both.

To do this, *American Indians and the Mass Media* presents a collection of scholarly articles by contemporary Native and non-Native writers, along with essays from Native writers who offer a combined perspective on contemporary media issues from the insider experience.

The introduction, by renowned Indian scholar Patty Loew, sets the stage for an exploration of American Indian media that does not shy away from the complexities of culture, media, law, and language. From historical examinations of key events and topics, to pop culture icons in film and on the Internet, and from legal considerations to news reportage issues, the rest of *American Indians and the Mass Media* considers the intersection of culture and Native media along four themes: (1) *historical analyses* of American Indians in communication and mass media traditions; (2) *contemporary viewpoints,* focusing on current issues exploring the production, distribution, and expansion of American Indian content in the mass media and mass communication; (3) *mediated images and social expectations,* looking at the relationships between culture, image, social expectation, and meaning; and (4) *interior views and authentic voices,* featuring essays from the American Indian journalists.

On the whole, sometimes these chapters take issue with previously accepted ideas about the image and reality of American Indian lives. In part I, chapters focusing on historical analyses explore some of the origins of some stereotypes and the contested origins from which they sprang. In chapter 1, "American Indian News Frames in America's Oldest Newspaper, *Publick Occurrences Foreign and Domestick,*" John P. Sanchez begins with a discussion of how the nation's first newspaper unfavorably characterized American Indians in the seventeenth century. Miranda Brady's chapter, "'Stories of Great Indians' by Elmo Scott Watson," examines how newspaper stories about particular American Indians became amplified and celebrated through the works of one well-known early-twentieth-century journalist. By the middle of the twentieth century, as Selene G. Phillips discusses in chapter 3, "'Indians on Our Warpath': World War II Images of Native Americans in *Life* Magazine, 1937–1949," bold photographic images in the nation's leading magazine reverberated with symbolic visions of danger and Indian identity. Against the preponderance of biased media targeted at them, American Indians launched their own newspapers in the nineteenth century, as I recount in chapter 4, "To Sway Public Opinion: Early Persuasive Appeals in the *Cherokee Phoenix* and the *Cherokee Advocate.*" I explore the language in the founding proposals for the first two Indian newspapers to show that reporting "news" played a subordinate role to more strategic rhetorical goals.

In part II, on contemporary viewpoints, even some of the most popular and accepted contemporary portrayals of American Indians come under incisive scrutiny, as authors give voice to troubling media representations. Ruth Seymour, in a benchmark study of how two leading newspapers referred to American Indians in the late 1990s, illustrates in chapter 5, "Names, Not Nations: Patterned References to Indigenous Americans in the *New York Times* and *Los Angeles Times,*" how small words can play a big difference in the ways that news stories deliver meaning. But just as with the first newspapers, when American Indians today create their own media, different, complex, and inherently more positive messages emerge, as Jennifer Meness shows in chapter 6, "*Smoke Signals* as Equipment for Living," her analysis of a groundbreaking Indian-produced film. Yet news coverage in the Midwest, where the American Indian presence looms larger that in some other areas of the country, also points to troubling issues, as Lynn Klyde-Silverstein discusses in Chapter 7, "The Fighting Whites Phenomenon: An Interpretive Analysis of Media Coverage of an American Indian Mascot Issue." Here, she interprets ways in which reportage about a team that satirized the popular abuse of Indian names for sports mascots took on a decidedly biased view. Tension also escalates in media coverage of community attempts to remove a familiar but pejorative word referring to Indian women from public spaces. In chapter 7, "The 'S'-Word: Activist Texts and Media Coverage Related to the Movement to Eradicate 'Squaw,'" co-authors Stacey J. T. Hust and Debra Merskin expose ways that media reports can demean this issue.

Part III, on mediated images and social expectations, builds upon the discussions in the previous two parts of the book, augmenting what we have learned of history and specific media performances, with expanded discussions about the intersection of culture, media, and meaning. In chapter 9, "Buying into Racism: American Indian Product Icons in the American Marketplace," Victoria E. Sanchez illustrates how the abuse of American Indian identities has also become commonplace in the American marketplace, as she connects underlying consumerism with historical stereotyping to illustrate how virulent the marketing of false images has become.

Considered to be the dean of current American Indian journalism, Paul DeMain delivers—in chapter 10, "The Notion of Somebody Sovereign: Why Sovereignty Is Important to Tribal Nations"—an incisive analysis of the concept of sovereignty and its implications for identity and media. Combining history, personal narrative, and his work as a journalist, DeMain gives complexity to the reality of living sovereignly, against the ideal of what it means to be independent. Expanding further on this core concept of American Indian identity, legal scholar andré douglas pond cummings gives a historical account in chapter 11, "A Shifting Wind? Media Stereotyping of American Indians and the Law," that incisively connects the intersection of specific laws, mediated events, and stereotyping. Examining sovereignty primarily as a legal precept, cummings's analysis emphasizes the power of legal text in framing media portrayals.

Rounding out this book in part IV, on interior views and authentic voices, are short essays giving insider perspectives on covering Indians in the mass media. In chapter 12, "American Indians at Press: The Native American Journalists Association," journalist and editor Mark Trahant provides a hopeful look into the future of Native journalism. In chapter 13, "Cherokeespace.com: Native Social Networking," Indian filmmaker and scholar Roy Boney offers a provocative essay that stakes out new parameters for an Indian presence in cyberspace. Journalist Juan Avila Hernandez offers insight in chapter 14, "Native Americans in the Twenty-First-Century Newsroom: Breaking through

Barriers in New Media," into some of the challenges facing American Indians entering journalism and how some Native initiatives have been trying to address the problems. Journalism professor Ray Chavez, in a previously rendered short memoir, closes our collection with a reflection on his earliest experiences as a reporter. This account, in chapter 15, "Joining the Circle: A Yakima Story," relates that, even as an Indian journalist, Chavez had to learn how to win the trust of the Yakima people he sought to interview. (Although the river and city in Washington State remain "Yakima," the nation recently adopted "Yakama" as its preferred spelling.) With this essay, we look back, from a more positive outcome, to the challenge faced, and failed, by the first U.S. newspaper as chronicled in the book's first chapter. Media stereotypes and misrepresentations flourish in the absence of honest, respectful engagements with the subjects of their attention.

Call and response extends an invitation—through words, or song, or dance—to participatory action. This is our call, our response, and our invitation. These authors are diverse in their topics, approaches, and styles. But this book aims to stand the test of time, as it places themes about media resources, power, and the representation of American Indians under intense scrutiny and, perhaps, opens renewed debates. In a most comprehensive way, *American Indians in the Mass Media* endeavors to chart some of the seminal issues concerning American Indians and the media, from past portrayals to contemporary icons, in a manner that explicates the new and the nuanced.

American Indians and the Mass Media offers bold, evocative, and informed perspectives designed to help instruct scholars, journalists, and students of culture and history from all walks of life to engage in this lively, participatory engagement.

NOTE

1. Josephy 1994, 8. A number of scholars have weighed in on the estimation of precontact populations in the Americas, including Thornton (1990) and Haines and Steckel (2000). For an in-depth discussion of some of the challenges in making these estimates, see Henige (1998).

Acknowledgments

This book marks a transition, from the end of one long road to the beginning of another. We recognize this project as a labor of love and faith and acknowledge the many people along the way who have helped us. We appreciate the anonymous external reviewers, who were unfailingly generous with their insights, knowledge, and support for this project. We thank our acquisitions editor, Alessandra Jacobi Tamulevich, who patiently shepherded this project through many phases. We could not have asked for a better champion. Other OU Press staff have been invaluable to us as well. We appreciate the meticulous care our copyeditor, Laura Oaks, gave the text, allowing us to polish our prose and concepts even further. Steven Baker managed the manuscript's passage through the production stages, and his calm persona proved to be a great support for us. The cover design evolved over many iterations and discussions, and we appreciate all of the talents in production and design that made this happen. And, for all of the OU Press personnel we did not meet, we are grateful for their professionalism and dedication as reflected in this book.

For Meta, the Gaylord College of Journalism and Mass Communication has been a wonderful incubator for this book, starting with the hosting of several symposia on "Native Americans and the Media," first launched by Charles Self and Fred Blevens. Joe Foote, whose love for Oklahoma and for journalism have animated those who have served under his leadership at Gaylord College, has been a solid supporter of this project, as well. OU graduate students Mikaela J. Sullivan and Rebekah A. Husted were amazing aids before some critical manuscript deadlines and during other phases. Their willingness to read, copyedit, and help organize files was much appreciated. Gaylord College librarian Catherine "Cat" Bark Troy employed her archivist and librarian skills to help with graphics and microfilm collections, and staff from the Oklahoma Historical Society provided valuable resources and expertise. Much of this work would have been impossible without the generous support of the Gaylord family, whose research endowment supported Meta's time and access to resources in very material ways.

We are particularly proud of the cover art contribution of Kolton Belt, a teenage student at the Takini Indian School, on the Cheyenne River Sioux Reservation in Cheyenne River, South Dakota. His original drawing featured within the computer screen is a modern-day example of "ledger art," a type of graphic communication popular among Plains Indians after their forced relocation to reservations after 1860. As animal skins became unavailable to American Indians, ledger artists among them began to record significant events on the often lined and sometimes used pages of the books white accountants would keep and bring to Indian lands for assessments. We can imagine this representation of ledger art offering viewers insight into how important events might have been depicted on hides before the reservation period and transmitted on horseback from one community to another. Bracketed within a computer screen, the cover art reminds us of the continuum of American Indian media, from origins to the Internet.

Last, but not least, we appreciate greatly the authors who contributed their essays to this book. Their work provides some of the most original thinking and creativity concerning all aspects of American Indians and the media. We are grateful for their willingness to share their insights in this volume.

American Indians and the Mass Media

Introduction

Finding A New Voice—Foundations for American Indian Media

PATTY LOEW

If art imitates life, the world has long gazed upon a surrealistic portrait of Indigenous people. It is a canvas painted by outsiders, textured initially through trader journals, missionary reports, and government documents and later through dime novels, Hollywood Westerns, and mainstream media accounts. The palette is predictable. Indian life is colored by tragic, reactive, and paradoxical events: Native Americans are people whom the federal government attempted to subdue and subjugate, exterminate, or assimilate, and who, at the very least, exist mainly in opposition to mainstream culture. However, these are not true Native portraits. These are the representations of white colonists, military leaders, government workers, and missionaries whose lives intersected with Native Americans.

In 1983 I was working at an ABC affiliate in Portland, Oregon. I remember a colleague alerting me to a court decision involving my tribe, the Lake Superior Ojibwe, that was coming across the wire. "Court Gives Indians Unlimited Rights to Hunt and Fish," the wire headlines read, a gross misinterpretation of what really had transpired. The 7th Circuit Court of Appeals had not "given," but had merely affirmed rights reserved by the Ojibwe more than a hundred years earlier. And despite the implication that the decision affected all Indians (there are twelve Indian nations in Wisconsin), the ruling involved only the Ojibwe. Furthermore, the rights were not unlimited; they were, in fact, extremely restricted.

For readers who are unfamiliar with how wire services operate, let me explain that reporters contribute stories to them, which are then picked up by newsrooms around the world for reprint or broadcast. Should a factual error make its way into the original report, the mistake is repeated *ad infinitum* to all corners of the world. Even today news accounts refer to the Ojibwe as having been "given" the right to spear fish.

I have come to view certain historical documents, such as the multivolume *Jesuit Relations,* which preserves missionary accounts, as "wire service reports of Native history." Thousands of books and scholarly papers about the Indigenous nations of the Great Lakes, for example, have built upon this seminal work begun in 1611 and published in 1902. In it, missionaries describe everyday life among their would-be converts, detailing the beliefs, customs, and ceremonies of nearly fifty Native communities. There are lurid accounts of torture and cannibalism, religious zeal and martyrdom—stories collected from "Christian savages worthy of belief"—that captivated the European aristocracy, who were the series' primary subscribers.[1] That these field notes, often based on hearsay, were heavily edited both in Quebec and in Paris, and sensationalized in order to raise funds for the missions, is often overlooked.

Sensationalism is a recurring theme in the depiction of Native Americans. Consider news coverage of the Indian War Campaigns (1867–1890), compromised by the symbiotic relationship between the military and western war correspondents. After the Civil War ended, the military was downsized, and the careers of individual officers along with it. A commander who had enjoyed the rank of brevet general, for example, found his commission reduced to colonel or lieutenant colonel. Worse yet, the demotion often came with an assignment to a bleak western outpost. More than one military officer saw favorable news coverage as a way to advance his career and return to the civilized East. Many freely shared their field reports with reporters. Likewise, journalists were heavily dependent upon the commanding officers of the western forces. Native warriors saw no distinction between combatants and noncombatants riding with the cavalry. Western war correspondents were Indian fighters first, journalists second. They relied upon their commanding officers not only for stories, but also for their lives.

Objectivity back then had not yet emerged as a journalistic ideal among newspaper reporters. Journalists were paid on the basis of "space"—the more column inches they published, the more money they received. Space writers obviously were thus inclined to embellish major stories and overdramatize minor ones. The consequences of poor journalistic ideals are tragically evident in the events that unfolded in the 1890 massacre at Wounded Knee.

Space writers, along with whites who would profit by attracting more troops to the Dakota frontier, helped create a mass hysteria. They bombarded Congress and the president with requests for more soldiers. When those arrived, a large number of Lakota became alarmed and fled to the Badlands. The press responded by trumpeting the reaction as an "outbreak," and the major dailies moved their correspondents into place. When Colonel J.W. Forsyth was ordered to round up Big Foot's band of Miniconjou, who had left the agency to join the others in the Badlands, only three of the twenty-one correspondents at Pine Ridge went with him to witness the confrontation. As the Lakota were being disarmed, a shot was fired. When the "battle" was over, more than two hundred Lakota—most of them women, children, and elderly—lay dead. The government awarded twenty Medals of Honor, the most of any single military encounter during the western conflicts, to the soldiers involved in the massacre.

One of the three reporters present on the scene, William Kelley of the *Nebraska State Journal,* became caught up in the fighting. The correspondents at Pine Ridge had previously made an agreement to rotate top priority on the telegraph wire. Kelley, a business office employee with no previous reporting experience, was scheduled to file his dispatches first that day. Ironically, the world learned about one of the most tragic encounters between whites and Native Americans from perhaps the least qualified correspondent to tell the story.

"Indians on the warpath" imagery dominated the worldwide news coverage of Wounded Knee II, the 1973 takeover of the massacre site by members of American Indian Movement. The nightly news audience saw a modernized U.S. cavalry with tanks and automatic weapons, but the Indians—some brandishing shotguns and riding ponies—had remained pretty much frozen in time. Network news cameras gravitated to activists who "looked" Indian (beads, feathers, and fringe) and their non-Indian sympathizers sporting Plains Indian headbands and names like Dancing Cloud Woman. However, news coverage of the siege also brought attention to the grim realities of everyday Indigenous life: poverty, dilapidated housing, and other social ills. The old stereotype of "Indian as Victim" was reborn.

In a 1979 journal article, James and Sharon Murphy described mainstream accounts of Native People as tales of "neglect and stereotype."[2] In the decades since the article and their subsequent book, *Let My People Know* (1981), appeared, some things have changed, notably the proliferation of tribal media. Gaming dollars have economically revitalized some Native communities, as is evident in the impressive number of tribal newspapers, radio and television stations, and websites available across the United States today. However, other things have remained the same. Indian casinos have inspired a new stereotype: the Rich Indian. Many mainstream Americans believe that all Indian nations have prospered because of gaming, when in reality just one-third of Indian tribes host high-stakes gambling and only a handful make what can be described as serious money from it.

Mainstream reporting on these enterprises often lacks context. Stories rarely mention sovereignty, a core concept, nor the National Indian Gaming Act, which contrary to public opinion, limited, not allowed, Indian gaming. Often reporters question why the tribes do not pay taxes or why Indians have "special rights." Consider one editorial from Wisconsin's official newspaper, the *Wisconsin State Journal:* "What do you call a race-based gambling monopoly that pays virtually no taxes and won't reveal its financial records?" the writer inquired. "If the owners of these casinos were Sicilian-Americans instead of Native Americans, . . . the word 'Mafia' might come to mind."[3] The mistaken notions that Indian nations are taxable organizations, subordinate to the states in which they reside, and that their rights are held by virtue of race, not sovereignty, continues to find favor.

The chapters of *American Indians and the Mass Media* explore the misrepresentation of Native people by the mainstream media, but also the contemporary insurgent redefinition of Indigenous people and cultures by Native Americans themselves. The essays and articles contained here, written by academics and professional communicators, most of whom are Native Americans, examine historical events, imagery, and expression within the context of popular culture. Familiar topics, like Indian mascots, find fresh examination, as in Victoria Sanchez's "Buying into Racism," which connects mascots to ethnostress and low self-esteem among Native observers. "Names, Not Nations," by Ruth Seymour, explores the power of words. The problem of language speaks to root issues that confront Native peoples today: invisibility, lack of understanding about sovereignty, and confusion on the part of mainstream America over the nationhood of American Indian sovereign governments. Longtime news editor Paul DeMain's "The Notion of Somebody Sovereign" is an essential read for anyone who truly hopes to understand contemporary Native communities. Together, these fifteen essays represent a gallery of insights about Native America, creating multiple realistic and recognizable portraits of Native people themselves. It is an exhibition that is long overdue.

NOTES

1. See, e.g., Christophe Regnaut, "A Veritable Account of the Martyrdom and Blessed Death of Father Jean de Brebœuf and of Father Gabriel L'Alemant, in New France, in the Country of the Hurons, by the Iroquois, Enemies of the Faith," *Jesuit Relations*, 34:31 (item 69). The series appears in French and English renditions, both now available online, as is an index for all volumes. See, e.g., http://puffin.creighton.edu/jesuit/relations/relations_34.html (accessed August 15, 2011).

2. Murphy 1979.

3. "Casinos Give Too Little Back," editorial, *Wisconsin State Journal*, 17 June 1997, 9A.

Part I
Historical Analyses

1

American Indian News Frames in America's First Newspaper, *Publick Occurrences Both Forreign and Domestick*

JOHN P. SANCHEZ

American Indians have been a part of the American newspaper media on this continent since the very first American newspaper was published in Boston in 1690. However, in the twenty-first century it is not uncommon still to find news frames that are culturally insensitive to American Indians in use as part of the daily American mass newspaper media experience. This chapter examines the very beginnings of American Indian ethnocentric cultural perceptions found in the first newspaper frames in America.

In the United States, many public school curricula include introductions to American Indian cultures, and colleges and universities across the country offer undergraduate and graduate studies in American Indian cultures, including classes taught by American Indian professors. Even with all these opportunities in the education system for gaining knowledge, the most common approach to learning about American Indians in the United States remains information in American mass media.[1] But why do the mass media in the twenty-first century seem to remain focused on American Indian imagery that is stuck in the eighteenth century? When did this all begin, and what will it take to change it to a more accurate and more contemporary view of American Indian cultures today?

THE BEGINNINGS OF THE NEWSPAPER MASS MEDIA IN AMERICA

The first recognized newspaper in America, *Publick Occurrences Both Forreign and Domestick,* was published on September 25, 1690, in Boston.[2] The first issue filled only three 6-by-10-inch pages with news of events and happenings

Numb. 1.

PUBLICK
OCCURRENCES

Both *FORREIGN* and *DOMESTICK.*

Boston, Thursday *Sept.* 25th. 1690.

IT is designed, that the Countrey shall be furnished once a moneth (or if any Glut of Occurrences happen, oftener,) with an Account of such considerable things as have arrived unto our Notice.

In order hereunto, the Publisher will take what pains he can to obtain a Faithful Relation of all such things ; and will particularly make himself beholden to such Persons in Boston whom he knows to have been for their own use the diligent Observers of such matters.

That which is herein proposed, is, First, *That Memorable Occurrents of Divine Providence may not be neglected or forgotten, as they too often are.* Secondly, *That people every where may better understand the Circumstances of Publique Affairs, both abroad and at home ; which may not only direct their Thoughts at all times, but at some times also to assist their Businesses and Negotiations.*

Thirdly, *That some thing may be done towards the Curing, or at least the Charming of that Spirit of Lying, which prevails amongst us, wherefore nothing shall be entered, but what we have reason to believe is true, repairing to the best fountains for our Information.* *And when there appears any material mistake in any thing that is collected, it shall be corrected in the next.*

Moreover, the Publisher of these Occurrences is willing to engage, that whereas, there are many False Reports, maliciously made, and spread among us, if any well-minded person will be at the pains to trace any such false Report so far as to find out and Convict the First Raiser of it, he will in this Paper (unless just Advice be given to to the contrary,) expose the Name of such person, as A malicious Raiser of a false Report. *It is supposd that none will dislike this Proposal, but such as intend to be guilty of so villanous a Crime.*

THE Christianized *Indians* in some parts of *Plimouth,* have newly appointed a day of Thanksgiving to God for his Mercy in supplying their extream and pinching Necessities under their late want of Corn, & for His giving them now a prospect of a very *Comfortable Harvest.* Their Example may be worth Mentioning.

Tis observed by the Husbandmen, that altho' the With-draw of so great a strength from them, as what is in the Forces lately gone for *Canada,* made them think it almost impossible for them to get well through the Affairs of their Husbandry at this time of the year, yet the Season has been so unusually favourable that they scarce find any want of the many hundreds of hands, that are gone from them ; which is looked upon as a Merciful Providence.

While the barbarous *Indians* were lurking about *Chelmsford,* there were missing about the beginning of this month a couple of Children belonging to a man of that Town, one of them aged about eleven, the other aged about nine years, both of them supposed to be fallen into the hands of the *Indians.*

A very *Tragical Accident* happened at *Water-Town,* the beginning of this Month, an *Old man,* that was of somewhat a Silent and Morose Temper, but one that had long enjoyed the reputation of a *Sober* and a *pious Man,* having newly buried his Wife, The Devil took advantage of the Melancholly which he thereupon fell into, his Wives discretion and industry had long been the support of his Family, and he seemed hurried with an impertinent fear that he should now come to want before he dyed, though he had very careful friends to look after him who kept a strict eye upon him, least he should do himself any harm. But one evening escaping from them into the Cow-house, they there quickly followed him, found him *hanging by a Rope,* which they had used to tye their Calves withal, he was dead with his feet near touching the Ground.

Epidemical *Fevers* and *Agues* grow very common, in some parts of the Country, whereof, tho' many dye not, yet they are sorely unfitted for their imployments ; but in some parts a more *malignant Fever* seems to prevail in such sort, that it usually goes thro' a Family where it comes, and proves *Mortal* unto many.

The *Small-pox* which has been raging in *Boston,* after a manner very Extraordinary, is now very much abated. It is thought that far more have been sick of it then were visited with it, when it raged so much twelve years ago, nevertheless it has not been so Mortal, The number of them that have around colonial Boston. The fourth page was blank. The publisher, Benjamin Harris, a London-born writer who had also been a publisher in England, promised to publish monthly only "honest accounts of news and information as they occurred" and to "cure the spirit of lying" that prevailed in the colonies at that time. On September 29, 1690, only four days after its maiden issue appeared, Boston officials as surrogates for the British crown officially closed down *Publick Occurrences,* ending the run of the first multipage newspaper in America. Their reasons for censuring Harris included his lack of permission from the Crown and of the necessary license needed to publish in the colonies.

A brief examination of the sole issue of *Publick Occurrences* shows that a total of thirteen news stories appeared in its few pages. More than half of them (eight) contained references to American Indians, verifiable proof that American Indians have been a part of American newspapers since that mass medium first existed on this continent.[3]

THE FIRST AMERICAN INDIAN NEWS FRAMES

Publick Occurrences also stands at the beginning of mass media news frames in America. Gamson and Modigliani have defined news framing as "a central organizing idea or storyline that provides meaning to an unfolding strip of events."[4] As news media consumers we begin to accept the news frames of stories that we consume in the print and broadcast media as "reality," most of the time without serious reservations about how accurate these frames really are.

A content analysis of articles in *Publick Occurrences,* in the sequence they were published, reveals a preponderance of negative frames over positive ones, including some negative characterizations that remain vivid today. Over time, colonial and later news consumers would begin to accept as reality the story frames that we first see presented here, without questioning their accuracy.

The first news story, or story of any type, in *Publick Occurrences* is seemingly a laudatory story about American Indians. (This and all further examples given are shown as originally written and published, in colonial English with all misspellings and typographical errors.)

> THE Crisftianized Indians in fome parts of Plimouth, have newly appointed a day of Thanksgiving to God for his Mercy in fupplying their extream and pinching Neceffities under their late want of Corn, & for His giving them now a profpect of a very Comfortable Harveft. Their Example may be worth Mentioning.

This first news story contains references to Christianity, God, and Indians and tells the reader about a promising fall harvest. It says that there is a newly appointed day of thanksgiving and that these Christianized Indians from Plymouth should be recognized for the day.

The second news article reports that two young boys from the town of Chelmsford are missing and that it is believed that Indians have taken them. The Indians are described negatively here:

> While the barbarous Indians were lurking about Chelmsford, there were miſſing about the beginning of this month a couple of Children belonging to a man of that Town, one of them aged about eleven, the other aged about nine years, both of them ſuppoſed to be fallen into the hands of the Indians.

American Indians appear for the third time when Harris reports that Indians and Frenchmen have attacked a small ship on its way to Virginia, according to one of the sailors who was able to get away, and describes the attack and the seaman's escape:

> That a Veſſel of ſmall Bulk bound from Briſtol to Virginia, having been ſo long at Sea, till they were preſt with want, put in at the Penobſcot inſtead of Piſcataqua, where the Indians and French ſeized her, and Butchered the Maſter, and ſeveral of the men: but that himſelf who belonged unto the Ships Crew, being a Jerſey-man, what more farourably uſed, & found at length an advantage to make his Eſcape.

This news story frames American Indians and the French forces as killers and, with a surviving eyewitness account, heightens the sense of reality in the report.

The fourth news story to mention American Indians reports on events involving Canadians, New Yorkers, and the Five Nations of the Iroquois:

> The chief diſcourse this month has been about the affairs of the Weſtern Expedition against Canada. The Albanians, New-Yorkers and the five Nations of Indians, in the Weſt, had long been preſſing of the Maſſachuſers, to make an Expedition by Sea, into Canada, and ſtill make us believe, that they ſtayed for us, and that while we aſſaulted Quebeck, they would paſs the Lake, and by Land make a Deſcent upon Mount Real.

In this story the Albanians (from Albany), New Yorkers, and the Five Nations of Indians are described as all working together in a military campaign against the French in Quebec.[5] Though only three sentences long, the news frame conveys the valuable information that Indians could sometimes be allies of the British colonists, not always adversaries.

The fifth story involving American Indians marks a noticeable shift in content. Here, the Maqua (Indians from the Iroquois Confederacy) are mentioned as allies in a military campaign, charged with having canoes ready to move General Fitz-John Winthrop's army across Lake Champlain. However, plans fell through:

> The Honourable General Winthrop was Head of thefe, and advanced within a few miles of the Lake; He there had fome good Number of Maqua's to joyn his Forces, but contrary to his Expectation, it was found that the Canoo's to have been ready for the Tranfportation of the Army over the Lake, were not prepared, and the other Nations of Indians, that fhould have come to this Campaign, fent their Excufes, pretending that the Small-pox was among them, and fome other Trifles.

This story contains several distinct references to American Indians. The first news frame in this regard, seen in the excerpt above, indicates that Indians are not reliable: the Maqua did not have canoes prepared, as promised, for Winthrop's army; and many of the other Indian forces did not arrive to assist the army when expected. Their excuses given for not showing up are characterized as pretense or "trifles." The remainder of the article proceeds to report that the Maqua were dispatched into the French territories to fight for Winthrop and that they did meet with some success, killing some French forces and returning with some prisoners. However, this good report is curtailed, as the story goes on to relate that the Indians then used these French prisoners in such a "barbarous manner that no Englishman could approve." The story ends with a condemnation of those "miserable salvages"—the very same Indians General Winthrop had depended upon to assist his army in a military campaign:

> And if Almighty God will have Canada fubdu'd without the affiftance of thofe miferable Salvages, in whom we have too much confided, we fhall be glad, that there will be Sacrifice offered up to the Devil, upon this occafion God alone will have all the Glory.

The next news article focuses only on American Indian activity, reporting on a battle between American Indians in alliance with the French (referred to in this story as French Indians, thus enemies at this time), and the Maqua (in alliance with the English). In this story a French captive escapes from the fort and then informs the French forces that the Maqua are approaching:

> Another late matter of difcourfe, has been an unaccountable deftruction befalling a body of Indians, that were our Enemies. This body of French Indians had a Fort fomewhere far up the River, and a party of Maqua's

returning from the Eaſt Country, where they have a great rate purſued and terrified those Indians which have been invading of our North-Eaſt Plantations, and Killed their General Hope Hood among the reſt; reſolved to viſit this Fort; but they found the Fort ruined, the Canoo's cut to pieces, and the people all either Butchered or Captived.

The seventh news story containing American Indian material reports that two English captives being held by Indians and the French at Piscadamoquady have escaped. It also reports that a Captain Mason (an English officer), in full view of the French, mutilated and killed two captured Indians and threw another overboard. This report clearly describes the execution of American Indian prisoners (in this case, allies of the French) by an English officer. Later, after the French informed their Indian allies what had happen at the hands of Captain Mason, Indian allies of the French retaliated and "barbarously butchered" forty English captives that they were holding:

Two Engliſh Captives eſcaped from the hands of the indians and French at Piſcadamoquady, come into Portſmouth on the ſixteenth Inſtant & ſay, That when Capt Maſon was at Port Real, he cut the faces, and ript the bellies of two Indians, and threw a third Over-board in the ſight of the French, who informing the other Indians of it, they have in revenge barbarouſly Butcher'd forty Captives of ours that were in their hands . . . whereupon twenty Kennebeck Indian Warriors went to look further after the buſineſs, who never yet returned. Which gives hope that they may come ſhort home but upon this the Squaws are ſent to Penobſcot, and the men ſtand on their Defence.

The remainder of the article reports more detailed information about the fighting between the English and the French, as well as about the clashes between French Indians and the Maqua Indians. In the latter part of the article, we see one of the first instances of an "unnamed source." Also in the passage quoted above, the word "squaw" here makes its first appearance in American journalism.

The eighth and last news story in *Publick Occurrences* that refers to American Indians contains much more in-depth information about military maneuvers that benefited the colonists and were designed to repel the French and French Indians. Here, the French forces attack auxiliary Indians—American Indians friendly to the English and colonists—and during an attempt to repel the French, the English forces instead receive a surprise attack by French Indians and lose the battle:

From Plimouth Sept. 22 We have an Accounts, that on Friday the 12th Inſtant, in the night, our Force Landing privately, forthwith ſurrounded Pegypſcot Fort; but finding no Indians there, they March d to

Amonofcoggin. There on the Lords-day, they kill'd and took 15 or 16 of the Enemy, and recovered five Englifh Captives, mostly belonging to Oyfter-River; who advifed, that the men had gone about ten days down to a River, to meet with the French, and the French Indians; where they expected to make up a Body of 300 men.

DISCUSSION: BIAS, FRAMING, AND NEWSPAPER CONVENTIONS

Some of the news frames that were used to describe American Indians in *Publick Occurrences* in 1690 can still be found in the American mass media in the twenty-first century. On assessing positive and negative values exhibited toward American Indians in the eight news stories from *Publick Occurrences* that reference them, it can be seen that they fall within either positive or negative news frames.

Frame 1. Positive   shared Thanksgiving celebration
Frame 2. Negative   "barbarous" and lurking
Frame 3. Negative   "butchered" the ship's master and several of the men
Frame 4. Positive   collaboration of citizens of Albany and New York and members of the Five Nations of the Iroquois
Frame 5. Negative   Indians "pretend" smallpox at home has prevented promised support of colonists; several prisoners are used in a manner "too barbarous for any English to approve"
Frame 6. Negative   the people all either "butchered" or "captived"
Frame 7. Negative   Indians have in revenge "barbarously butchered" forty captives
Frame 8. Neutral   Indians take some French captives and are now sending a force farther afield, outcome uncertain

This summary reveals that only one of the eight news frames that include American Indians can be considered entirely positive in referencing them. Only one story falls into a neutral category and cannot be considered negative or positive in referencing American Indians. The remaining five of these eight news stories exhibit framing images that are negative or insensitive toward American Indians. Thus, negative imagery makes up the majority of all the news frames referring to American Indians in the first recognized newspaper in America. One other notable ethnocentric perception arose in the newspaper media with the publication of *Publick Occurrences*: the monolithic images of the good Indian and the bad Indian. From the news stories contained in *Publick Occurrences* one can see that Indians are considered good Indians when they can be referenced as allies, friendly, and "our" auxiliary Indians. They are considered bad Indians when they go against the status quo in the

Boston of 1690: these are French Indians, butchers, lurking, lying about having smallpox, undependable, "salvages," abusing French prisoners in a manner "too barbarous for any English to approve"—even though in the same story, these Indians have gone on a military excursion into French Territories at the request of General Winthrop, where the general himself felt unprepared to venture. Instead of being hailed as a brave people for undertaking a military feat that a well-trained English army would not attempt, these Indians are featured in this news story as savages.

True, *Publick Occurrences* represents the first attempt in America to publish a newspaper, which means that its content should not be judged by twenty-first-century journalism standards.[6] Still, on learning that the majority of the frames referencing American Indians in the newspaper's sole issue exhibit a negative or insensitive attitude toward them, it seems justifiable to say that a generally negative position against American Indians prevails in *Publick Occurrences*. This, despite Harris's promise in the first words of his newspaper to report with truth and honesty:

> That fome thing may be done towards the Curing, or at least the Charming, of that Spirit of Lying, which prevailf amongft us wherefore nothing fhall be entered, but what we have reafon to believe is true, repairing to the beft fountains for our Information. And when there appears any material miftake in any thing that is collected, it fhall be corrected in the next.

One source of the power of the print media is the ability to create mental images with words. This first American newspaper exerted its power of persuasion during a time when words were the most powerful mode of understanding and knowing.

Over time, these insensitive ethnocentric perceptions of American Indians would come to represent a reality to European settlers and eventually to more recent citizens who absorbed the images from stories in the media of their eras. The power of the media to create insensitive, ethnocentric, and inaccurate media perceptions was as true in 1690 is it is today in the twenty-first century.

DISCUSSION QUESTIONS

1. What is the most recent American Indian news story that you can remember reading in a newspaper or seeing on television? What kind of pictures or images of American Indians did you see in that story?
2. *Publick Occurrences* is recognized as the first newspaper in America. What kinds of words are used in that first newspaper to describe American Indians? In what types of twenty-first-century media do those descriptive

words for American Indians continue to be used? Do any of these words appear in school newspapers when competitions are being held that involve schools that have American Indian sporting mascots? In what other kinds of media might you also find these words still being used?

3. The presence of American Indians in stories in *Publick Occurrences* proves that they have played a part in the American newspaper mass media since the very beginning. Why were there so many news stories referring to American Indians in this first American newspaper?

4. If you were an American Indian in 1690, how would you have felt had you read *Publick Occurrences?* If you were an American Indian today, how would you feel on reading such words to describe your people in a modern daily newspaper?

5. When you think of American Indians, where have you learned most about them—from newspapers, radio, television, movies, educational broadcasters like NPR and PBS, public schools, college/university classes, graduate school? What do you really know about American Indians?

NOTES

1. Sanchez 2009.

2. Sloan and Williams 1994, 1–2. The author recognizes that Boston in 1690 was a colony under the rule of the English crown. However, by 1690 the continent was known as America, and thus the author acknowledges and accepts that with Boston as its venue, *Publick Occurrences* can be recognized by historians of American journalism, newspapers, and mass communication as first American newspaper. America is named after Amerigo Vespucci, the Italian explorer who proposed the then revolutionary concept that the lands that Christopher Columbus had sailed to in 1492 were part of a separate continent. A map created in 1507 by Martin Waldseemüller was the first to depict this new continent with the name America, a Latinized version of Amerigo. http://www.loc.gov/wiseguide/aug03/america .html (accessed July 10, 2011).

3. Sloan and Williams 1994.

4. W. A. Gamson and A. Modigliani, "The Changing Culture of Affirmative Action," in *Research in Political Sociology*, edited by R. G. Braungart and M. M. Braungart, 3:137–177 (Greenwood, Conn.: JAI, 1987).

5. In New York State, the first city to be so designated was New York City, which received a royal charter in April 1686. Albany, with a population of about 500 people (one-fourth the size of New York City), received its municipal charter from Governor Thomas Dongan three months later, on July 22, 1686. The so-called Dongan Charter incorporated Albany, fixed its boundaries, established a municipal government, and endowed the city corporation with a number of special rights and privileges.

6. Jim Vrabel, *When in Boston: A Time Line and Almanac* (Boston: Northeastern University Press, 2004).

2

"Stories of Great Indians" by Elmo Scott Watson

Syndication, Standardization, and the Noble Savage in Feature Writing

MIRANDA J. BRADY

This chapter explores the career and work of the journalist Elmo Scott Watson, whose syndicated column "Stories of Great Indians" was influential in standardizing discourse about American Indian people in the popular press of the early twentieth century. Watson's stories were published as entertainment, but he and his colleagues also promoted their educational value. In particular, Watson hoped that by using the identity construct of the noble savage, his stories would help to correct negative misconceptions about American Indian people in newspapers and other popular texts.

"Now I will show you how a chief can die!" shouted Satank of the Kiowas to the soldiers as he tore off the shackles in which they were leading him away to prison. "I call upon Those-Above to witness that I die like a man unafraid." . . . The next moment he fell to the ground riddled with bullets. As he fell he was singing his death song. He gave one last defiant warwhoop, then died.

Elmo Scott Watson, "Satank Shows How a Kiowa Chief Can Die"

The epigraph above is taken from "Stories of Great Indians," a syndicated feature series written by the popular columnist Elmo Scott Watson (1891–1951) for the Western Newspaper Union in the 1920s.(See the appendix to this chapter for titles discussed below.) It was not unique in its subject matter as Watson frequently focused upon subjects who fit neatly into the archetype of the noble savage in an effort to use his appealing story platform to dispel what he believed to be prolific misinformation about American Indians.[1] According to Watson and the Western Newspaper Union ads that pitched his series to local newspapers around the country, feature writing, although distinct from the

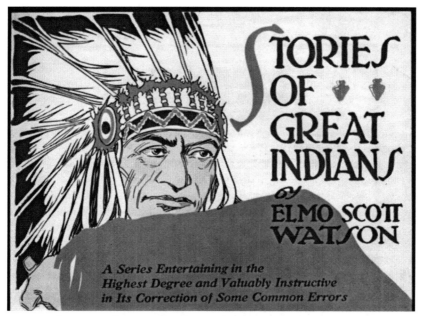

STORIEŚ OF GREAT INDIANŚ by ELMO SCOTT WATŚON

*A Series Entertaining in the
Highest Degree and Valuably Instructive
in Its Correction of Some Common Errors*

Cover art for *Stories of Great Indians* by Elmo Scott Watson. Courtesy of the
Newberry Library, Chicago.

increasingly professionalized, "objective" news stories of the early twentieth
century, nevertheless served an important educational function. As journalists began to adopt standards of professionalization, formulas for successful
feature writing also took shape. Successful feature discourse would resonate
easily with readers and provide them with educational entertainment to fill
their expanding leisure hours.

As a successful journalist and author, an active member of several professional societies, and a journalism educator at three institutions in the course
of his career, Watson was one of the notable figures who helped to establish
these formulas for his profession. We can look to the man and his work as a
significant landmark in the development of American journalism. His career
grew along with the newly accepted standards of his profession, and he spent
a lifetime reflecting on the history and hubris of his field. His writings on
American Indians, which spanned his long and productive career, can similarly inform our understanding of the history of popular sentiment about Native identity and its relationship with journalism during his time.

It has been argued that the professionalization of news in the late nineteenth and early twentieth centuries led to the disappearance of the "tall
tale" from newspapers as standardized, more "objective" news language and
formats emerged.[2] Although the "ideal of objectivity"[3] can indeed foster a

dangerous presumption that newspaper stories are to be understood as objective truth, the paradigm of strict objectivity still does not comfortably fit more entertaining newspaper content. Even though they supposedly were banished from the new, professionalized news that reproduced the same discursive formations from town to town across the breadth of subscriber coverage, tall tales persisted in the pages of American newspapers. They were relegated to syndicated feature stories. The emergent technologies and the "internal rules" of the discourses themselves allowed these tales to be easily reproduced.[4] Perhaps tall tales were dismissed as innocuous because they were considered mere entertainment. But such stories were popular and widely circulated and became part of the intertextual backdrop with which people made sense of their lives. Feature writers might have assumed more entertaining writing styles, but they also adopted the professionalized standards of journalists, as well as the legitimacy these standards lent and took their jobs seriously. As media scholars, we should treat their role in shaping ideas about race and identity with the same seriousness.

In the passages reproduced and analyzed here I examine the historical and disciplinary position of Watson and his syndicated feature "Stories of Great Indians" to explore the development of professional journalism and its intersections with the noble savage identity construct in the popular press of his time. Focusing on one of the many series he wrote that included the noble savage archetype, I discuss Watson's career and the conventions of his profession in order to illustrate the ways in which his work was reflective of its era. His stories and their historical context prompt the question, What does it mean that readers were entertained by such discourses, and to a large extent, continue to be so?

While newspaper content experienced a serious shift during the professionalization of journalism during the latter half of the nineteenth century and into the twentieth, journalists like Watson continued in the pursuit of a good tall tale, producing grand narratives that would "make subscribers stick!"[5] The compelling question here is not whether newspaper stories about American Indian people measure up with reality but rather how reality is constructed and how the making of meaning occurs.[6] Discursive formations about American Indian people can tell us much more about those who created them than about the subjects of the stories themselves.[7]

FROM EXPERIENCE TO ADVOCACY

Watson's career is a perfect exemplar of developments in his field during his time. He was not only a syndicated writer but an instructor who disseminated journalistic practices in his classes at the University of Illinois and Northwestern University, and finally as the chair of his department at the University of Denver.[8] He was an active member of several journalism societies, serving as president of the Society of Professional Journalism, editor of the *Publisher's Auxiliary*, and a longtime member of the Blue Pencil Club, a professional writer's group. He was commended by his peers for his work, perhaps most notably for *Modern Feature Writing* (1935), a collaborative volume with his Northwestern University colleague Harry Franklin Harrington.[9] Watson's other book-length publications include *History of Auxiliary Newspaper Service* (1923), *Rural Jobs in Journalism* (1945), *The Illinois Wesleyan Story: 1850–1950* (1950), and *The Professor Goes West* (1954, published posthumously).[10]

In *Modern Feature Writing* (1935) Harrington and Watson state that "probably the soundest advice which may be offered the beginner on the threshold of print is to turn the microscope upon his own experience, to capitalize on what interests him profoundly and intimately" (5). Watson's career supplies ample evidence that he had lived what he advised. He was born only two years after the Massacre at Wounded Knee (1890), and the event profoundly affected his professional and personal interests, as is evident in his later work (1940, 1943). One Western Newspaper Union promotional mentions that "the Indian has been the author's hobby," attributing his interest in stories about American Indian people to his upbringing near a Kickapoo village in Illinois.[11] However, Watson was much more than a casual hobbyist. His criticism of the United Sates government and of journalists themselves for inciting the violence at Wounded Knee suggests that he was driven to dispel what he perceived as misinformation and unfair assumptions about Native people (1940, 1943).

He also believed that the promotion of the "good Indian" (a positively inverted stereotype) in the popular press might help in the "correction" of "some common errors" about American Indian people.[12] He chastised the education system for not including more historical information on American Indian heroes such as Dull Knife and Standing Bear. Recognizing the ideology that informs "school histories," he suggested, "Some day, perhaps, he [the American Indian hero] will get justice—not justice in the restoration of his land which most of us admit we stole from him and did it pretty crudely, but justice in what we say about him." He continued,

> Perhaps, then, there won't be so much in our school histories about some of the blundering generals of the Civil War and more about Crazy Horse and Gall, Cornstalk and Little Turtle. We may even put Black Hawk, Osceola, King Phillip, Tecumseh and Captain Jack under the classification of patriots along with some of the Revolutionary statesmen and soldiers.

As part of his efforts toward this end, Watson ensured that these "good Indian" heroes were made to fit neatly into narratives that were easily accessible to the average reader of stories offered by the Western Newspaper

Union. Perhaps in order to encourage his readers to relate to American Indian people, Watson mapped Eurocentric values onto his stories of their lives and deeds, as seems to have been typical of news coverage about American Indians at that time. These Eurocentric constructs of American Indian identity tell us much about the writers that created them and the public that received and accepted them.

THE CONSTRUCT OF THE NOBLE SAVAGE IN WESTERN NARRATIVES

"The good Indian" or noble savage was certainly not an identity construct unique to Watson's stories. The term "Indian" as applied to Indigenous people throughout the Americas has persisted from the time of Columbus, and the noble versus ignoble savage "binary" has consistently been used to categorize Indians as a people rather than more nuanced distinctions between nations, tribes, or individuals in popular texts of the twentieth century.[13]

Several factors led to the proliferation of the iconographic noble savage. It was after the "Indian problem" in the eastern states had been "resolved" and with the rise of tourism and westward travel, mass production, and commodification of Native cultures that the noble savage became popularized.[14] Common themes in this popular construct are of a masculine American Indian who acts as a spiritual consultant or guide or friend of the white man; the brave warrior, who is technologically primitive but physically strong and often sexualized; and the friend or child of nature.[15] In story lines of the era, he is primarily represented in historical contexts that suggest he is nonmodern and lives in the past. These themes appear to have been confused with late nineteenth- and early twentieth-century popular needs to reconcile pressing problems of mass emigration, industrialization, science, and the value of human ingenuity. The consequent imperialist nostalgia reflected a sense of mourning at the loss of innocence, of which one representative was the iconographic noble savage of the past.[16] Along with many others of his generation, Watson seems to have longed for the unexplored frontier. At a time when older generations still remembered participating in frontier settlement and in the Indian Wars, Watson fetishized their adventure stories.

Keeping with the paternalist sentiment of salvagers, who attempted to preserve the trappings of Native cultures under the assumption that they would cease to exist, we can situate Watson's work during an ambivalent time: he was attempting to interpret the country's history and sense of loss while pandering to a wide audience with familiar stories. In what could be considered a kind of salvage journalism, Watson diligently attempted to record the great achievements of American Indian individuals before they were forgotten. He used the construct of the noble savage to portray an American Indian hero who was a masculine leader, living in the past, individualistic, talented, intelligent, and exceptionally brave, but who was still destined for extinction—like Satank in the epigraph. Watson often combined this identity construct with elements from other popular narratives such as Greco-Roman epideictic speech and biblical stories. For example, he writes, "About the best we can do in estimating the Indian is to take him just as he was, a pretty fine sort of savage man—certainly as good as many of the Homeric Greeks and the Romans—and give him his place in history" (1922a).

An excerpt from one of Watson's columns for "Stories of Great Indians" illustrates his distillation of American Indian characters with accepted biblical narratives: "The white man's history records Captain Jack only as a treacherous murderer. Had he been a white man, perhaps it would have pronounced him a martyr" (1922b). He describes Shabbona and Spotted Tail as "friends" of the white man (1922m, 1922o). Sitting Bull becomes "The Indian Sphinx" (1922n). He suggests of Chief Rain-In-The-Face that he was "a man utterly indifferent to pain, danger or death" (1922d). Sequoyah is "the Cadmus of the Cherokees," a reference to his invention of his nation's alphabet (1922l); Osceola is the "Indian Hamlet" (1922g), and Chief Joseph the "Xenophon" of the Indians (1922f). He refers to Chikchikam Lupalkuelatko as "the Leonidas of the Modocs," after the Spartan leader at Thermopylae (1922k). He calls Pontiac the "Indian Napoleon" (1922h) and refers to Chief Red Jacket as "Sage of The Senecas" (1922e). In addition to the stories, illustrations for Watson's series also exemplified the iconographic Indian. A drawing of a classic noble savage in headdress adorns each installment of "Stories of Great Indians."[17]

But even as he paternalistically imposed European, Greco-Roman, and Christian images and metaphors upon Native American people, Watson also suggested that his Indian subjects were less developed socially. He appealed to his more skeptical readers in passages like the following:

> Some readers may think I have played these Indians up too much as heroes, and be impelled to write to the editor and tell him what they think of the stories and the man who wrote them. To get a jump on them I will say this. . . . To the old-timer who has seen Indians on the warpath and witnessed some of their cruelties, who says: "If that young feller had seen some of the things I've seen them red devils do!" . . . Common fairness shouldn't allow us to judge the Indians by our standards. He was a savage, at just about the stage in civilization the white man was just a few centuries back. The Apache Indian, usually rated the worst of them all, didn't have much on the Spanish Inquisition. About 300 years ago the Puritans were burning witches in the name of religion. The Germans are said to have done some beastly things in Belgium. (1922a)

Even so, staying with the framework of the Greek tragedy or Shakespearean play, Watson's stories often start by describing the noble deaths of his heroes—as with Satank—again reinforcing the idea that American Indians were destined to extinction.

Despite his valorization of the past, Watson frequently stresses the importance of a modern perspective, as suggested obliquely in his evocation of a cantankerous "old timer" in the excerpt above, in his dismissal of "old-fogies" in *History of Auxiliary Newspaper Service* (1923), and in the title of his co-authored volume *Modern Feature Writing* (1935). Watson was not an apologist and seems at times to exhibit signs of a social Darwinist perspective as he places American Indians in the past, which would account for the demise of their people and culture. In one Western Newspaper Union ad he expands on this topic: "He's gone now and no amount of railing against the destiny which ruled that the white man should dominate the red, can bring him back. Sometime the yellow race may do the same to the white and then the law of compensation will have worked out" (1922a).

Watson's use of past tense in most of his descriptions as with the examples above, reinforced for his readers the determinism presumed by the dominant cultural perspective at that time. However, despite his adherence to standard notions of modernity and progress, he saw himself primarily as a creative individual from whom original thought flowed. Like many writers, he believed himself to be an arbiter of an experience that was in fact "constructed by ideological codes"—to borrow a phrase from Grossberg et al.—even while he worked within the conventions of his trade.[18]

DISCIPLINE, INSTRUCTION, AND STANDARDIZATION OF JOURNALISTIC CONVENTIONS

Looking at the standards and practices within which Watson was operating can tell us a great deal about the reasons his stories took shape in particular ways. Many historians attribute modern journalism's standardized language to the rise of the Associated Press in the later nineteenth century and of the wire story at the turn of the twentieth, or to positioning and branding and issues of class.[19] As the examples given from Watson's series illustrate, the discourses in syndicated features themselves acted as standardizing mechanisms. The "internal rules" that organize, classify, and control such discourses,[20] as well as their writing conventions, make only some narratives possible while excluding other possibilities. Watson's "great Indians" were not new inventions, but they worked to reinforce particular notions of Indian identity rather than alternative constructs, and they did so in accordance with the successful formulas of his burgeoning industry. However, while standardized discourses and syndication may have made the newspaper business more efficient, there is evidence, even in Watson's work, that many newspaper readers resisted their homogenizing effects.

Just as there were anxieties about mass-production of goods in the post-industrialized world of the 1920s,[21] there also arose concerns about mass-produced, syndicated newspaper content, in the categories of both entertainment and news. Watson's own booklet *History of Auxiliary Newspaper Service* (1923) suggests that doubts regarding standardizing effects existed even before Associated Press stories were used by many newspapers.[22] The booklet celebrates "auxiliary press" services' preceding wire-story innovations such as ready-print pages, mats, and plates; yet it also dismisses the "old-fogeyism" that laments standardization and the disappearance of a local tone in news coverage (1923a, 12).[23] Watson reassures readers that their communities should no more be deprived of common news stories than of a common diet with the next town over (1923a, 12, 44–45). But the anxieties expressed by the "old-fogeys" seem to reflect not only fear of the homogenization of their local papers, but the infiltration of outside discourses into their communities. Regardless of whether the technologies that made this standardization possible were ready-print pages or wire stories, the old-fogeys' apprehension touches on the idea that the very words themselves could act as technologies of normalization.

Investigating Watson's role as an agent in reproducing professional conventions can denaturalize the discursive formations that constitute his stories and tell us more about his field. Michel Foucault has argued that while authors often may believe they are making individual choices in their "author-function," they are always working within the discursive formations that have been made available to them as well as the particular logics of their discipline. Everything from "simple mundane remarks" to the entire "oeuvre" only makes sense in so far as it is consistent with already established knowledge formations.[24] They even dictate what is outside of or resistant to those discourses. In this sense Watson's work would have followed the conventions of his field, including those prescriptions for successful feature items described in his own *Modern Feature Writing* (1935) with Harry Franklin Harrington. There the authors suggest that features should command attention with "entertainment, emotional or informational value" (15). From his "Stories of Great Indians" series, published a decade before, it is apparent that Watson took each of these elements seriously.

For Watson and Harrington in *Modern Feature Writing* it was imperative to write stories that would be welcomed and entertaining among a wide range of readers. Those readers might be "your friends and neighbors and relatives— that young couple with whom you played bridge last Wednesday night"(76). The authors advised, "Be sure you have something people want" (59). Of Watson's stories, Western Newspaper Union boasted, "They cannot fail to create a following," and the Union likewise advertised its own wide appeal:

> You will find in our service, features which cover every variety of editorial requirement excepting those of a purely local nature, whether it be material appealing to women, children, farmers, wage earners, automobile owners and dealers, lovers of sports, devotees or casual readers of

fiction, the all-embracing crowd which enjoys humor and humorous pictures, or others entirely too numerous for mention.[25]

Further sage advice in *Modern Feature Writing* included "Make your story step lively" (67). In other terms, "The technique of that exciting game of Hare and Hounds may be applied effectively to the making of an article intended to catch a reader, and to keep him active on the trail" (67). In his actual feature columns Watson relied heavily on grand narratives that he knew would appeal to his readers including stories of great men, the old frontier, and adventure. It is also clear from some of his other projects, such as *The Professor Goes West* (1954), about Major John Wesley Powell, that he applied the great-man narrative often, adapting it to the "great red man" and occasionally even "the great woman."[26]

Watson seems to have believed that along with offering wide appeal and adventure, his stories should serve the important function of educating his readers.[27] He described his series as "entertaining in the highest degree and valuably instructive in its correction of some common errors" (1922a). This statement speaks volumes about the assumptions that were held for such stories, regardless of the fact that they were not considered hard news. In keeping with the deeply embedded protestant work ethic of this country,[28] readers were encouraged to utilize the enjoyable content for self-education, investing their labor in their pleasurable edutainment.

As Foucault has suggested, institutions ensure that discourse is "within the established order of things" by giving it power and by establishing and reproducing what is normative within systems of knowledge.[29] As discussed, Watson's position as a well-established syndicate writer, a member and leader of several professional societies, an author writing on the topic of writing itself, and an instructor of journalism suggest he was an agent of those normalizing technologies that regulate what is and is not acceptable in the field. In addition, he is also remembered as a frontier historian,[30] which demonstrates the overlap of academic fields and entertainment. In each of his capacities, Watson acted to reproduce those systems of knowledge, the legitimacy of journalism, and discourses about the noble savage.

LATER REFLECTIONS: WATSON AFTER THE WAR

Despite Watson's "instructive" intentions, it was not until later in his career that he questioned the problematic ideology that could be reproduced through newspaper writing. In the 1940s he argued that newspaper coverage had facilitated the slaughter of Indian men, women, and children at Wounded Knee in 1890, and events (like the coming of the railroad and westward settlement) that ultimately allowed for further development and access to resources like the Black Hills.[31] It may also be prudent to point out that by 1943, during the height of World War II and a struggle with a fascist regime, Watson's "great man" default became eroded as he witnessed an entire nation and beyond swayed by the exciting stories of otherness which incited genocide. He had borne witness to and taken part in similar nationalistic discourses. Was it possible that he was troubled by journalism's role in swaying public opinion for nationalistic goals? When it had become apparent that appeals to nationalism by fascists could be made through those apparatuses of public opinion, one must ask whether Watson found the potential of their standardizing effect problematic.

Whereas Watson was not reflexive about the grand narratives apparent in his feature stories of the 1920s, his interest in American Indian issues as well as what he perceived as misconceptions about them led him to become more critical of the productivity of newspapers (Watson 1940, 1943). He reflected back on the United States' own relations with American Indian people just as the power/knowledge/discourse relationship was becoming apparent in Europe. While some of his "instructive" pieces in the popular press worked to right what he considered to be misconceptions about American Indian people, his work in professional and scholarly publications condemned outright the system that reproduced the "jingoism" that facilitated violence against them (1943). As exemplified by his articles published in *Journalism Quarterly* in the 1940s, he began to see journalism not as an isolated institution but in its capacity to reproduce discursive formations by extending them into micro-moral domains.[32]

CONCLUSIONS: STANDARDS AND TECHNOLOGIES

Perhaps what is most interesting in looking at Watson's work is not just the potential of emergent technologies to standardize journalism and discourse, but the ways in which discursive formations also worked to standardize technologies. As an example, the construct of the noble savage was persistent in news features of the early twentieth century as a result of a culmination of socio-historical circumstances. It was a popular, normalizing discourse and was part of a rising nostalgia expressed by a generation living through post-industrialization in the first decades after the end of westward expansion.

There were reasons the same narrative structures appear repeatedly in the writings of Elmo Scott Watson, a man who schooled others on how to succeed in his profession and who reproduced such discourses through syndication. The narrative structures of tall tales were not merely embedded and stereotyped, but were also professionalized just as journalism itself became a profession. For beginners, instructional guides such as Harrington and Watson's *Modern Feature Writing* also acted as normalizing mechanisms by reproducing the conventions of the discipline. As journalism was made more efficient, it increasingly became standardized, limiting the normalized discourses that were acceptable within the discipline and available to describe American Indian people. Watson became professionalized alongside the journalism he practiced, and later in his life he also came to question its productivity. He understood the "informational" function of his feature stories and the entertainment in which it was packaged. Looking to Watson's work and the reasons it appealed so widely, we can better understand those tall tales about American Indian people and the ways in which they are a persistent foundation of a much longer story.

DISCUSSION QUESTIONS

1. What can Watson's feature stories tell us about American culture in the early twentieth century?
2. Why did many journalists begin to question the standard of objectivity during the latter part of the twentieth century?
3. Why do scholars critique both negative and positive racial stereotypes such as the ignoble savage and the noble savage?
4. How can discourse shape how we think about race?
5. Can you identify the positive and negative racial stereotypes from Watson's feature stories in popular cultural texts today, such as television shows and films?

ACKNOWLEDGMENTS

I thank the Newberry Library's D'Arcy McNickle Center for American Indian History in Chicago and the Committee for Institutional Cooperation for a graduate fellowship that made this article possible. I also thank John Sanchez, Jeremy Packer, Matthew McAllister, Chris Russill, and the anonymous reviewers of the Communication History Interest Group of the International Communication Association for their helpful advice.

APPENDIX. "STORIES OF GREAT INDIANS"
AND OTHER WORKS OF ELMO SCOTT WATSON
CITED IN THIS CHAPTER

Watson's works mentioned in this chapter have been cited, in the text and in the notes, according to the dates shown here. Most of these were accessed through the Newberry Library's Ayer Collection, which contains the Elmo Scott Watson Papers, 1816–1951, the bulk of these from the years 1920–1951. An inventory of the Watson papers is available at http://www.newberry.org/collections/FindingAids/watson/Watson.html (accessed June 10, 2008).

"Stories of Great Indians"

1922a. "Stories of Great Indians." Western Newspaper Union. Ayer Collection: Elmo Scott Watson Papers, Box 5, Folder 47. The folder contains the following stories in the series:

1922b. "Captain Jack, The Martyr of the Modocs."

1922c. "Chief Logan, The Cayuga, His Immortal Speech."

1922d. "Chief Rain-in-The-Face Got Undeserved Fame."

1922e. "Chief Red Jacket: Sage of the Senecas."

1922f. "Joseph, The Nez Perce, The Indian Xenophon."

1922g. "Osceola, The Seminole, The Indian Hamlet."

1922h. "Pontiac, The Ottawa, The Indian Napoleon."

1922i. "Satank Shows How a Kiowa Chief Can Die."

1922j. "Satanta of the Kiowas, As 'Orator of the Plains.'"

1922k. "Scar Face Charley, Leonidas of the Modocs."

1922l. "Sequoyah, The Cadmus of the Cherokees."

1922m. "Shabbona, A Pottawatomie: 'White Man's Friend.'"

1922n. "Sitting Bull Who Was the Indian Sphinx."

1922o. "Spotted Tail, Sioux Friend of the White Man."

Later Works

1923a. *History of Auxiliary Newspaper Service in the United States*. Champaign: Illini Publishing Company.

1923b. "Tales of the Old Frontier." Western Newspaper Union. Watson Papers, Box 5, Folder 49. 1923b.

1936. *A History of Newspaper Syndicates in the United States, 1865-1935*. Chicago. 1936.

1940. "The Indian Wars and the Press, 1866–1877." *Journalism Quarterly* 17:301–312.

1943. "The Last Indian War, 1890–91—A Study of Newspaper Jingoism." *Journalism Quarterly* 20:205-219.

1945. *Rural Jobs in Journalism*. Chicago: Science Research Associates.

1949. Letter to Ms. Kuhn, November 10 Watson Papers, Box 7, Folder 88.

1950. *The* Illinois Wesleyan *Story: 1850–1950*. Bloomington: Illinois Wesleyan University Press.

1954. *The Professor Goes West*. Bloomington: Illinois Wesleyan University Press.

n.d. "Stories of Great Scouts." Western Newspaper Union. Watson Papers, Box 5, Folder 48.

Collaborative Works

Harrington, Harry Franklin, and Elmo Scott Watson. 1935. *Modern Feature Writing*. New York and London: Harper.

Watson, Elmo Scott, and Julia Watson. n.d. "The Major's Right Hand Woman." Unpublished draft. Watson Papers, Box 7, Folder 76.

NOTES

1. Worth noting is that these stories frequently described the "inevitable" deaths of great Indian leaders, who always faced their grim fates bravely.

2. Carey 1989.

3. Schudson 1978.

4. The term "internal rules" is from Foucault 1972.

5. "Features Which Make Subscribers Stick!" (1922). Western Newspaper Union, May 13. Accessed through the Newberry Library Ayer Collection: Elmo Scott Watson Papers. Box 5, Folder 47.

6. Coward 1999.

7. Deloria 1998.

8. Appendix, 1922a, Inventory.

9. One reviewer wrote of Watson's *History of Auxiliary Newspaper Service*, "The work is done well. The booklet is carefully prepared. It is an attempt to compass an educational force in community life that has been overlooked by others"; see Fred L. Holms, *Mississippi Valley Historical Review* 11 (1924): 295–296.

10. An expanded version of Watson's *History of Auxiliary Newspaper Service* was published in 1936 under the title *A History of Newspaper Syndicates in the United States, 1865-1935*.

11. "Stories of Great Indians: Newspaper Values in Names," Western Newspaper Union, 1922, accessed through the Newberry Library's Ayer Collection: Elmo Scott Watson Papers, Box 5, Folder 47.

12. The term "good Indian" is from Weston 1996. Watson's advocacy of "corrections" (and subsequent matter quoted in the paragraph) appears in "Stories of Great Indians by Elmo Scott Watson," 1922a.

13. On the "good Indian," see Weston 1996. The "binary" of the noble versus ignoble savage is from Berkhofer 1979. See also Bird 2001a, 2001b.

14. See Phillips 1998.

15. Bird 2001b, 75.

16. Hinsley 1981, Phillips 1998 (on social issues); "imperialist nostalgia," Rosaldo 1989.

17. When his protagonist was a white frontiersman, Watson also drew upon the image of the ignoble savage in order to further immortalize his hero. Not surprisingly, Watson's white subjects in the "Tales of the Old Frontier" series are likewise compared with Greek heroes as they escape from attacks by ignoble savages. See, for example, "A Frontier Ulysses" (Watson 1923b). A more archetypal ignoble savage is shown lurking outside a white settlement with shotgun in hand, on the cover of "Tales of the Old Frontier" (Watson 1923b).

18. Grossberg et al. 2006, 207.

19. Carey 1989; Czitrom 1982 (rise of AP and the wire story). Schudson 1978 (positioning, branding, class issues).

20. Foucault 1972, 220.

21. Nye 2003; Phillips 1998.

22. See also Harter 1991.

23. Watson's argument was a convenient one as he wrote for the Western Newspaper Union Service, which at one time dominated the market of auxiliary newspaper services.

24. Foucault 1972, 223.

25. ("Features," 1922, Ayer Collection). Similarly, the Western Newspaper Union suggests in another ad that while not the "bread and meat of the newspaper menu," feature stories acted as the "salads, the apple pie, the ice cream and other delicacies that make the meal palatable and appetizing" ("Stories . . . Newspaper Value," 1922, Ayer Collection). It is worth noting that American Indian people are not among those included in the ideal audience list.

26. One of Watson's favorite characters was John Wesley Powell, the epitome of the American hero. Powell had been promoted to the rank of major after fighting for the Union during the Civil War. Despite losing an arm, he was said to have been the first white man to explore the Rocky Mountains, Grand Canyon, and Colorado River. He gained quite a bit of fame as a result of his explorations and work for the U.S. Geological Survey, and he was eventually appointed as head of the federal Bureau of American Ethnology. *The Professor Goes West* (1954), released after Watson's death by his wife Julia, was an extension of his book *The Illinois Wesleyan 1850–1950* (1950). Watson was not the only writer fascinated with Powell's heroic persona. To Watson's credit, other historians were similarly celebratory of Powell's accomplishments, including William Culp Darrah, who published another history of the hero's adventures (*Powell of the Colorado*, Princeton University Press, 1951) shortly before Watson's was released; and Wallace Stegner, whose "Jack Sumner and John Wesley Powell" had appeared in *Colorado Magazine* 26 (1949), 61–69 (a copy is filed in the Ayer Collection with Watson's papers, Box 7, Folder 88). Watson and his wife also collaborated on a piece about John Wesley Powell's wife, Emma Dean Powell. It seems appropriate that the Watsons

were writing about another husband and wife team. Emma helped her husband recover from the war injury that had taken his arm and accompanied him on field trips to collect geological specimens (Watson and Watson n.d., 6). "Emma's name," they wrote, "isn't covered on the monument, but it should be said that without his right-hand woman, John Wesley Powell could not have won his enduring fame" (6).

27. "Features," 1922, Ayer Collection.

28. See Weber 1958.

29. Foucault 1972, 216.

30. Appendix, 1922a, Inventory.

31. Watson 1940, 1943. For a similar perspective on the press's ability to incite anxiety during the Indian Wars see Coward's *The Newspaper Indian* (1999). He more specifically points to issues of political economy such as the interests of Horace Greeley, editor of the *New York Tribune,* in westward expansion, and Greeley's motivations for eliminating American Indian people as he developed his investments toward that end. Coward makes reference to Watson's work, including "The Last Indian War, 1890–91—A Study of Newspaper Jingoism" (1943).

32. Watson 1940, 1943. Ironically, while Watson (1943) attributed the inflamed relations between U.S. soldiers and American Indians to the uncritical patriotism reflected by newspaper writers, he did not chastise other national social institutions (namely Powell's Bureau of American Ethnology) for their treatment of American Indian people. He critiqued their symptoms, but he did not diagnose the connections (discursive and systemic) between such institutions and the power relations they yielded.

3

"Indians on Our Warpath"

World War II Images of American Indians in Life *Magazine, 1937–1949*

SELENE G. PHILLIPS

Life *was a pervasive force in American life from its founding in 1936 until weekly publication ceased in 1972. A number of studies have focused on the magazine's positive historic contributions, but none has analyzed images of American Indians presented in its stories and advertisements. This chapter analyzes the content, both visual and textual, of more than six hundred images of American Indians that appeared in Life from 1937 through 1949. Even well-intentioned presentations prove not to have been free of negative stereotypes of Native Americans. Imagery became more positive after the United States entered the war, but stereotypes continued to infuse even well-intentioned presentations throughout the era that was surveyed.*

I was out in Arizona for eight years and nobody paid any attention to me. They might ask me what I think of the way they treat Indians out there, compared to how we are treated in Chicago. I'd tell them the truth and Arizona would not like it.

Ira Hayes (1923–1955), Statement, Flag Day, 1953,
Chicago, Illinois

Associated Press photographer Joe Rosenthal, whose pictures appeared in *Life,* captured what became arguably the most famous picture from World War II, "Raising the Flag on Iwo Jima." On February 19, 1945, the Fifth Marine Division assaulted that island's Mount Suribachi. In the hour of victory Ira R. Hayes, a nineteen-year-old Pima man from Arizona, was one of six soldiers to raise an American flag on the summit. As a result he became the most recognized American Indian soldier of the war. But this was only part of a story that was packaged and disseminated for propaganda. Hayes was not the only American Indian who raised a flag on the summit that day. Two Flatheads, Louis C. Charlo and James R. Michels, had helped raise a first flag earlier, before an order came that it should be replaced by a larger one.[1]

Hayes, Charlo, Michels, and thousands of American Indians fought on battlefields next to white soldiers during World War II, but their stories and the tales of the now-famous Code Talkers were not headline news. At the time, few knew how the Marines had used bilingual Navajo Code Talkers to send messages in their Native language to aid classified communication efforts; the army had likewise employed other Native speakers for the war effort, including Cherokee, Choctaw, and Comanche.

Although American Indian soldiers were seldom in the news, the war brought them into face-to-face contact with a large number of mainstream Americans for the first time. This contact changed how many viewed them, shifting American Indians in the public mind from the role of savage enemy, of being part of the "Indian problem," to a new recognition of American Indian rights.[2] However, an analysis of the images of American Indians in *Life* magazine during the years surrounding the war demonstrates that this transformation was only temporary.

"IMAGINARY INDIANS"

Historically, American Indians have been subjected to false stereotyping.[3] The journalist Walter Lippmann, writing in the 1920s, commented that when someone identifies a "foreigner," a certain image comes to mind. Stereotyping saves time and requires little effort and helps make sense of the unknown. We notice traits and selectively choose images to "fill in the rest of the picture." After centuries in which the word "Indian" has been part of our written and spoken languages, it is almost impossible to encounter the word without envisioning specific mental images. "Our stereotyped world is not necessarily the world we should like it to be," Lippmann noted. "It is simply the kind of world we expect it to be." In this sense, realities are defined, then observed.[4]

Writing more than fifty years later, Robert F. Berkhofer, Jr., defined the mainstream image of the American Indian as a white conception. Christopher Columbus, believing he was meeting people of the (East) Indies, wrote that Indians were fierce, thieving cannibals.[5] Imagery from the era of initial European contact with North American peoples, an imagery that arose from the dominant and ruling class of the time, has endured into the present. Stereotyping is thus an American legacy. Most Americans today, for example, expect American Indians to be and look like historical Plains Indians on reservations, despite the fact that the majority of Native individuals now live in urban areas. Daniel Francis has proposed that retention of this kind of outdated imagery is a result of guilt and anxiety that non-Natives have about the legitimacy of their own presence in North America.[6] He sets this view revealingly in a Canadian context in a discussion regarding the results of European conquest in Canada: the Canadians' dilemma has been whether to get rid of Indians or become one with them.

Euro-Canadian civilization has always had second thoughts. We have always been uncomfortable with our treatment of the Native peoples. But more than that, we have also suspected that we could never be at home in America because we were not Indians, not indigenous to the place. Newcomers did not often admit this anxiety, but Native people recognized it. . . . As we have seen, one way non-Natives choose to resolve this anxiety is to somehow become Indian.[7]

In a similar vein Philip J. Deloria has detailed the American practice of "playing Indian."[8] He studied ads from the popular press that featured American Indian imagery, showing how they reflect mainstream Americans' self-doubts about their status as imposters. Most images in these ads situated American Indians historically, thus reinforcing the received idea that Native peoples have vanished from present-day American reality.[9]

LIFE'S HISTORY: A MEDIA MILESTONE

The first issue of *Life,* dated November 23, 1936, was an immediate success. No magazine had ever sold 500,000 copies in its first year, and *Life* sold more than that in its first few weeks.[10] The magazine's founder, Henry Robinson Luce, wrote that readers would see life, the world, great events, the proud, strange things, machines, armies, multitudes, shadows in the jungle, the moon, man's work, paintings, towers, discoveries, things thousands of miles away, things hidden behind walls and within rooms, things dangerous, the women that men love, and many children. Readers were "to see and to take pleasure in seeing; to see and be amazed; to see and be instructed." Luce also wrote, more soberly, that readers would "watch the faces of the poor." *Life*'s audience was neither the nation's poor nor its American Indians. Both these groups were subjected to observation by the magazine and thus assigned an implicit status of "otherness."

The poor of that era did not purchase many products at all. *Life*'s identity, however, was equated with its ads and promotions. Industrialization had increased consumerism, resulting in a need for more advertising to control costs. Advertisers reflected buying patterns. Editorial decisions reflected the need to maintain a specific audience. Images were crafted to attract and represent middle-class values.[11] Staff photographers knew what editors were likely to publish and planned their shots accordingly.[12] By most accounts, *Life* was extravagant. No expense was spared to obtain an exciting or appealing picture.[13] Money was spent reinforcing myths of the American dream, and American journalistic ideals of objectivity were sometimes set aside.[14] In the years prior to the Japanese attack on Pearl Harbor on December 7, 1941, *Life* was preparing Americans for the war in Europe. "It was going to be a dandy war," recalls writer James Brady, "the kind little boys who don't know anything just love to read about and see the pictures."[15] This vein of optimistic patriotism would continue through the postwar boom in consumerism.[16]

Life's demise as a prominent weekly news magazine in 1972 has been blamed on everything from television to niche marketing. *Time's* editor-in-chief at that moment, Hedley Donovan, told employees that declining profits, shrinking advertising, rising production costs, and postal rate increases had sealed *Life's* fate.[17] It has also been argued that management abandoned the magazine's "visual mission."[18] The last weekly issue appeared December 29, 1972. America was changing, and *Life* had fallen behind.

IMAGES OF AMERICAN INDIANS
IN THE WORLD WAR II ERA

During the Great Depression in the 1930s, unemployment was high, and unemployment in Indian reservations was higher.[19] Historians have credited World War II with changing American Indians' lives more than any other event besides the establishment of reservations in the previous century.[20] The Indian Citizenship Act of 1924 had subjected American Indians to selective service, and they served in proportionately higher numbers than some other racial groups.

World War II brought movement away from reservations and created an increase in employment for American Indians. The Alcoa aluminum plant hired Iroquois, for example, and the National Gypsum mining company hired Seneca. A New York State Board of Social Work report declared that the war had taken care of unemployment on New York reservations.[21] Like their non-Native counterparts, American Indian women worked in war industries. Opportunities for education and job skills increased. Young American Indian men and women increasingly purchased goods and services from white society.[22]

President Franklin D. Roosevelt appointed John Collier commissioner of Indian affairs in 1933, a position he held until 1945. Collier lobbied for an all-Indian military division but did not succeed. However, the Indian Reorganization Act of 1934 (sometimes called the Indian New Deal) returned some land to tribes, although the U.S. House objected to self-governance.[23] This long-awaited reversal of the Dawes Act of 1887 (amended in 1891 and 1906) restored common holding of reservation land after years of disadvantageous private allotments, but American Indian communities were still poor. Some Bureau of Indian Affairs funding was transferred to war efforts, and some American Indian land was appropriated by the War Department.

As late as 1940 some states prohibited American Indians from voting, but Native troops' participation in the war increased a push for suffrage.[24] Despite the Indian New Deal the gap between American Indian poverty and the mainstream white lifestyle had not been bridged.[25] In the postwar era

American Indians' economic security would be deeply affected by congressional attempts to reverse New Deal initiatives such as dams and highway construction, to decentralize the Bureau of Indian Affairs, and to extend "termination" policies that encouraged tribes to abandon claims to their reservations in exchange for full citizenship and financial settlements.[26]

Journalists, for their part, had historically treated American Indians poorly in the press.[27] Their outlook changed with World War II. *American Legion Magazine* fed stereotypes but was generally positively disposed:

> The red soldier is tough. Usually he has lived outdoors all his life, and lived by his senses; he is a natural Ranger. He takes to Commando fighting with gusto. Why not? His ancestors invented it. . . . We could use more like 'em. At ambushing, scouting, signaling, sniping, they're peerless. Some can smell a snake yards away and hear the faintest movement; all endure thirst and lack of food better than the average white man.[28]

Ernie Pyle's last news reports before his death in 1945 refer informally but respectfully to the Navajo Code Talkers' efforts to maintain their tribal customs even in distant war zones:

> Before the convoy left the far south tropical island where the Navajos had been training since the last campaign, the boys put on a ceremonial dance. The Red Cross furnished some colored cloth and paint to stain their faces. They made up the rest of their Indian costumes from chicken feathers, seashells, cocoanuts, empty ration cans and rifle cartridges. Then they did their own Native ceremonial chants and dances out there under the tropical palm trees with several thousand marines as a grave audience.[29]

The Code Talkers provided an alternative to stereotypes of American Indians as belligerent savages. Two hundred Navajo comprised the first Code Talkers unit in 1942, and by the end of the war more than four hundred had served. One veteran of the unit recalled, "Our Navajo language had been coded and used very successfully in the Pacific in the battles with the Japanese forces."[30] Their relationships with non-Native soldiers also helped to change prejudiced attitudes. "One of my friends was in the [same foxhole] as I was," another veteran remembered. "He was a Mormon from Salt Lake City, Utah. He gave me his parents' address and a note to send to them if he got shot."[31]

Native veterans believed that life would improve after military service, yet problems persisted after the war. Fame did not change Hayes's life. He petitioned Washington for Pima rights, but unsuccessfully. After the brief period when he was honored, he went back to "being just another Indian."

Discouraged, he died at age 33, of alcoholism and exposure to winter cold, at home on his reservation.[32] American Indian veterans and workers became expendable as the war effort ended; veterans felt excluded or uncomfortable in white society and also (like many other returning soldiers) among their own people at home. Native women lost their jobs to white women, and Native men lost their jobs to white men.[33]

"Nowhere," the writer Raymond William Stedman has pointed out, "does there seem to be a place for individual Indians possessing both strengths and weaknesses in the manner of real people."[34] *Life* was not that site: its editors and advertisers served as cultural historians recording acceptable and popular images of their time.

> Even if new meaning is given the idea of the Indian, historians of the future will probably chronicle it as part of the recurrent effort of Whites to understand themselves, for the very attraction of the Indian to the White imagination rests upon the contrast that lies at the core of the idea. Thus the debate over "realism" will always be framed in terms of White values and needs, White ideologies and creative uses.[35]

White Americans continue to struggle with and redefine their identity, which lies firmly in their conception of American Indians. Meanwhile the mainstream American definition of American Indians remains perpetually in flux, despite how American Indians define themselves. American Indians themselves continue to have little leverage for eradicating negative stereotypes.

World War II did strengthen American Indians' abilities to stand up for their rights. Alaskan Natives opposed "No Natives Allowed" signs and a "Nigger Heaven" sign in a Nome theater balcony that was reserved for Eskimos.[36] But stereotypes persisted, if in new guises. American Indians were admired for possessing traits previously feared; Native soldiers proved to be excellent "warriors"; many were nicknamed "chief." The Indian Commissioners' report in 1944 had highlighted their outstanding service record. Seventy-five Purple Hearts had been awarded to Native soldiers.[37] By the end of the war 25,000 American Indians had joined the armed services, and 10,000 had died proving their patriotism.[38]

LIFE AND WARTIME ADVERTISING

American Indians have been a fringe audience in the mass media, too small to attract the attention of advertisers preoccupied with mass audiences.[39] After a decline in the late 1930s, mass media advertising increased during the 1940s, despite the war. The decade immediately after the war inaugurated a golden age of advertising.[40] Compared to *American, Time, Saturday Evening Post,* and *Newsweek, Life* had a relatively high frequency rate of ads among its pages.

American had the highest rate at 33 percent of pages per issue; *Life* had 26 percent. Advertising agencies and big businesses made money during the war. The percentage of ads per issue increased from 1940 to 1950.[41]

The war did pose some challenges to American advertisers. Some received tax breaks for supporting war efforts.[42] One famous war ad for the New Haven Railroad Company encouraged passengers to stand for servicemen.[43] But owing to the heavy concentration of effort in manufacturing war items, many products were temporarily off the market or rationed. Madison Avenue designed ads asking consumers to "Go away, but don't go away forever."[44] Homemakers yearned for goods and worked outside the home as the major labor force.[45]

A SURVEY OF NATIVE AMERICAN IMAGES IN LIFE, 1937–1949

Methodology

The study reported in this chapter examined 678 issues of *Life* published from January 4, 1937, through December 26, 1949. These represent roughly the four years immediately preceding active U.S. involvement in World War II (1937–1940), the four years of active U. S. engagement in the war (1941–1945), and the first four years after the war (1945–1949). The United States entered the war on December 7, 1941, and the war ended on August 27, 1945.

Life was selected for analysis because it was a popular magazine during the war era. It represented Americana and "had no equal."[46] Qualitative content analysis was chosen as a method for observing changes in attitude and images toward American Indians over the series of issues surveyed. It was hypothesized that images found in the issues would reinforce stereotypes of Native peoples as a dangerous and vanishing race (as described by Brian Dippie) and would show instances of non-Natives "playing Indian" (as outlined by Philip J. Deloria).[47]

In the analysis the term "American Indian" includes Alaskans, Hawaiians, and Mexican Americans as well as Indians of the continental United States.[48] "Item" refers to a complete news article or a complete ad. Many items contained several images. For inclusion in the survey of issues from *Life* an item had to generate an image of Americans Indians themselves (that is, not merely an image of an Indian artifact, such as a totem pole) that merited the classification of "other." An "ad" is a paid announcement published for the purpose of promoting a sale of goods, a product, or service. "News coverage" or "news article" refers to an item generated by an editorial board, such as a report of a recent, historic, or significant event. The news coverage category was subdivided into editorials, movie reviews, and letters to the editor. "Image" refers to any drawing, caricature, or photograph of Native Americans, even if the subject depicted is a non-Native dressed as an American Indian. "Text" refers to any typewritten copy accompanying an item. "Playing Indian" refers to non-Natives dressed like American Indians. "Icon" refers to a sign, representation, or image that stands for its object by virtue of resemblance to American Indians.

Findings: Positive Images Are Misleading

During the interval studied, *Life* editors annually chose 10,000 photographs for publication, from 500,000 available.[49] That amounts to a total selection of approximately 130,000 photographs over the the thirteen years' worth of issues surveyed. Only 145, or .11 percent, of these photographs could be classified as showing American Indians. In total, 333 American Indian photographs, drawings, and icons appeared, across 240 items. Of those, 49 percent were ads, 20 percent were news stories, 1.5 percent were movie reviews, 1.2 percent were letters to the editor, and .6 percent were editorials. These figures do not add up exactly to the original totals, because some items used both drawings and photographs.

There were 69 news stories. When the texts of those stories were analyzed, 51 (74%) were about contemporary American Indians and their issues. Eighteen (26%) were about American Indian history. But when the stories' images were analyzed, the results were reversed. In other words, a contemporary news article was often accompanied by a historic picture. Of the images accompanying news stories, only 19 (27.5%) were images of a contemporary nature; 50 (72.5%) were historical images. Nearly three-fourths of contemporary news stories featured "vanishing" imagery.

At first glance, many ads appeared positive. In-depth analysis revealed another story. Seemingly positive thematic images placed Native Americans a "safe" geographic or psychological distance from the reader. This distance included non-Natives "playing Indian." The analysis also considered evidence for American Indians as icons, as landscape figures, and as "other." American Indians as "other" were subcategorized as "worthy" and "unworthy" in terms of how they were portrayed in each instance.

In all of the 333 images, "playing Indian" occurred 40 times (12% of the time). In many of these instances, the image exhibited what psychologists have termed "hostile humor."[50] The instigator of this type of humor perpetrates a psychological attack against the target of the humor; those who participate in the humor can be said implicitly to endorse the attack. A common theme in many of these images was white people dressed up as American Indians; this turned out almost always to be somehow at the expense of American Indians. Typically, the model, actor, or icon is shown dressed in a silly or comical fashion, always in some way mocking actual modes of American Indian dress, behavior, or culture. The comical image invites readers join in the fun, and by doing so they reinforce and endorse the image's (and the magazine's) subtle attack against American Indians. What appears on the surface as an amusing or trivial depiction is in fact an assault in which humor serves as the weapon.

The most frequent instance of "playing Indian" was Clicquot Club Soda ads, at 54. This beverage brand, known for the quality of its ingredients, existed from 1885 until Canada Dry bought the company in 1965. The company's logo presented a character, Klee-ko, whose name (echoing the French pronunciation of Clicquot) lent a certain exoticism to the brand's image. The company advertised in *Life* 18 times in 1940. Klee-ko, obviously not Inuit, "played Indian" with his fur parka and pants, snow boots, and mittens. The "copy" (text) for the ad once read, "When quality decides the call, This Eskimo is paged." The smiling "little fellow" was a "sunny youngster." Despite his white complexion, the adjacent copy read: "Ever since he came down from his ice-floes, more than fifty years ago, the Clicquot Club Eskimo Boy has been a family friend in millions of homes."[51] In these instances Eskimo culture was equated with wholesome quality. Patrons could even acquire a Klee-ko doll.[52] No Clicquot ads appeared in 1942 or from 1946 through 1948. In 1942 the news article "Alaska U.S. Frontier Waits for War" appeared, and a 1944 news photograph of a dark, unsmiling "Eskimo boy" sharply contrasts with the Klee-ko of happier times.[53]

One 1941 ad for Dole pineapple juice, positions a photo of a doll-like figure near a glass of juice. Like Klee-ko, the actor (character) wears stereotypically Native costume: in this case, a Hawaiian lei, hula skirt, and bikini top. As if to deny the "playing" role, copy reads, "I'm from Hawaii, the land of lovely flowers and gorgeous sunshine. This glass of Dole Pineapple Juice reminded me of home." Further signaling that "home" is an exotic native paradise, the ad's backdrop seems to suggest that real Hawaiian women would seem unreal there. All the women are portrayed as scantily clad, except one. The lei maker sits on a mat, wearing a short-sleeved shirt and long pants. Her fully clothed body contrasts with the Dole artist's other, sexy images. Her photograph appears ingenuous against the surreal Hawaiian "princesses."[54]

"Playing Indian," in the sense of a popular childhood pastime in the era surveyed, turns up in images that use "playing Indian" as an advertising ploy. One image from the *Life* sample shows a fully headdressed white youth, "Big Chief Billy, though quite brave," awaiting a Band-Aid. In another, a white child receives a cake after informing his aunt of Fels-Naptha Soap Chips. "Whoopee!" he cries. "Is it all for me?" The aunt replies, "Yes, you little Indian!" In a third instance, a white child pulls his sister's hair while whooping and dancing, his pep the result of Bosco iron. In another, a happy baby with a feathered headband crawls near copy that reads, "Whoopee! I got the Injun sign on Prickly Heat! Your little Indian will whoop with joy." One news photo shows an African-American child dressed as an Indian in a parade.[55]

White men and women "played Indian" in this fashion as well. One man is shown wielding a tomahawk and dancing "on the warpath" due to unsatisfactory zippers. In another image, two smoke around a totem pole. A majorette performs vertical splits for the legionnaires. A dancer says, "I was a Red-skin . . . until I stopped using those harsh, scratchy tissues and switched to Kleenex, the softer tissue that never irritates delicate skin." A white Pocahontas spares John Smith because he has Venus Velvet Pencils. A "sister" in "Igloo Land" snuggles up to a Gem razor user.[56] Others variously "playing Indian" in images from the survey include football players dressed in sealskins and fox-fur parkas to look like their "Alaskan namesakes"; actors, California delegates, college students, Admiral Nimitz, a summer reader, Abott and Costello, Joan Davis for CBS and for Roi-Tan cigars, and white Eskimos for Yes tissues. A cowboy and Indian play at a "million-dollar cottage" in a New York Life Insurance Company ad.[57]

Nonthreatening American Indian icons appeared in the abstract. Treatment of the Ottawa chief Pontiac (1720–1769) offers a perfect example. The historic leader, a comfortable distance away in time, was metaphorically resurrected to represent one of General Motors' automobile lines, even before Pearl Harbor brought the United States into the war. GM's Pontiac ads represented a progression of co-opting another culture for propaganda. In two ads appearing before the United States entered the war the icon representing the chief was a minimal part of the design area, smaller than a dime. In an ad from less than a year after the United States entered the war, the icon has grown to six by eight inches. Letters across the black silhouette read, "Pontiac is working as a subcontractor, too!" The Native imagery promoted other war efforts as well. Copy read, "Today, as these words are being written, thousands of Pontiac men and women are devoting their full and exclusive efforts to speeding the progress of our subcontracting operations along." Fine print reads, "Seeking to cooperate fully in the war effort, Pontiac has voluntarily censored this advertisement." The ad portrays the historic Pontiac as being compliant with, condoning the new war effort. The icon has become transformed from a tiny trademark to a warrior with a cause. Chief Pontiac is angry, and he is making weapons. The ad refers to GM factory workers as "Pontiac men and women," positioning them in a "playing Indian" role. In a later wartime ad the icon, larger still, more than eight inches long, the icon silhouette has been dropped for a portrait effect, reminiscent of the "Indian-head" nickel then in circulation. This was the only ad in the sequence that shows Pontiac's face, which evoking forceful movement. The copy reads, "This is the symbol of Pontiac. It stood for good cars before Pearl Harbor. . . . It will stand for good cars again."[58] As Francis concludes,

> The point is not that General Motors presented a false image of Pontiac. That may or may not be. The point is that the company appropriated an actual historical character and turned him into a commercial icon of the industrial age. A figure who once led an unprecedented resistance against White civilization is now a symbol of that civilization. An

important part of Native history is at once trivialized and domesticated. Pontiac is not an isolated example.[59]

Logically Pontiac should have represented rebellion, not loyal patriotism. Instead he was used as an image symbolizing unity.

Ads for Ronson cigarette lighters, also called Ronson Redskin Lighter Accessories, claimed the product to be the world's greatest of its kind and also promoted flints, fuels, and wicks. During the war Ronson also produced ammunition around the clock. Eleven Ronson ads in the *Life* issues surveyed feature an R-shaped body with a Native (Plains-style) headdress.[60] This versatile icon promoted the war and advertised war bonds. One Ronson Redskin chief holds a gift package of flints. Others variously go skiing, cling to the top of a pole, peer from a boat's crow's nest, ride a unicycle, and water-ski. Every R-shaped icon smokes a cigarette and uses a Ronson lighter. Two of these ads advise readers, "Hold Your War Bonds." Like GM's Pontiac ads, these turn a previously savage warrior against U.S. forces into a soldier for the American cause. Two of the ads promote the radio show *Ronson on the Air* and the radio program *20 Questions* on the Mutual Network.[61]

Many of the tourism ads and news items in the *Life* issues surveyed show American Indians incorporated into background physical landscapes. In a news item focused on New Mexico two women see to blend with pueblos and are unmentioned in copy that reads, "Taos has long been a cynosure for artists attracted by the intense color of the country, the authentic Indian types." Artists also drew Hawaiians as figures in the exotic (to statesiders) landscape of their homeland. Millard Sheets, a Californian artist, served as a war artist correspondent for *Life* and for the U.S. Army Air Forces (the precursor of today's U.S. Air Force) in India and Burma. He had specialized in coverage of the West Coast urban poor and in wartime depicted the famine and death he saw. His faceless Hawaiian women gathering flowers for leis and seem to merge with their surroundings.[62] Willard Andrews drew a New Mexico Native as if hovering above the pueblos, as if a part of the mountains.[63]

Founded in 1925, Wembley Ties was named after the English mill town where the company's fabric originated. Fourteen of Wembley's brightly drawn color ads appeared in the issues of *Life* surveyed, standing out vividly against otherwise black and white pages. Six of these ads mention colors named after American Indian tribes. American Indian are shown in the backgrounds of these ads as figures in a landscape. The headline for the "Cherokee Red" tie touts the entire product line, "Colors of America's Great Outdoors." A Native woman, child, and man are shown around an open fire, and adjacent copy reads, "Select Cherokee Red in Wembley's new wartime all-wool fabric." Two other headlines read, "The Colors of America's Frontiers." A Native hunter on a painted pony, bow drawn and chasing a buffalo, is assigned to "Buffalo Brown." Two American Indians preparing to dine on their catch beside a campfire, with a canoe beached nearby, represent "Champlain Blue." Two other headlines read, "Colors of America's Historic Trails." A "Tamiami Green" Native islander sits under a palm tree. Two men portage a birchbark canoe in the "Mohawk Red" ad.[64]

The last Wembley ad in the *Life* issues surveyed outlines British guards, Arctic people, and woodlands. Copy reads, "In the Arctic—Northern Lights gleam. And Wembley captures their brilliant sparkle in Iridescent Ties running the whole range of color tones to go with every suit color and every complexion!" But the Arctic complexions are not shown. Backs to the reader, the figures blend with the landscape, while British guards majestically ride toward the reader.[65]

The only other ethnic- or race-themed colorways in Wembley ads in the issues surveyed are assigned to Irish "Killarney Green" and Spanish "Toreador Red." Wembley, now Wemco, Inc., of New Orleans, is now the world's largest manufacturer of neckties, producing 8.3 million a year. Company insensitivity continues, as its New Orleans–themed website design from 2003 touts a former stock clerk's rise to a successful career by describing his original status in the company as "the lowest man on the totem pole."[66]

American Indians' otherness was also used to the exotic. This "other" imagery created a notion of the "worthwhile Indian": Klee-ko and Hawaiians served drinks to non-Natives; Hawaiians made leis, and American Indians lured tourists to unique places. Fifteen of the *Life* ads surveyed from the four years prior to the United States' entry into World War II incorporate American Indian imagery designed to promote tourism, hotels, travel, railroads, steam liners, and bus lines. These ads present Indians as "other," with "strange" and "weird ceremonial dances." Travelers are promised an array of new thrills, including living history, a "great adventure," a "different life," a "fairytale Totemland," cocktail and observation lounges in "Indian motif," welcoming Hawaiian leis, and "eighteen Indian pueblos." One ad shows a tourist taking a snapshot of a headdressed Native as he takes a snapshot of her. Copy reads, "Perhaps the old Chief won't surprise you with a candid-camera shot, but you'll certainly get a more life-like 'close-up' of America on a Greyhound trip!"[67]

Like the company's ads for its pineapple juice, Dole Pineapple's ads for other pineapple products in the *Life* issues surveyed seem at first glance to be positive and unambiguous. Dole often employed well-known trained artists. One of these, the Mexico City author and ethnographer Miguel Covarrubias, is known to have been knowledgeable about Indigenous culture, yet his "Hula girl" for Dole wears only a hula skirt and lei.[68] The well-known advertising firm N. W. Ayer and Son commissioned work from the world-famous lithographer Robert Riggs, who drew from memory and photographs of his South Pacific travels in the 1920s. About 17 of these works were intended for the *Saturday Evening Post*; most were not used, but *Life* readers could send in a Dole product label to request a "Pineapple Harvest" lithograph "suitable for framing." Copy juxtaposed "ancient rulers" against bare-breasted "Gracious Island hostesses" who "offer their holiday guests royal hospitality in the modern manner." Another reads "Hawaiian Hula girls know 'swing.'"[69] Sexy Hawaiians were worthy, because they were pretty and served nice drinks.

Other worthy American Indians appeared, in the *Life* issues surveyed, in five Vermont Maid Syrup ads from Penick and Ford, Ltd., Inc. of Burlington, Vermont. Although inaccurate at times and consistently situating Natives historically, these unusual ads did attempt to educate readers about American Indian traditions, but not always in a sensitive manner. In three of the ads a Frenchman is shown handing a kettle to American Indians. Copy reads:

> The Indians taught maple-sugar to the French settlers who, in return, furnished the metal kettles to replace crude Indian utensils. The Indians were the first to discover that syrup could be made from the sap of maple trees. But their crude methods could not match the flavor of our Vermont Maid Syrup.[70]

Another ad in this series reads,

> First ceremony of the Ojibwa maple sugar festival was the mixing of new maple sugar with some from the season before. The Indians first discovered maple sugar. They realized the value of having a uniformly delicious flavor. But they didn't know the right way to get it![71]

The accompanying illustration shows five Ojibwe men sitting on a blanket with a tent or a tipi in the background, tending a kettle set over a fire.

With more accuracy than most, one Vermont Maid ad shows Native women preparing syrup in a woodland setting. Copy reads,

> Having no metal kettles, Indian women made maple syrup by repeatedly dropping hot stones into bark vessels containing maple sap. Long before the white man, the Indians found that delicious syrup could be made from maple tree sap. But their primitive methods could not produce the uniform flavor of our Vermont Maple Syrup.[72]

Copy in this series of ads does credit American Indians with discovering maple syrup, but the noble Indians portrayed are primitive and ignorant of superior technology and methods. Civilized people of European background are stated to have perfected the most desirable processes. The not-very-subtle message is that without colonization, American Indians would not have gained the knowledge to best use the natural fruits of their land. This message was repeated in each ad, even though many American Indians had enjoyed abundant agrarian lifestyles before the arrival of European settlers.

A memorable Southern Pacific rail line ad from a 1944 issue of *Life* combines a respectful image with an insulting headline and belittling copy. The headline reads, "Indians on Our Warpath," and Navajo, Hopi, Pima, and Apache are said to be "working on our right of way—the railroad's warpath." The accompanying copy implies that the war is not really American Indians' fight and questions their citizenship.

> Their grandfathers fought to halt the white westward trek. When tracks of the first continental railroad were being laid down, raiders were a constant threat to workers' right of way.
>   But descendants of these first Americans today have a common cause with all Americans. Many are serving in the armed forces. Indians are raising food crops, buying war bonds, and helping to keep the war trains rolling![73]

The illustration here, which shows Native men carrying a railroad tie, represents "worthy" American Indians helping the war effort. This rare positive image is accompanied by demeaning copy that terms their ancestors "raiders" and a "threat." The copy continues in a scarcely less insensitive vein: "These patriotic Redmen came from the reservations and from scattered hogans in answer to our wartime call for extra manpower."

A second theme of Native American "otherness" depicts American Indians as dangerous and bearing weapons. In these instances space is carefully maintained between middle-class readers and the stalwart American Indians displayed, who are kept close enough to be admired and far enough away not to seem to threaten safety. Five sophisticated ads for the National Life Insurance Company of Vermont that appeared in the *Life* issues surveyed depicted American Indians and scenes from Vermont history in this fashion. The artist commissioned for the series, Roy F. Heinrich, created about one hundred drawings for the project. National Life still grants permission for these drawings to appear in books, magazines, and texts.[74] One ad reads, "The Indians often marked the Vermont trails by tieing saplings to the ground, bent in the direction to be followed."[75] The adjacent drawing has little to do with insurance protection, but the viewer may interpret the message to mean that American Indians too needed protection from the dangers on life's trail. Though the scene and copy portray a nonviolent chore, the two stoic American Indians in the illustration wear "war paint" and flex strong and dangerous muscles as they work.

Another National Life ad in the *Life* series, framed around the same motif of protection, refers to a story of the Algonquians, the French, the British, and the French explorer Samuel de Champlain. The explorer stands in front of his men, flanked by two American Indians. Copy reads, "Champlain, the French explorer, was the first white man known to have looked upon what is now

"Indians on our Warpath," from *Life* Magazine, May 8, 1944.

Vermont. . . . Vermont, for a long time a buffer state between the Algonquins and the Iroquois, and between the French and the British, had to fight from its earliest days for home protection and independence."[76]

Two of the National Life ads in the *Life* series relate the story of Native Americans offering assistance to the family of the third white child born in Vermont. The illustration and the copy center around the modern topic of insuring and protecting newborn children. "The Indians erected a lean-to to protect Mrs. Johnson and her baby," runs the copy—yet the drawing shows only watchful Natives with painted faces surrounding the mother as she prepares to give birth.[77]

A fourth Vermont national Life ad in the series in the *Life* issues surveyed reads, "Jemima Sartwell, taken captive in an Indian raid and separated from her two young daughters, whom the Indians had taken to Montreal, persuaded her captors to sell her in the city, hoping that she might find and rescue her children. After many hardships as a drudging servant, she located her children and fled with them to Vermont." The illustration for this story shows American Indians bargaining with a colonist.

Like Vermont Maid Syrup ads, the Vermont National Life ads attempt to enlighten but nevertheless reproduce negative stereotypes. Dangerous American Indians stand between the women and their safety. The subtle message conveyed that is modern middle-class people need insurance to protect them from lurking Native threats.

In a 1939 ad for the Greyhound interstate bus line, an American Indian holds a staff that could pass for a spear as he peers down at a bus traveling across the page beneath his position, not unlike a hostile Native scout in a period cowboy and Indian movie. Another travel ad, designed to promote Carlsbad Caverns in New Mexico, shows a Native man holding a torch and a dead elk, suggesting that hunting weapons have been used just offstage.[78]

In three ads for alcoholic beverage companies that appeared in the *Life* issues surveyed, Native men stand ready to attack, brandishing a tomahawk or club. Two Haig & Haig Scotch ads read, "It was 1773 when the Boston Tea Party took place—when a group of citizens, disguised as Native Americans, dumped cargoes of tea into Boston Bay."[79] Here the reader is treated to a scene of white Americans "playing Indian" in an aggressive rather than comical incident. An ad for Gambarelli and Davitto American Vermouth coopts, in very offhand terms, a legend about an eminent American Indian:

> The story of Pocahontas and how she saved the life of John Smith is American folklore. Concerning the romance that followed, you will never see mentioned how, as the stone axe was about to fall, she appealed for John Smith's life by holding aloft a treasured bottle of native wine, surprisingly like G&D American Vermouth. . . . Whether her father, chief Powhatan, was annoyed to see his private stock raided, or whether the executioner actually got the wine, we shall never know— but John Smith was saved.[80]

Instead of depicting Native Americans with accuracy and respect, copywriters for Gambarelli and Davitto enhanced and subverted a potentially violent fable, highlighting the image of the Native executioner and his axe.

One could argue these alcoholic beverage ads had an educational dimension. But the stories of the Boston Tea Party and of Pocahontas' were mythologized. The ads present armed Native males ready for violence, even though the Boston "Indians" are ersatz. Both stories represent adaptation of an "other" culture to purposes never intended by its originators. The Boston Tea Party "play" on Native American costume and weapons is obvious. In the Pocahontas story the "play" is complex. Her legend in history evokes and sanctions white men's desire for permission to take New World lands for themselves; her clemency toward Smith can be seen as signaling Native consent. If Haig & Haig and Gambarelli and Davitto had truly sought accuracy about the history of their industry, they would have been obliged to report stories about how American Indians were deceived and betrayed through trade in alcoholic beverages—but that would not have been likely to sell more of their product.

Another "other" category was that of the unworthy American Indians, too ignorant to deserve full American citizenship or to manage their own land. One tactic used to portray this unworthiness was ridicule of Native use of rudimentary or pidgin English; another was to portray Native speakers as simply inarticulate. Three Nicholson File Company ads that appeared in the *Life* files surveyed illustrate this kind of stereotyping. In one, a spear bearer "assures himself of many square meals by outsmarting giant tortoise with harpoon made from Nicholson File." In another, Eskimos approve of the files, which they want to use on a walrus tusk, with an "Ugh." Accompanying copy reads, "More articulate are the hundreds of letters [received] from file users throughout the industry." The third Nicholson ad reads, "Twenty years ago resourceful and ingenious Osage Indian hit on idea of grinding down Nicholson File until edge was razor sharp. Found it ideal for giving braves of tribe traditional 'hair cut and shave' around the forelock." An older Osage is shown shaving a younger man—though at first glance he appears to be scalping him.[81]

In a tourism ad, a Puritan named Pilgrim Pete who has taken his companion Tomahawk to a Statler Hotel says in an aside, "I've dodged this Indian since Sixteen-Twenty-Four." At dinner and bedtime, Tomahawk says "Ugh." Awaiting a bath, he manages a little more: "'Ugh,' said the red man, 'my turn now.'"[82] The shirtless Tomahawk wears two feathers and fringed pants, except at Thanksgiving dinner, when he dons a loincloth. He foolishly sets up a tipi over his is hotel bed before lying down to sleep.

A more elaborate script mimicking pidgin English features in an ad for Bosco chocolate syrup. A child proclaims: "Indian fix-um paleface! Heap big glass of Bosco and milk at my wigwam. Best-um chocolate flavor makes milk extra good. Bosco full of iron besides! Yippee!" A soap ad reads, "The Indian says 'ugh' to 'B.O.,'" and continues: "The only time we say 'Ugh' is when people don't use Lifebuoy for 'B.O.'" A tobacco ad states, "Kentucky Club, like totem poles." Copy for an ad for Wildroot hair tonic reads "Ugh! Scalp no good! Won't pass fingernail test." Here, tomahawk poised, an American Indian man stands over an anxious white man, grasping his victim's scalp, which he complains is "gummy as a race track after a rain." A caption for a news picture reads, "Man-on-the-street program turns into man-in-the-tepee interview"—an interview in which an American Indian man answers questions only with "Ugh." A summer reading textbook is advertised under the title *Chief Read Heap Much*.[83] The pidgin English and foolish behavior seem innocent, but the underlying hostile humor depicts American Indians as too ignorant to communicate well, and thus undeserving of full American citizenship and identity.

Ads also ridiculed Native bodies. A Pacquins hand cream ad reads, "As old as an OLD SQUAW . . . that's how my hands made me feel!" Similar to Kleenex, Jeris hair tonic copy reads, "This is a Zuni Indian, a man of social importance in his community. He thinks his hairway most distinguished. We don't agree. We like the modern way, the 'Jeris-Way.'" An Ingram shaving cream ad reads, "Even weathered old faces like his"—the reader views an aging Native man—" feel almost as smooth as his—a Native baby—"after a cool, cool Ingram shave."[84] Messages were that readers would not want American Indians' wrinkled hands, old faces, and ungroomed hair.

CONCLUSION: AN INDUSTRY OF HOSTILITY

Before World War II, railroads and cities competed for tourists. In the earlier part of the century, highway construction, new factories, and increased availability of disposable personal and family income had prompted the tourism industry to entice travelers to remote locations like the American Southwest and Northwest. Friendlier, landscaped American Indian imagery in tourism ads had made dangerous, faraway places seem safe. Industrialization and the war created a watershed moment when white middle-class Americans encountered American Indians face to face. During the war, fleeting instances where positive images of American Indians appeared in the mass media reinforced a sense of unity and democracy in action. Yet negative imagery persisted in *Life*. Stereotypes upheld *Life*'s construction of the world. In *Life*'s narrative, minorities' lives, especially American Indians' lives, were not discussed. Instead, they sustained "other" status.[85]

Life editors, advertisers, and readers repeatedly mocked American Indians. Seemingly innocent and positive ads packed a powerful punch using hostile humor. Current event news stories were accompanied with historic figures, evoking "vanishing Indians." Photographs, seemingly an accurate and true portrayal, often depicted non-Natives "playing Indian." Clicquot ads evoked "Eskimos" without any Inuit. American Indians appeared as icons. The strange or ignorant were unworthy of full citizenship, the land, or equal consideration. Worthy American Indians were attractive to look at, helped with the war, or provided some type of service to non-Natives.

The long-standing tradition of using American Indian culture to promote products continues. American Indian culture sells sports teams, Jeep Cherokees, Cherokee clothing, Land O'Lakes butter, and Mohawk carpets. A 1992 mid-northern Indiana television commercial featured a white male dressed as an American Indian who said "ugh." The commercial appeared several times before protesters caused it to be pulled. The car dealer apologized, but before the commercial had aired, it had passed review by the car dealer, the television station, and a production crew, all apparently insensitive to American Indian issues. If it sells without offending a majority of the audience, it stays.

American Indians are often described as the most invisible minority.[86] Many people would never use the term "pickaninny," but think nothing of using "redskin" or "squaw."[87] Imagery appearing in other *Life* issues and other popular national magazines like *Time* and *Saturday Evening Post* merits further examination. Further study may indicate how imagery has shifted. Research may provide inroads to decreasing mainstream America's commodification of American Indian culture.

Despite the progress made during World War II, despite how Native women worked in factories, despite how Native men served and died to help the cause, despite how their imagery helped corporate America to sell mainstream products, despite Ira Hayes's notoriety, American Indians' contributions made little more than a dent in the negative stereotypes that appeared in *Life* magazine immediately after World War II. Many racial and cultural groups have been mistreated and discriminated against in American history, but few can repeatedly demonstrate how little progress was made in the twentieth century.

DISCUSSION QUESTIONS

1. Why does the author refer to photographic images of American Indians as "imaginary?"
2. How might a magazine such as *Life* influence readers' perceptions of American Indians differently than a newspaper would?
3. What advertising examples as described in this chapter ridiculed American Indians? What images or concepts contributed to this dismissive treatment?
4. Were there parallels between the depictions of American Indians in *Life* magazine and stereotypes applied to other ethnic groups?
5. Describe the impact World War II had on the development of images and stereotypes of American Indians in *Life*.

ACKNOWLEDGMENTS

This chapter is dedicated to the memory of the author's cousin, Sgt. Donnie Allen, Jr., USMC ret. (1968–2008), of Lac du Flambeau, Wisconsin.

NOTES

Epigraph: *Chronicles of Indian Protest* 1971, 278.

1. Rosenthal photo: *Life*, February 23, 1945. Charlo and Michels: *Famous Pictures: The Magazine,* "Raising The Flag on Iwo Jima," http://www.famouspictures.org/mag/index.php?title=Iwo_Jima (accessed November 23, 2008). Photos of the original flag-raising were suppressed by General Alexander Archer Vandegrift; see Parker Bishop Albee, Jr., and Keller Cushing Freeman, *Shadow of Suribachi: Raising the Flags on Iwo Jima* (West Port: Praeger, 1995).

2. Sheffield (2004, 82) outlines a similar change but not a total paradigm shift in Canada.

3. For the term "Imaginary Indian" see Francis 1992). See also, on stereotyping, Weiser 1978, 93.

4. Lippmann 1921, 54–55, 59, 69.

5. Berkhofer 1978, 3, 5, 7.

6. Francis 1992, 107–108.

7. Francis 1992, 223–224.

8. P. Deloria 1998.

9. For more, see Dippie 1982.

10. Tebbel and Zuckerman 1991, 169, 170.

11. Megan Fath, "Visuals of *Life*," Master's thesis, Kent State University Honors College, May 2000, 53 (ads, promotions), 7 (buying patterns), 13 (middle-class values).

12. Feeney, 1997, 2; Wendy Kozol, "Documenting the Public and Private in *Life*: Cultural Politics in Postwar Photojournalism," Master's Thesis, University of Minnesota, 1990, 53.

13. Hamblin 1977, 35, 175.

14. For example, African Americans' contributions to the war did not gain them increased coverage. See Sentman 1983, 504.

15. James Brady, "Fifty Years Ago," *Advertising Age,* August 21, 1989, 39.

16. Fath, "Visuals of *Life*," 17.

17. Hamblin 1977, 309.

18. See Doss 2001.

19. Bernstein 1991, 16–17.

20. Parman 1994, 107–122.

21. Hauptman, 1986, 5.

22. Bernstein 1991, 59.

23. Bernstein 1991, 7.

24. Keyssar 2000, 254; V. Deloria, Jr. 1985, 111–112.

25. Bernstein 1991, 20; Berkhofer 1978, 175, 179, 184.

26. Parman 1994, 123–124.

27. For example, see Watson 1943.

28. Donald Culross Peattie, "Braves on the Warpath," *Reader's Digest* 43, no. 255 (July 1943):78.

29. Ernie Pyle, "Release to PM's Thursday" (No. 69) Newswire from Okinawa, April 26, 1945, Ernie Pyle Collection, Lilly Library, Indiana University, Bloomington, Indiana.

30. Gorman 1990, ix.

31. Sidney Bendoni, quoted in Kawano 1990, 23.

32. *Chronicles of American Indian Protest* 1971, 267 ("just another Indian"); Nabokov 1999, 333.

33. See also Townsend 2000.

34. Stedman 1982, 249.

35. Berkhofer 1978, 111.

36. Cole 1992, 431, 441.

37. Washburn, 1973, 965.

38. Nabokov 1999, 332.

39. Wilson and Gutierrez 1985, 39.

40. Ross K. Baker, "Shooting with Blanks," *American Demographics,* February 1988, 64.

41. Brown 1981, 20.

42. Stole 2006, 185.

43. Nelson Metcalf Jr., "Writer Recalls Famed World War II Ad: Ad Council's 50-Year Retrospective Will Include New Haven's Heart-Tugger," *Advertising Age,* June 3, 1991, 24.

44. Baker, "Shooting with Blanks", 64.

45. See also Honey 1984, 2.

46. Baughman 2001, 41.

47. Dippie 1982; P. Deloria 1998.

48. These groups were included to observe how Indigenous Peoples were treated.

49. Wainwright 1986, 174.

50. See Sigmund Freud, Sigmund. *Jokes and Their Relation to the Unconscious,* edited and translated by James Strachey (New York: W. W. Norton, 1960).

51. Clicquot and Klee-Ko: *Life,* March 3, 1941, 107 ("paged"); (sunny, young); August 2, 1943, 58 (family friend).

52. Vintage Doll Collector.com, "Advertising Dolls," http://www.vintagedoll collector.com/advert.htm; accessed November 23, 2008.

53. *Life,* "Alaska U.S. Frontier Waits for War," January 19, 1942, 66, and January 17, 1944, 62.

54. Dole pineapple juice: *Life,* August 25, 1941, 88 (reminds of home); June 5, 1939, 71 ("princesses").

55. *Life,* October, 16, 1939, 107 (Band-Aid, Chief Billy); July, 8, 1940, 45 (Naphtha soap); January 20, 1941, 4 (Bosco iron); July 16, 1945, 6 (prickly heat, Mennen Baby Powder); March 4, 1940, 94 (African American child).

56. *Life,* June 17, 1940, 73 (zippers, Talon, Inc.); January 12, 1942, 16 (totem pole, Penn Tobacco Co.); September, 29, 1941, 37 (majorette); March 24, 1941, 98 (Kleenex); March, 22, 1943, 84 (Pocahontas; for more see Green 1975); April 3, 1944, 104 (Gem).

57. *Life,* October, 3, 1938, 9; December 5, 1938, 6; August 21, 1939, 24; June, 16, 1947, 120; October 27, 1947, 41; September 29, 1947, 152; February 16, 1948, 13; September 19, 1949, 16; November 14, 1949, 11; March 14, 1949, 129; and July 18, 1949, 85.

58. Pontiac: *Life,* January 22, 1940, 8; September 29, 1941, 20 (dime-sized); November 23, 1942, 7 (larger, aids war effort); July 16, 1945, 43 (later, very large, portrait).

59. Francis 1992, 171–172.

60. Ronson, R-shaped figure: *Life,* March 20, 1944, 12; July 10, 1944, 91; August 7, 1944, 92; December 18, 1944, 7; February 5, 1945, 101; May 14, 1945, 108; August 6, 1945, 80; September 24, 1945, 116; October 29, 1945, 46; August 5, 1946, 104; October 8, 1946; 128.

61. Ronson radio shows: *Life*, August 5, 1946, 104; October 8, 1946, 128.

62. *Life*, June 27, 1938, 26 (Taos); December 19, 1938, 3 (Hawaiians). Wikipedia, "Millard Sheets," http://en.wikipedia.org/wiki/Millard_Sheets; and Ruth Chandler Williamson Gallery, "Millard Owen Sheets," http://web-kiosk.scrippscollege .edu/Art2800$25152, accessed November 22, 2008. The Redfern Gallery, "Millard Sheets," http://www.redferngallery.com/BuySheets.htm; and Renowned Art, "Millard Sheets," http://renownedart.com/artist.php?a=Millard+Sheets, accessed November 22, 2008. *Life*, December 19, 1938, 3 (Sheets's women with flowers).

63. *Life*, February 27, 1939, 64 (Andrews).

64. Burl Veneer's Tie Blog, http://burlveneer.blogspot.com/, accessed November 6, 2008. *Life*, February 5, 1945, 53 (Cherokee Red); September 3, 1945, 54; October 1, 1945, 64 (Champlain Blue); August 5, 1946, 48 (Tamiami Green); October 28, 1946, 20 (Mohawk Red).

65. *Life*, October 2, 1939, 8 (Arctic scene, Iridescent).

66. Largest manufacturer: Frenchcreoles.com, "Ties," http://www.frenchcreoles .com/Louisiana%20Superlatives/louisiana%20superlatives.htm, accessed November 23, 2008. "Lowest on totem pole": Best of New Orleans, http://www.bestofnew orleans.com/dispatch/2003-10-20/cover_story.html, accessed November 6, 2008.

67. *Life*, March 22, 1937, 65; and April 18, 1938, 64 (ceremonial dances); February 27, 1939, 64; April 18, 1938, 64; March 22, 1937, 65; November 28, 1938, 62; March 22, 1937, 65; May 24, 1937, 88; March 7, 1938, 68; March 27, 1939, 82 (adventure, fairy Totemland, Indian motif lounges, leis, pueblos); March 28, 1938, 72 (Greyhound; camera duo).

68. Covarrubias: see Ruby Lane, "Antique Goodies," http://www.rubylane.com/ shops/molotov/item/4774; and Wikipedia, "Miguel Covarrubias," http://en.wiki pedia.org/wiki/Miguel_Covarrubias, accessed November 23, 2008. *Life*, April 17, 1939, 4 ("hula girl").

69. *Life*, N. W. Ayer and Son: Douglas Frazer, "Robert Riggs," http://www.frazer fineart.com/SearchE2.asp?At=RobertRiggs; and The Annex Galleries, "Robert Riggs," http://www.annexgalleries.com/cgi-bin/gallery.cgi?Robert-Riggs++9935, accessed November 23, 2008. *Life*, October, 17, 1938, 2 (Dole lithograph offer); January 23, 1939, 58 ("hostesses"); March 20, 1939, 70("swing").

70. Vermont Maid syrup: *Life*, September 24, 1945, 22; November 12, 1945, 124; October 4, 1948, 21 (kettle scene).

71. *Life*, March 4, 1946, 8 (five men, kettle).

72. *Life*, December 12, 1949, 102 (women).

73. *Life*, May 8, 1944, 57 (Southern Pacific).

74. National Life Insurance Company, "Art," http://www.nationallife.com/pub lic/histarchive/art_intro.asp; and "Robert F. Heinrich," http://www.nationallife .com/public/histarchive/art_heinrich.asp (accessed November 23, 2008). Heinrich's work appeared in *Life, National Geographic, Newsweek, Saturday Evening Post,* and *Time.* He illustrated for Chevrolet, Ford, Dodge, Buick, Chrysler, and Cadillac.

75. National Life: *Life*, October 14, 1940, 2 (sapling).

76. National Life: *Life*, February 26, 1945, 4 (Algonquians).

77. National Life: *Life,* July 16, 1945, 2; August 27, 1945, 4 (aid to mother, infant).

78. *Life*, February 27, 1939, 63 (Greyhound; man views bus); March 27, 1939, 82 (Carlsbad; man with torch, elk).

79. *Life*, August 7, 1939, 65; and April 1, 1940, 55 (Haig & Haig).

80. *Life*, August 20, 1945, 56 (Gambarelli and Davitto).

81. *Life*, Nicholson Files: *Life*, March 19, 1937, 77 (harpoonist); January 25, 1937, 2 (men with walrus tusk); March 22, 1937, 71 (older man shaves youth).

82. *Life*, November 10, 1947, 49 (Statler Hotels).

83. *Life*, January 20, 1941, 4 (Bosco syrup); September 18, 1944, 109 (Lifebuoy soap); January 12, 1942, 16 (Kentucky Club tobacco); November 27, 1939, 94 (Wildroot hair tonic); "Man on the Street," March 3, 1947, 64 (news picture, tipi dweller); September 29, 1947, 152 (*Chief Read Heap Much*)

84. *Life*, January 31, 1944, 44 (Paquins hand cream); September 24, 1945, 16 (Jeris hair tonic); April 23, 1945, 70 (Ingraham shave).

85. Kozol, "Documenting the Public and Private in *Life*," 140 (minorities undiscussed); "Berkhofer 1978, 196 ("other" status).

86. Wilson and Gutierrez 1985, 127.

87. Stedman 1982, 241.

4

To Sway Public Opinion

Early Persuasive Appeals in the Cherokee Phoenix and Cherokee Advocate

META G. CARSTARPHEN

American Indian newspapers can trace their origins to two inaugural mass media efforts: the Cherokee Phoenix *and the* Cherokee Advocate. *More than simply seeking to report the news of the day, these two pioneering publications were rhetorical communication tools, as described in their originating proposals, intended to negotiate new understandings of their people. This chapter offers a perspective that positions these early Cherokee newspapers as "transactional" agents for the Cherokee Nation during critical periods in its history.*

> In a republican nation, whose citizens are to be led by reason and persuasion and not by force, the art of reasoning becomes of first importance.
> Thomas Jefferson, U.S. President 1801–1809

NEW BEGINNINGS: A HOME FOR A NEW PRESS

Customized to accommodate both the English and the Cherokee languages, the first printing press to arrive in 1835 in what is modern-day Oklahoma nearly disappeared underwater before it published its first page. Had it sunk with the boat that carried it along Oklahoma's Arkansas River, the region's first newspaper could have vanished as well.[1] But the press was rescued and eventually was established within a geography that national political and social contexts had created. By 1907, some sixty-three years later, all territorial ambiguities would be settled, as the permanent defining borders for some American Indian tribal nations, as well as the states of Arkansas and of Oklahoma, would become established by treaties and U.S. constitutional processes.[2]

What it meant to be an Indian, an "other," an Oklahoman, and an American would become shifting and contested notions over the next six decades of the nineteenth century. At the heart of this vortex of definitions were the print

After a forced relocation to Oklahoma, the Cherokee Nation started a new newspaper in 1844, the *Cherokee Advocate*. Courtesy of the Oklahoma Historical Society, Newspaper Collection (7624-38 Cherokee Advocate 1844–1877).

media of the day, especially newspapers, as they chronicled the experiences and the expectations of their audiences. The fusion of those who created the newspapers, the content they crafted, and the audiences who consumed it comprised a communication stance vital to understanding the role these early newspapers contributed to culture and social memory.

The *Cherokee Advocate,* historically, has most often been characterized as the "heir apparent" to the first American Indian newspaper, the *Cherokee Phoenix.* Published from 1828 through the spring of 1834, the *Cherokee Phoenix* gave witness to a series of tumultuous events for the Cherokee Nation, ending its publishing career when Georgians destroyed the newspaper offices in a last crippling act designed to hasten the removal of Indians from highly sought-after lands in Calhoun County, Georgia, and in North Carolina.[3]

Certainly, the *Phoenix* and the *Advocate* shared similar historic roles in their inceptions as the official publications for the Cherokee Nation. But as individual newspapers, defined as much by their different places in time and geography as well as by their nonidentical names, these publications were strikingly distinct in their rhetorical messages. A critical reading of the prepublication editorial intentions of these papers, expressed in their promotional "prospectus" announcements, reveals that principal among their goals was an agenda to move and persuade key and multiple audiences, not just to inform them. The *Cherokee Phoenix* and the Cherokee Advocate, the first Indian newspapers, reflect strategic, persuasive communication efforts, intentionally offering more than traditional news and journalism.

A PERSUASIVE PATH: CHEROKEE AGENCY
AND THE NEWSPAPER

In 1835 the Reverend Samuel A. Worcester, a white Congregationalist missionary who had spent his adult life living in the lands of the Cherokee Nation,
joined his expelled neighbors during their forced removal from Georgia in the
mass exodus that became known as The Trail of Tears. Instrumental in helping
to bring the press to the new territory, Worcester used it initially to publish
the *Cherokee Almanac* and various religious materials. However, the Cherokee
National Council resolved to institute a newspaper and passed legislation on
October 25, 1843, to authorize it under the editorship of twenty-five-year-old
William P. Ross, a Cherokee. On September 26, 1844, the *Cherokee Advocate*
published its first issue, becoming the first true newspaper to be published
in an area that had been recently constructed as both Indian Territory and
"unassigned" territory.[4] During its first series, the weekly newspaper appeared
continually until September 28, 1853, when it ceased publication—although it
would resume in two more iterations during the nineteenth century.[5]

Nearly a generation before the debut of the *Cherokee Advocate,* another
young editor, twenty-four-year-old Elias Boudinot, had issued a flyer, announcing the debut of the first Indian newspaper. Locating both Cherokee
newspapers in the traditions of journalism history illustrates precisely why
they functioned more as strategically designed advocacy media for their
founders, than as news vehicles. As such, these publications are early, largely
unrecognized models of the use of media to respond to social conditions and
to articulate opposing views—tactics that are recognized as part of public relations practices today.

Credited with coining the term "public relations" in the 1920s, communication strategist Edward Bernays recognized the power of persuasive messages to define social movements and groups. Scholarship has linked his
work in promoting the growth of public relations in the twentieth century to
antecedents in post–Civil War trends in industrialization, as public groups
began to voice their opposition to the power of large corporations.[6] Since its
formal recognition as a cohesive set of practices, the term "public relations"
has evolved in definition, enlarging upon concepts involving information
exchanges among multiple audiences, or publics, and the development of
long-term relationships. Current definitions emphasize public relations as a
"management function" whose goal is to sustain and maintain "mutually ben-
eficial" relationships between an organization and the multiple groups with
which it shares a stake.[7] Yet if one takes a long view of the conceptual roots of
public relations and its potential influence upon U.S. societal discourse, it is
important to examine the Cherokee newspapers. Subsidized primarily by the
Cherokee government, both newspapers were deliberately crafted by a people
determined to manage their image and their future.

EARLY CHEROKEE NEWSPAPERS AS
TRANSACTIONAL AGENTS

The birth of the *Cherokee Phoenix* has been seen as part of a historical continuum, a groundbreaking addition to the linear account of newspaper history. A first for American Indian media, the *Cherokee Phoenix* on the surface appears to be a reasonable facsimile of contemporaneous periodicals, featuring such structural commonalities as headlines, a masthead, and short articles imported from other newspapers. But despite the inclusion of outside material, the core content of the *Cherokee Phoenix* was all its own, intentionally constructed to persuade as well as inform. Subsequently, the *Cherokee Advocate* sought to achieve these same broad goals.

As such, the *Cherokee Phoenix* and the *Cherokee Advocate* operated as metaphorical media, symbolic of the ways these media interacted with public audiences in addition to how they were functionally designed. This transactional view examines the interaction and exchange that was proposed by both papers. Looking at the potentially symbolic, or metaphorical, roles of media, one scholar posits that they can serve in three roles: as conduits, as languages, and/or as environments.[8] As a conduit, the newspaper would simply be the vehicle for news and information from other sources. As a language, the newspaper could be seen as subordinating content to such structural elements as headlines, images, and page positioning. Or, as an environment, the newspaper could create a context for presenting news and information, serving as a site of contestation and discussion for the issues of its day. As rhetorical actors, both the *Cherokee Phoenix* and the *Cherokee Advocate* attempted to serve all three of these roles. Seen through these lenses, these newspapers were metaphorical agents, performing their representational roles through the agency of a print publication.

It was not until the twentieth century that the philosopher and pragmatist John Dewey would reassert, as a philosophical dictum, the ways in which an informed public can support a strong democracy. Dewey held that people with shared interests can work together cooperatively for social good. The notion of a "circle of citizens" with shared concerns led to his definition of what it meant to be a "public."[9] By extension, it is easy to argue that such a public stays connected through the civil exchange of discourse and ideas, achieving an intellectual and potentially action-oriented consensus. From this view, the alliance of individuals that forms a public is an ever-changing constellation, made as pliant and variable as the issues that confront them.

The pragmatism of the notable American philosopher William James, a contemporary of Dewey's, has been perceived by the historian Scott Ewen as underlying the foundations of contemporary public relations practice within this expanded notion of societal discourse. In Ewen's view James and others helped establish how social discourse could be the key tool in the pursuit of a

Front page of the *Cherokee Phoenix*, published in 1828, the paper's first year of publication. Courtesy of the Oklahoma Historical Society, Newspaper Collection (30-820 Cherokee Phoenix 1828–1834).

malleable truth, one that existed in a "perpetual state of flux."[10] Ewen further interprets James's perspectives through the modernist sensibility of the early twentieth century, as influenced by the social, political, and economic forces of an increasingly industrialized society: "As long as people accept the value of each other's truths . . . those truths assume the character of legal tender. They are passed from person to person without thought or comment like dollar bills."[11]

This exchange provides early evidence of what I call a transactional theory of diversity in mass communications, an analysis that finds such oppositional exchanges inherently rhetorical, confrontational, and strategic. This transactional exchange marks the essential rhetorical nature of public relations, a process that Heath has described as a "wrangle" in the marketplace of "ideas, preferences, choices, and influences."[12] In fact, some scholars cite this ability of organized groups to counter powerful opposition with communicative acts of protest as examples of early public relations practice.

However, for these Cherokee newspapers, the ability to manifest the competence to argue and exchange ideas was not merely a protest against specific material conditions. Certainly, had conflict not existed between the U.S. government and the Cherokee Nation, perhaps the first Cherokee newspaper could have been published entirely in its own language, with an occasional bilingual nod to curious English readers. For instance, its purposes might have been designed more provincially to serve the needs of its citizens, the way that small-town newspapers focus intently on their own environs.

Instead, the Cherokee editors were purposeful and pragmatic in creating their early newspapers, exhibiting measured rhetorical skill in assessing their intended audiences. They sought a dynamic and ongoing exchange of information that would permit white audiences a controlled view of Cherokee life, while providing a forum where the Cherokee Nation could monitor the thinking of their Anglo neighbors.

A full century after the first Cherokee newspapers had begun publication, Dewey's notion of the role of public discourse in supporting democracy and James's sensibility of a "truth exchange" articulated the strategic, transactional agenda that the Cherokee Nation had displayed in establishing a newspaper. Like no other medium available to it at the time, a newspaper—when distributed broadly—offered a space within which the Cherokee Nation could participate fully in transactional communication. As metaphorical spaces more significant than their conventional journalistic business of writing and reporting news, the *Cherokee Phoenix* and the *Cherokee Advocate* would serve also as transactional spaces where members of the Cherokee Nation could exchange its truths and barter against the fallacies, deceptions, and prejudice of opponents in a comparable marketplace of ideas. The Cherokee newspapers would also serve as rallying points for their supporters, whose contributions to their cause would build up enough invaluable moral currency that their detractors would be silenced by the wealth of their alliances. To a people who had achieved a nearly total level of literacy through the invention and use of its own syllabary, the practical need for a newspaper to enhance intergroup communication would have been useful, but not urgent. But as rhetorical tools, these newspapers were invaluable.

NEWSPAPERS AS NARRATIVES, NEWSPAPERS AS HISTORY

Publick Occurrences, Both Forreign and Domestick, which debuted briefly in Boston, Massachusetts, in 1690, is now widely viewed as the first example, in what would become the United States, of the newspaper as a "watchdog," guarding the public's rights to express social and political freedoms. Printer and publisher Benjamin Harris managed to publish only one issue of *Publick Occurrences* before it was abruptly shut down because of its criticism of the colonial government.[13] Although no independent Indigenous voice was given a place in that early journalistic effort, the Indigenous presence was certainly, if obliquely, a part of its pages as a result of the paper's vivid descriptions of Indian attacks upon colonists.

Two centuries later, the ability of territorial newspapers to give voice to the Indigenous populations remained similarly flawed. In their study of journalism in the emerging United States during the nineteenth century, Winfield and Hume investigated the patterns of historical referents, or commonly understood objects of the American experience, that selected newspapers used. The rationale for this approach was that certain words and phrases that were used repeatedly, such names of as prominent leaders and allusions to war, helped sustain public memory; among these were patterns that excluded Native Americans, African Americans, women, and newly arrived immigrants from the news appearing in the majority press.[14]

Clearly, in the absence of real news about groups marginalized socially and politically, the remaining historical record of such groups became invisible or distorted. Existing as an extension of those who owned them, early U.S. newspapers often carried the partisan voices of the printers or editors who chose to create them.[15] And although a standard of "objectivity" eventually came to symbolize the professional aim of the modern newspaper, that construct was not always an element of the American newspaper.[16] Consequently, opinionated views and information that attempted to influence public opinions were part of popular newspaper content. Perhaps more damaging were newspaper reports that relied upon provocative depictions of American Indians as savage and uncivilized. Thus a newspaper for the Cherokee in 1828—the first American Indian newspaper created and published in the United States—evolved in the context of a long colonial publishing history that eviscerated the Indian symbolically and thematically.

What united the newspaper editors of both the *Cherokee Phoenix* and the *Cherokee Advocate* was a singular purpose: to allow the Cherokee Nation a voice in the national debate about the "Indian problem." Nevertheless, rhetorical analyses of both prospectus announcements show that the names, the stated *intentions,* and the proposed *content* of these newspapers represented one cultural voice with decidedly different agendas. These differences reflected the historical shifts in the lived experiences of the Cherokee Nation.

LANGUAGE, TRANSLATION, AND A MODEST PROPOSAL

For the Cherokee, technology and invention helped make the notion of a printed newspaper leap from idea into actuality. The orality of the Cherokee language had no direct translation into English words, despite centuries of direct contact with European settlers. Thus the lack of a translation agent rendered these languages mutually unknowable except through close contact and verbal exchanges. This slow pace of one-on-one instruction changed dramatically when the self-taught Cherokee scholar Sequoyah created a code, or syllabary, based upon the pronunciation of Cherokee syllables, that could then be combined and recombined to form written words.[17] Beginning in 1809, motivated by a desire to unlock the secrets behind the "talking leaves" of the written language he saw among white contemporaries, Sequoyah had created a fully developed Cherokee writing system by 1821.[18] As a result, he not only developed competent readers of his bilingual system within days but provided a model that was adapted for writing and reading other Indian languages.[19]

The plan to launch a newspaper solidified on November 15, 1826, when both the Cherokee National Council and National Committee approved funds to build a "printing office" in New Echota, Georgia.[20] Earlier that year, on May 26, 1826, Elias Boudinot had delivered a speech at the First Presbyterian Church in Philadelphia as part of a national speaking tour. This circuit was designed to elicit financial, spiritual, and political support for the Cherokee Nation's continuing progress in the "arts of civilization," including the publication of a national newspaper.[21] Boudinot proved remarkably effective at fundraising. By 1827 the General Council of the Cherokee Nation was able to purchase a printing press and Cherokee typeface for the publication of a national newspaper, with Boudinot as its editor. The groundbreaking first issue of the bilingual periodical, known as the *Cherokee Phoenix,* appeared on February 21, 1828. Within its pages, Boudinot pledged to print the official documents of the Cherokee Nation and tracts on religion and temperance, as well as local and international news.[22]

In the early stages of planning a newspaper in that era the editor and/or publisher usually circulated a prospectus, or public announcement of intent to publish. This statement gave voice to the publisher's aims and ambitions in a way that would, it was hoped, set the proposed publication apart from other competing newspapers. The prospectus also gave details about subscriptions and contact persons, or "agents," through whom potential audiences across the country could learn of the newspaper's subscription prices and advertising opportunities.

When the *Cherokee Phoenix* circulated its prospectus in 1827, it bore the signature of its first editor, Elias Boudinot,[23] who by then had became the face of the Cherokee Nation through a series of lectures and speaking engagements. In a short 521 words, the *Cherokee Phoenix* prospectus laid out its stated intentions, or plans, by announcing its name, by describing the sections or regular departments that would comprise its content, and by discussing its use of language.

A headline in large, 48-point type at the top of the circular announces that a weekly newspaper to be published at New Echota in Georgia will be called the *Cherokee Phoenix.*[24] Even without immediate commentary or explanation, the title, which invokes a magical creature from Greek mythology, stood in strong contrast to the more declarative names of earlier papers, such as the *Pennsylvania Journal* or the *South Carolina Gazette.* In this symbolic naming, it seems, the Cherokee founders of the new newspaper fully intended it to be something more than a chronicler of contemporary events—rather, a witness to a new regeneration. A few sentences later the prospectus evokes the mythical image again as it refers to the newspaper as "this feeble effort of the Cherokees to rise from their ashes." Despite this modest pretense of weakness, the proposed contents were to be quite robust and promised to include "Laws & public documents; Manners and customs; Progress in Education, religion and arts of civilized life; Principal and interesting news of the day; and Misc. articles to promote Literature, Civilization and religion among Cherokees." With its heavy attention to such weighty topics as law, literature, and religion, the *Cherokee Phoenix* was clearly positioning itself as a participant in the intellectual discourse of its times, not merely a chronicler of sensationalist topics in crime and social deviance.

However, even before it laid out details about the paper's content, the prospectus highlighted the paper's intended unique position as a dual-audience newspaper—the fact that the columns would be filled "partly in English, partly in Cherokee." Although the prospectus does not state in what proportion the two languages will appear, the language presenting this idea balances them as if in a new partnership of meaning. The editor even hints at a kind of communicative parity by promising that "all matter which is of common interest will be given in both languages and [in] parallel columns."

A new publication of this kind might be expected to promote its intention to report the news of the day as a reason for potential subscribers to support it. But the prospectus for the *Cherokee Phoenix* claims more complex reasons for its existence. With the combination of its evocative name, its bilingual intentions, and its sophisticated content, the *Cherokee Phoenix* announced that the "great and sole motive in establishing this paper is the benefit of the Cherokees." But its audience would have everything to do achieving this success: the prospectus states in unequivocal terms that the support of the paper "must principally depend" upon those proven to be friends of the Cherokee. As he ended his appeal, editor Boudinot clearly tied the well-being of the Cherokee Nation to investment in the future paper from friendly whites:

> In closing this short Prospectus, the Editors would appeal to the friends of Indians, and respectfully ask their patronage. Those who have heretofore manifested a Christian zeal in promoting our welfare and happiness, will no doubt freely lend their helping hand.

Positioned as vehicle for transactional communication between the Cherokee Nation and the hostile United States, the *Cherokee Phoenix* stood poised to negotiate differences through an argument of shared values, faith, and laws. A little more than a year after its first issue appeared in September 1828, the *Cherokee Phoenix* extended its name in its issue of February 11, 1829, to become the *Cherokee Phoenix and Indian Advocate*,[25] paving the way for a new chapter in American Indian media.

THE NEXT GENERATION:
THE *CHEROKEE ADVOCATE* PROSPECTUS

With legal rhetoric and official signatures, the 1830 Indian Removal Act began the slow process of forcing the removal of targeted American Indian nations from their southeastern homelands in the emergent United States. By 1838–39, resistant Cherokee were forced to leave at gunpoint by the U.S. Army, joining the arduous Trail of Tears to face resettlement in unknown lands west of the Mississippi.[26]

In 1843, as the *Cherokee Advocate*'s editor, William P. Ross, prepared his prospectus for circulation, he wrote nearly one-third more than Boudinot had for the prospectus launching the *Cherokee Phoenix* fifteen years before. Ross elaborated an expanded argument about the rationale for the proposed new newspaper. Without the flourish of a bold headline, the prospectus for the *Cherokee Advocate* began more simply, with a straightforward announcement of its intention: "There will be issued at TAH-LE-QUAH, Cherokee nation, about the middle of August next, the first number of a weekly newspaper to be called the CHEROKEE ADVOCATE."[27]

As the announcement showed, the site for the new Cherokee newspaper was no longer the traditional Cherokee home in Georgia but a new capital city in what would decades later become the state of Oklahoma. Significantly, this new paper did not reclaim the more figurative title of its past, nor its emblem of the phoenix, but instead adopted the more activist portion of the original newspaper's title, *Cherokee Advocate*. In this way, the new paper seemed to be positioning itself as part of what it anticipated to be a potentially explosive discourse. For if it expected to be the "advocate," for whom would it be speaking and against what opposition?

Early in his prospectus, Ross seems to anticipate these questions and works to construct a notion of advocacy that includes speaking for, and to, different audiences. He begins by relaying the interests of the Cherokee National Council in authorizing the newspaper to provide for "the physical, moral and intellectual improvement of the Cherokee people." As the *Phoenix* prospectus had pledged earlier, now the *Advocate* too made known its intent to provide content that will be seen as socially uplifting for the Cherokee.

Closely behind this aim was the anticipated role of the newspaper to provide a legal education to its readers that was tinged with the political realities of its times. Promising to offer more than a reprint of laws and bills, the *Cherokee Advocate* committed to an engagement and debate about the Law, promising

> defence of those rights recognized as belonging to [the Cherokee Nation] in Treaties legally made at different times with the United States, and of such measures as seem best calculated to secure their peace and

happiness, promote their prosperity, and elevate their character as a distinct community.

Here, Ross actively promises to defend the role of laws designed to support the Cherokee as a nation unto itself. Building upon this goal, the prospectus further argued for advocacy beyond its own community boundaries, anticipating an audience who, too, would need to be intelligently prodded to new understandings:

> It will, therefore, be the aim of those having charge of the ADVOCATE to enlighten public sentiment, as far as possible, as to the feelings, wishes and proper expectations of the Cherokees.

As with the *Phoenix,* this prospectus for the *Advocate* also stressed the importance of having outside supporters for the newspaper:

> In commencing and sustaining a public journal in the Nation, its success must depend very much upon the kind feelings, liberality and patronage of the citizens of the United States.

But here, the *Advocate* makes a statement that is barely a request and certainly far in tone from a plea. Rather, the brunt of its argument for soliciting readers does not lie in an appeal to their sympathetic charity but rather to their hidden curiosity. Recognizing the Cherokee position as new inhabitants of a region that must have seemed foreign even to the more established communities of white Easterners who had settled there as well, the *Advocate* seemed to position itself as a conduit for supplying the "unknowable": information about the inner lives of the Indians. Adding another level of meaning to its title, the prospectus offers its readers not only keys to unlock the "mystery that shrouds" the origins of the Cherokee but insights into the character of other Indian nations:

> Our location, and station we occupy relative to the Creeks, Chickasaws, Choctaws, Osages, Senecas, Delawares, and other Indians, are such as will enable us at all times to furnish the readers of the paper with the latest and most correct border news.

Evidently aiming to position the Cherokee Nation ahead of other Indian groups within a new, emerging social order, the prospectus for the *Cherokee Advocate* pledged to use its pages as translator and mediator between Indians and others. Unlike that of the *Phoenix,* the *Advocate*'s prospectus gives no specific promises about the type of articles or topics it will cover. Nor does it commit to publishing in both the Cherokee and the English languages, even though its printing press was equipped to do so. Instead the *Cherokee*

Advocate publicly offers itself as witness, arbitrator, and a leader in the continued fight for Indian wholeness. Using the medium of the newspaper as its weapon of choice, the Cherokee Nation embarked on a renewed persuasive campaign with the *Cherokee Advocate* to influence hearts and minds of a new generation.

ONE CULTURE, TWO APPROACHES

When the *Cherokee Phoenix* debuted in 1828, seven years after the Cherokee syllabary was fully developed, it appears that despite the success of Sequoyah's translation schema, the Cherokee saw no urgency in publishing a newspaper. The syllabary language system greatly boosted Cherokee literacy rates and, one can assume, enhanced the Cherokee's already effective internal communication networks. What made a newspaper a matter of tactical necessity was the continued hostility in the surrounding world to Indians in general and to Cherokee specifically as Anglo settlers threatened Native American survival. Although both the *Cherokee Phoenix* and the *Cherokee Advocate* positioned themselves as newspapers from the Cherokee, designed to help the Cherokee, the path to this type of aid was clearly through persuasive means. Both newspapers actively sought audiences outside their own national borders and directly appealed to the sympathies of white audiences for political, financial, and social support. Both announced their intentions to present constructed representations of Cherokee life and manners through strategically selected articles about their government, their appreciation of Western culture, and their devotion to a Christian belief system. For the *Cherokee Phoenix,* when accommodation seemed the prudent approach, the newspaper focused on constructing a narrative that argued for the benefits of assimilation. But for the *Cherokee Advocate,* after the trauma of the Cherokee Nation's forced removal from its homeland, the focus was on educating its various audiences about Cherokee sovereignty.

CONCLUSION: IDENTITY TRANSACTIONS AND PERSUASIVE MILESTONES

So long as the *Cherokee Advocate* newspaper is perceived simply as the historical heir to the *Cherokee Phoenix,* as a periodical in the tradition of emerging newspapers that cropped up across the United States' expanding West, its full significance lies muted. While part of its identity rests in the newspaper traditions from which it sprang, the *Cherokee Advocate* was much more than an heir. Examined through the framework of persuasive communication approaches, both of these early newspapers, the *Phoenix* and the *Advocate,* can be read as strategically designed advocates for the Cherokee Nation. Both tried to provide the conduit, language, and environment in which to transact more favorable social and political conditions for the Cherokee people. That they were not able to sway public opinion single-handedly to more enlightened perspectives and actions concerning American Indians remains a truth that is part of the complex record of their times. But the inability to overcome dominant, more powerful discourses through their narratives does not represent a failure on the part of these newspapers to participate in the dynamic persuasive exchanges of their era. In the best rhetorical concepts of a persuasive discourse that helps society sustain an exchange of ideas, the nineteenth-century Cherokee newspapers deserve more consideration for their role in transacting and negotiating arguments about American-ness, Indian-ness, and national identity.

DISCUSSION QUESTIONS

1. Why did the Cherokee create a newspaper? What conditions had to exist to make this undertaking feasible?
2. Select a major newspaper from the nineteenth century from an online archive. Can you find any mention of Indians? If so, how are they characterized?
3. What differences and similarities exist between the prospectus issued by Elias Boudinot for the *Phoenix* and the one issued by William P. Ross for the *Advocate*? Which would you find more convincing, and why?
4. Do an online search for the *Cherokee Phoenix* and the *Cherokee Advocate*. What is the status of these newspapers today? What can you discern about how their audiences and purposes have changed over the nearly two centuries since they originated?
5. What is the difference between public relations and journalism? Which best defines the intentions for the early Cherokee newspapers, in your opinion, and why?

ACKNOWLEDGMENTS

The author acknowledges the support of the Gaylord Family Professorship in making time and resources available to research this article, as well as the search assistance given by staff of the Oklahoma Historical Society's Research Center, including Susan Wentroth (newspapers and microfilm), Debra Spindle (Library Resources), Frank Davenport (Library Resources), Brian Basore (Research, Library Resources), and Chad Williams (newspapers and microfilm).

NOTES

1. According to a research report published in the late 1990s and funded through a grant given to the Oklahoma Historical Society from the National Endowment

of the Humanities, Oklahoma had a robust newspaper publishing history. The *Cherokee Advocate*'s September 1844 issue launched the developing state's first paper, with a documented 4,339 titles identified as of 1998. For more details see *Oklahoma Newspaper Genealogies Arranged Alphabetically by County,* compiled by Mary Huffman and edited by Angie Grimes, funded by the National Endowment for the Humanities (Grant #PS-20560-92) and the Oklahoma Historical Society, 1998.

2. Oklahoma became the forty-sixth state on November 16, 1907, incorporating within its borders sovereign Indian nations and moving away from its dual designation of Indian Territory and Unassigned Territory. See Strickland's (2005–2006) essay on "Sequoyah Statehood" for an in-depth discussion of the legal transitions partitioning land ownership in Oklahoma.

3. On the dates of publication see James P. Pate, *"Cherokee Phoenix," Encyclopedia of Oklahoma History and Culture,* http://digital.library.okstate.edu/encyclopedia, accessed July 3, 2011. Theda Perdue (1977) offers an in-depth analysis of how the traditional cultural mores of the Cherokee were misrepresented, misunderstood, or ignored in the efforts to present the Cherokee Nation as highly civilized. Therefore, much of the cultural reporting in the *Cherokee Phoenix* purporting to represent authentic Cherokee traditions is suspect.

4. The first actual publication issued from this geographic location, in 1836, was the *Cherokee Almanac.* Beating the *Cherokee Advocate* by two months was another publication, the *Cherokee Messenger,* which debuted in August 1844. Ceasing publication in May 1846, this hybrid publication developed more stylistically as a magazine and was produced independently of the Cherokee government by the Cherokee Baptist Mission. See Ray 1928.

5. The *Cherokee Advocate* appeared in three series through 1906, just at the brink of Oklahoma statehood, when the U.S. government discontinued it. For details about its first three series, see Starr 1967.

6. For an extended discussion of the roots of public relations, see Ewen 1996. Like traditional historical scholarship about public relations, Ewen's work positions it as a field that arose in response to corporate malfeasance. In an alternative view that highlights the role of public relations in a broader social context see Hon 1997.

7. See Wilcox, Ault, Agee, and Cameron 2001.

8. See Meyrowitz 1993, 56.

9. See Honneth and Ferrell 1998, 13.

10. See Ewen 1996, 39.

11. Ewen 1996, 40.

12. Heath 2000, 23.

13. See Bennett and Serrin 2005.

14. Winfield and Hume 2007, 126.

15. Sloan and Hedgepeth (1994, 65) note that colonial printer-publishers were overwhelmingly partisan in their political views even as they argued that they followed a policy of "newspaper neutrality."

16. For a thorough discussion of how early newspapers adopted the "inverted pyramid" structure for news reporting and the stance that news reporting should focus on facts, not opinion, see the excellent study *Just the Facts* (Mindich 2000).

17. Debo (1940) makes a nearly direct connection between the invention of the Cherokee Syllabary to the establishment of the *Cherokee Phoenix,* writing that "as a result of Sequoyah's great invention the Cherokees established a national newspaper in 1828." However, there is in fact an approximately seven-year gap between the invention of the syllabary and the debut of the newspaper.

18. See Jackson 1995, 69.

19. Jackson 1995, 69.

20. Passed on November 15, 1826, this act to appropriate funds to build a printing office followed measures passed within the previous month (October 18) to approve the hiring of Isaac H. Harris as Principal Printer and to endorse a detailed building plan for the printing officer (November 2). See *Laws of the Cherokee Nation* 1828.

21. "An Address to the Whites," E99.C5 B65, University of Georgia Libraries, presented in the Digital Library of Georgia, Athens: Digital Library of Georgia, 2001, accessed February 8, 2009, http://dlg.galileo.usg.edu/meta/html/dlg/zlna/meta_dlg_zlna_bdt001.html?Welcome. This speech became the text of a pamphlet by the same name printed in 1826 by William F. Geddes. On Boudinot himself see James W. Parins, *Elias Cornelius Boudinot: A Life on the Cherokee Border* (Lincoln: University of Nebraska Press, 2006).

22. A facsimile of the an early issue of the *Cherokee Phoenix,* including the distinctive bilingual masthead, can be viewed online courtesy of the Hargrett Rare Book and Manuscript Library, University of Georgia Libraries, http://www.georgia encyclopedia.org/nge/Article.jsp?id=h-611 (accessed June 10, 201). A microfilm version is available at the Oklahoma Historical Society, http://www.okhistory.org/ (accessed June 10, 2011).

23. Rev. Samuel Worcester was influential in helping to raise funds for this bilingual press and, according to some scholars, actually wrote the prospectus and printed it in Tennessee. See Murphy and Murphy 1981, 24-25. Although Worcester and Boudinot were close collaborators and friends, the younger man is seen as a strong, independent editor in his own right.

24. Elias Boudinot, "Prospectus, *Cherokee Phoenix*." *Cherokee Phoenix & Indians Advocate* (New Echota, Ga.), 1828–1834. Microfilm Roll No. 30,820.

25. See Murphy and Murphy 1981, 78.

26. See Riley 1976.

27. William P. Ross, "Prospectus Cherokee Advocate" [Tahlequah, Okla.], May 1, 1845–June 27, 1877, Oklahoma City: Oklahoma History Society, Microfilm Roll No. 7624-38.

Part II

Contemporary Viewpoints

5

Names, Not Nations

Patterned References to Indigenous Americans in the New York Times *and* Los Angeles Times, *1999–2000*

RUTH SEYMOUR

As journalists sit down to write stories about American Indians, they face lexical decisions distinct from those posed in coverage of other U.S. racial and ethnic groups. Are Indians a minority group, with common issues, voting patterns, demographics, and agenda? A race? Descendants of more than six hundred distinct ethnicities? Citizens of geographically imminent nations? Reportage from two eminent mainstream newspapers shows that even the most commonly accepted terms for groups of Indigenous people can subtly communicate political bias, factual inaccuracy, or disrespect. More thoughtful attention by journalists to several "small details" in their writing about American Indians could greatly enhance public understanding of American Indian rights and sovereignty.

Right off the bat, as they sit down to write stories about American Indians, journalists face lexical decisions quite distinct from those faced in their coverage of other ethnic groups. African Americans, for example, appear in newspapers as either black or African American. Latinos are called either Latino or Hispanic. But a staggering array of possible names confronts writers covering Indigenous America. In any given sentence, journalists choose from nouns and adjectives like American Indians, Yahi Indian, tribal leaders, the Indians, Native American communities, residents of the reservation, Indian tribes, the Goshute, the Lakota, full-blooded Native Americans, and many, many more.

And as the journalists choose words, they inescapably choose sides. Are American Indians a minority group, with common issues, voting patterns, demographics, and shared agenda? Are they a group at all? Are they a distinct race, or descendants of various ethnicities (more than six hundred, in fact)? Are they citizens and politicians of geographically proximate, sovereign nations? It is certainly fair to say that the scope of lexical possibility facing U.S.

journalists accurately reflects a broader public bewilderment regarding what and who the First Peoples of the North American continent are today.

In recent decades, many American Indians and mass media scholars have repeatedly criticized U.S. media for ignoring both the individuality and the sovereignty of Indian nations in favor of treating American Indians as a pseudo-race or minority.[1] It is within this context of public confusion over the status of Indigenous peoples in our multicultural society that the unusual spread of collective referents must be examined. Given the lack of public awareness of the legal status of many tribes as nations, what might otherwise be a writer's delight in the range of word choice becomes a rhetorical battle for cultural and political survival.

SELECTION AND ANALYSIS OF REPORTAGE ON AMERICAN INDIANS

The study described here involved a random sampling of one year's coverage of American Indians (March 1999–March 2000) in the *New York Times* and the *Los Angeles Times*. Five weeks during that interval were randomly chosen to provide a corpus of news items sufficient for simple statistical tests, and from these a total of fourteen stories were identified that both focused on American Indians and met a required length of more than 400 words. (Shorter stories were excluded because space constraints limit journalists' choices in phraseology.)

From these fourteen stories a tally was prepared of every word employed by journalists to describe Indigenous peoples of North America. (tables 1 and 2 present the range and frequency of appearance of the 181 referents found in the corpus of fourteen stories.) The words seemed sometimes to have been chosen by journalists for the sake of specificity, and other times for clarity; sometimes for ease, and other times for political convenience. Some choices were connotatively neutral, some insulting, and others merely disrespectful. But all had semantic implications.

The study also investigated some nuances and implications of four of the more common lexical choices made by journalists: a panoramic (generalizing) use of the designations "Indians," "American Indians," and "Native Americans"; fairly frequent and ostracizing use of "the Indians"; a versatile, cheerfully apolitical use of "tribes"; and strong avoidance, even exclusion, of the term "nation."

TABLE 1   Sampling of collective referents to Native Americans

Nominal	Adjectival
Indians	**Indians**
the Indians	Indian leaders
American Indians	Indian people
individual Indians	Indian tribes
two unemployed Indians	(heirs of) Indian account holders
last wild Indian	
Yahi Indian	**Native American(s)**
	Native American plaintiffs
Native American(s)	Native American leaders
full-blooded Native Americans	"entire Native American
the county's Native Americans	community"
the nation's Native Americans	Native American communities
	Native American civil rights
Tribe(s)	movement
Indian tribes	Native American feelings
unrelated tribes	Native American population
Hoopa and Klamath tribes	
Santee Sioux Tribe	**Tribal**
nationally recognized tribe	tribal leaders
a sovereign tribe	tribal governments
	tribal police
Tribal Referents	tribal President
tiny Skull Valley Band of	tribal members
the Goshute	tribal officials
many Lakota	tribal specialist
Oglala Lakota nation	tribal-state cooperation
the Lakota	tribal representative
Butte County Maidu tribes	tribal chairman
the Navajo in Arizona and	
New Mexico	**Tribal Referents**
the Oglala Lakota	Hoopa and Klamath tribes
the Oglala Sioux	Santee Sioux Tribe
Pine Ridge Sioux	nationally recognized tribe
the Yana	Oglala Sioux workers
the Oglalas	great Sioux chiefs Red Cloud
the Goshutes	and Crazy Horse

TABLE 2   All collective referents to Native Americans, by category

	Frequency	
	Number	Percentage
American Indian(s)	2	1.1
Indian	33	18.2
Native American	35	19.3
Reservation	4	2.2
Tribe	59	32.6
Tribal	28	15.5
Named tribes	20	11.0
Total	181	99.9

"INDIANS," "AMERICAN INDIANS," AND "NATIVE AMERICANS"

The government violated its duty to safeguard trust accounts for more than 300,000 American Indians, a federal judge ruled today.
New York Times, December 22, 1999

In Central California, the Census Bureau still lists some reservations as "rancherias," a Spanish-based term that may offend Indians.
Los Angeles Times, April 19, 1999

More than 550 Native Americans hiked under a blistering sun, stopping several times along the way to pray.
Los Angeles Times, July 4, 1999

Although the stylebooks of both newspapers permitted it, reporters only twice employed the phrase "American Indians" (not including another instance in which it seems to have been a journalistic paraphrase of a federal job title).[2] Instead of "American Indians," journalists at both papers consistently opted for "Native Americans" or "Indians." These two proper nouns and their adjective forms accounted for nearly 40 percent of collective referents to American Indians and greatly reduced mentions of specific tribes. Interestingly, the *Los Angeles Times* items sampled almost always used "Native American(s)" and the *New York Times* items almost always used "Indian(s)."[3]

It would appear that the hardiness and simplicity of "Native Americans" and "Indians" carried real appeal under deadline pressure. *(Shout from back of newsroom: "$&%?! Anyone know the plural of Oglala?!")* A further inducement toward a pan-tribal view of Indigenous Americans is likely historical, stemming from the relatively recent era of national civil rights movements. A pan-tribal stance was sometimes promoted by American Indians involved in politics and social service. Russell Means and Vine DeLoria, for instance, rose to national and international prominence in the 1970s as pan-tribal leaders decrying pan-tribal Indian oppression. And even prior to that, especially in urban areas, American Indian clubs and nonprofit service organizations encouraged cross-tribal socializing, employment training, health services, and cultural events.

So there is some lived American reality to the pan-tribal view. Still, what we are discussing here is U.S. journalism. And at least three problems arise for readers each time pan-tribal nomenclature is employed:

- First, the terms "Indian" and "Native American" are about as usefully descriptive as would be the term "European" for either an Italian child or Norwegian grandmother. It is only our greater familiarity with European cultures that makes it seem otherwise.
- Second, overuse of the pan-tribal terms in mass media reinforces any public ignorance of the realities of discretely existent sovereign nations within U.S. borders.
- Third, some instances of race-based overgeneralization seem to have been enabled into existence via sentences with pan-tribal frames.

For example:

> In Central California, the Census Bureau still lists some reservations as "rancherias," a Spanish-based term that may offend Indians.
>   *Los Angeles Times*, April 19, 1999

Silly Indians. Why would they object to their national territory being likened to a cattle pen? This sentence fell into a self-made trap as it attempted to describe 4.1 million American Indians (as of the U.S. Census of 2000) as a single group. Perhaps the writer simply muddled a modifier and actually intended something closer to "a Spanish-based term that offends *some* Indians."

Odd, though, that the wording here, as is, has its uses. For instance, it achieves a useful journalistic purpose by glossing over a need for more discussion. As illustrated below, the more precise modifier "*some*" would quickly open a can of questions by acknowledging individual discretion—and hence according greater legitimacy—to the taking of offense.

> In Central California, the Census Bureau still lists some reservations as "rancherias, a Spanish-based term that offends some Indians.

This hypothetical version, just above, also yields a slight pause at its close, and almost seems to bounce the spotlight back to the reality of American Indians corralled on reservations officially referred to as "ranches." It could easily force the reporter to answer an editor's questions (or even preemptively address reader confusion) about why only some American Indians find themselves offended at being likened to cattle, and about how on earth a Spanish-based term (of insult, yet!) came to be part of official U.S. Census Bureau operations. Consider: All of these potential nuances and demands on reporter knowledge and time were swept under the rug with one fast generalization—the notion of American Indians en masse.

As a breeding ground for this brand of opportunistic overgeneralization, "Native American" worked just as well as "Indian."

> Sensitive to Native American feelings, [President] Clinton spoke a word or two in the Sioux language during a speech, his attempt so appreciated that members of the audience cheered even when he announced he was about to try.
>
> *Los Angeles Times*, July 8, 1999

> Also, Indians fault him for not doing a better job of cleaning up the mess over trust funds, owned by perhaps as many as 500,000 individual Indians and held in trust by the Government.
>
> *New York Times*, July 8, 1999

It does not require syntactic analysis to realize that millions of American Indians are not of one mind and cannot be honestly described as such. Why does this happen to American Indians? Neither newsroom could have published similar sentences about most other social groups.

> Sensitive to white American feelings, Clinton spoke a word or two . . .
> Sensitive to women's feelings, Clinton spoke a word or two . . .
> Sensitive to African American feelings, Clinton spoke a word or two . . .
> Also, Jews fault him for not doing a better job . . .
> Also, women fault him for not doing a better job . . .
> Also, Asians fault him for not doing a better job . . .

This abuse of the allegedly "politically correct" term "Native American" may seem quite "politically correct" in itself, but these examples show that even consciously respectful terms can be degraded by writers' subconscious assumptions.[4]

Among examples of the dangers of panoramic vision, however, perhaps the most disheartening was this:

> Ishi became famous after his surrender in Oroville as the "last wild Indian in North America."
>
> *Los Angeles Times*, April 6, 1999

This sentence appeared midway through a story about the legal battle by Butte County tribes to reclaim and bury Ishi's remains.[5] The "last wild Indian" phrase is in quotation marks, but there is no source for the quote; hence these quotation marks are used to indicate journalistic use of a common expression. Here we witness the intrusion of ethnic insult into a news story—sans rationale.

My guess is that the reporter and numerous editors who approved this version would not have let pass, unattributed and without apology or cause, these very similar expressions:

She grew up to be a "stupid blonde."
He was the last "nigger" sold into slavery in South Carolina.
September 11 was worse than when the "Japs" invaded Pearl Harbor.

Our original point, here, is that the reporter's language avoids setting off newsroom alarm bells by hiding within the panoramic. No mere quotation marks could have shielded "the last wild Yahi" from some editor's delete key. It was the pan-tribal phrasing of "wild Indian"—which likely resonated as an expression with some informal history in American idiom—that allowed a racist insult passage.

"THE INDIANS": A UNIQUELY DEINDIVIDUATING PHRASE

In the fourteen stories examined for the study, it was apparent that both newspapers were willing to refer to American Indians in a way they never used to describe blacks, whites, or Latinos. In particular, the noun phrase "the Indians" was used 13 times (ee Table 2). Not one instance of "the blacks" or "the Hispanics" or "the Latinos" was found in corresponding analyses of coverage of those groups. But journalists somehow did feel free to write "the Indians." The phrase occurred with some regularity, in fact: in four of the fourteen stories (29%) and in 13 of 176 sentences (7.3%). At least four different reporters used the phrase (three staff bylines, plus one from the Associated Press).

Were it not such a semantically powerful and troubling construction, perhaps it would have gone unnoticed by when the tally of terms was compiled, and become merged with earlier counts of "Indians." But whenever it appeared, the phrase produced an almost unabashed "othering" effect. This deindividuating and delegitimizing power can easily be made apparent via substitution:

Presumably, the Indians would drop their plans for another ballot measure if a deal is struck.
Los Angeles Times, August 29, 1999

> One sticking point remains as to whether the Indians will allow workers to be represented by labor unions.
> *Los Angeles Times*, August 31, 1999

To (hypothetically) substitute other groups:

> Presumably, the whites would drop their plans for another ballot measure if a deal is struck.
> Presumably, the Latinos would drop their plans for another ballot measure if a deal is struck.
> One sticking point remains as to whether the blacks will allow workers to be represented by labor unions.
> One sticking point remains as to whether the Jews will allow workers to be represented by labor unions.

Before exploring semantic implications, let us note the reporting context. The four stories involved here were about two news events: a judge's ruling on federal "mismanagement" of American Indians funds (*New York Times*), and negotiations between casino operators and the governor of California (*Los Angeles Times*). First, in the casino negotiations and court proceedings being covered in these stories, American Indians participated as citizens of other nations seeking clarification and enforcement of existing international law (treaties). Second, a discrete number of American Indian individuals and nations was involved in the events of each story. (Some Native nations operate casinos and some do not; some are located in California, and some are not.) Third, not every member of every nation that operates casinos was participant in the negotiations with the governor. Nor was every American Indian represented by the class-action lawsuit against the federal government personally involved in the legal machinations. So, both in terms of international law and in terms of descriptive numbers, neither coverage context factually or consciously intended to include the panorama of American Indians in its sentences.

And, yet, there rises this multivalent "the."

Fairness and precision ask of us more specificity about the practice. In fact, we can distinguish three distinct ways in which journalists in the items studied employed the phrase "the Indians." Sometimes, the noun phrase was highly multivalent: it simultaneously pointed out specific individuals and yet instantly deindividuated those individuals. Other times, the noun phrase was hardly at all multivalent, seeming only to deindividuate. In these cases, "the Indians" seems to refer to an unspecified number of individuals, tribes, organizations, or business operators—perhaps even to all California American Indians. The third way of using "the" in front of a collective referent for American Indians or tribes is discussed below under the heading "Less Problematic Uses of 'The.'"

Highly Multivalent

The judge had ordered the Indians and the government to try to reach an out-of-court settlement and had withheld today's ruling for months while both sides worked on an agreement.
    New York Times December 22,1999

The judge wrote that the Indians might be disappointed he did not appoint a "special master" to oversee trust reform efforts but said his ruling was a "stunning victory" for the Indians nevertheless.
    New York Times, December 22, 1999

These sentences typify journalistic use of the phrase "the Indians" to describe some finite number of specific individuals acting on behalf of a larger group. But the (presumably unconscious) multivalence malignantly carries a sense of justified racialization: apparently, the most important fact about the plaintiffs is their race. This was not the case. The lawsuit was not a civil rights charge of discrimination; instead, it alleged that funds were wrongfully lost or stolen by federal agencies. Once again, a simple way to experience the oddness of highly multivalent descriptors is to imagine available alternative terms. The following hypothetical sentences would have been more true to the facts of the stories:

The judge had ordered the plaintiffs and government to try to reach an out-of-court settlement and had withheld today's ruling for months while both sides worked on an agreement.

The judge wrote that the account holders might be disappointed he did not appoint a "special master" to oversee trust reform efforts but said his ruling was a "stunning victory" for them, nevertheless.

As disturbing as they are, highly multivalent sentences could be considered the lesser of two evils in the journalistic use of "the Indians," as they actually do refer to a specific group of individuals and thus technically employ a demonstrative use of word "the."

Hardly Multivalent

Other uses of the phrase "the Indians" seemed only to generate deindividuation. In these sentences, it is difficult to identify a demonstrative or specifying function for the "the." In these sentences, the (likely unconscious) use of "the" before "Indians" simply produces the semantic effect of "social distancing" or constructing an "other." One way to experience the subtle difference between more and less multivalent uses of this noun phrase is to ask ourselves, as we read: "Who? Of which Indians do we speak, here?"

> The sources said that by lifting the curb on casino-style games for the Indians, the amendment would open the door to the tribes having such gambling as blackjack and roulette and sports betting—if not now, then at some future date.
> *Los Angeles Times*, August 29, 1999

> In the wake of a state Supreme Court ruling last week that struck down Proposition 5—the Indian gaming initiative overwhelmingly approved by voters in 1998—[Governor] Davis, legislative leaders and tribal officials began negotiations to allow the Indians to keep open the doors of their $1.7 billion-a-year industry.
> *Los Angeles Times*, August 29, 1999

> One sticking point remains as to whether the Indians will allow workers to be represented by labor unions.
> *Los Angeles Times*, August 29, 1999

> Presumably, the Indians would drop their plans for another ballot measure if a deal is struck.
> *Los Angeles Times*, August 29, 1999

My sense is that the most specific possible interpretation of "the Indians," here, is that the phrase refers to all members of any federally recognized tribe (there are more than six hundred such tribes, all eligible to operate gambling businesses) which happens to reside in California.[6] But even should we find ourselves comfortable with the panoramic scope of the phrase—which I am not—we must still ask, why the "the"?

Observe and compare:

> One sticking point remains as to whether the Indians will allow workers to be represented by labor unions.
> *Los Angeles Times*, August 29, 1999

> One sticking point remains as to whether Indians will allow workers to be represented by labor unions.

> Presumably, the Indians would drop their plans for another ballot measure if a deal is struck.
> *Los Angeles Times*, August 29, 1999

> Presumably, Indians would drop their plans for another ballot measure if a deal is struck.

The power of the "the" is subtle but palpable. With just three letters, the word somehow isolates American Indians and pushes them outside of both the presumed readership and "American" norms.

Less Problematic Uses of "The"

Of course, there were many sentences in the four offending stories (as well as in the other ten examined) that more carefully navigated this terrain. In the *Los Angeles Times* casino coverage, some sentences substituted the phrase "the tribes" for "the Indians" in sentences like those above. (The word "tribe," in and of itself, proves to be yet another highly multivalent noun; see discussion below.) When the complex concept of "the tribes" is substituted for "the Indians," the deindividuating impact seems lessened; the writer has chosen a specifying noun appropriate to coverage about several tribes in negotiation with a state government.

More specific referents than "tribes" were also employed, with yet better effect, including phrases like "Indian account holders" or "tribal leaders," as well as quantifying modifiers like "300,000 American Indians."[7]

> The government violated its duty to safeguard trust accounts for more than 300,000 American Indians, a federal judge ruled today.
> *New York Times*, Dec. 22, 1999

> Judge Lamberth's ruling came in a class-action lawsuit by Indian account holders who sought court-ordered fixes to the trust system, which holds about $500 million.
> *New York Times*, Dec. 22, 1999

> The compacts are subject to approval by the Legislature and could be changed by future governors, lawmakers and tribal leaders.
> *Los Angeles Times*, August 29, 1999

Finally, and perhaps counterintuitively, heightened specificity, in and of itself, was insufficient to protect journalistic prose from the insulting power of "the." Both newspapers produced examples of delegitimization and deindividuation—still via the "the" word—as they referred to members of specifically named tribes.

> The Oglalas continue to complain of a Government in Washington with misguided policies.
> *New York Times*, July 8, 1999

> But the flash point—the trigger that roused the Oglala Lakota on this desolate reservation to rally Saturday for the second angry week in a row—was beer.
> *Los Angeles Times*, July 4, 1999

"TRIBE(S)": ONE SIZE FITS ALL

Generally, the journalists who wrote the stories sampled for the study pre-ferred the collective referent "tribe(s)" and the adjective "tribal" over all other descriptors for American Indians (see Table 2). They chose "tribe(s)"/"tribal" as collective referent words three times as often they chose either "Native American" or "Indian" and more than four times as often as they chose to name specific tribes. In all, "tribe(s)" and "tribal" accounted for almost 50 percent of the collective referents used for Indigenous groups.

Why this popularity? One reason could be the term's incredible versatil-ity. "Tribe" and its plural and adjective forms can convey multiple kinds of meaning more efficiently than many other words. They can function in ways both demonstrative (pointing at certain groups) and definitional (distin-guishing, for instance, "tribal accounts" from "individual accounts"). They can stand in the place of broadly generalizing terms (like "Native Ameri-cans" or "Indians"). Further, "tribe"-derived referents work well in coverage of business, cultural, and governmental contexts. For writers, "tribe"-derived referents operate smoothly in almost any Indian-related context. Their ver-satility and multivalence make them highly appealing to present-day U.S. journalists.[8]

Unfortunately, however, this family of referents sometimes makes it hard for readers to discern (or perhaps even notice!) whether the noun describes a group of specified number or an uncountable agglomeration, or whether it is a national government or a loosely extended group of friends and clans. The terms' very versatility can create a blurring effect.

Demonstrative and Nondemonstrative Usage
of "Tribe"-Based Terms

When a specifiable number of Indian nations are joined in a given activity, the lexical choice of "the tribes" offers an attractively narrow middle road for reporters in need of a single collective referent for them all. "Tribes," in this type of demonstrative usage, treads elegantly between the too-unspecific "Native Americans" and the too-cumbersome need to name all participating nations.[9]

> They said they support the efforts of several tribes in Butte County to retrieve the remains from the Smithsonian Institution and bury them.
> *Los Angeles Times*, April 6, 1999

> The Smithsonian maintains that [as] Butte County tribes were not cul-turally affiliated with the Yahi, they cannot legally claim Ishi's remains.
> *Los Angeles Times*, April 6, 1999

But in other instances, the potential scope of the plural "tribes" breaches the line between finite and nonfinite reference; it then becomes difficult to say whether the writer intends to describe a specifiable clustering of nations.

> But in his effort to resolve the dispute, the governor has indicated that he would back such a constitutional amendment, thereby allowing the tribes to expand the types of games they now offer.
> *Los Angeles Times*, September 1, 1999

> The sources said that by lifting the curb on casino-style games for the Indians, the amendment would open the door to the tribes having such gambling as blackjack and roulette and sports betting—if not now, then at some future date.
> *Los Angeles Times*, August 29, 1999

In these sentences, "tribe"-derived words likely functioned for the writer as a nonrepetitive substitute for the overtly generalizing "Native American(s)" or "Indian(s)"—with the added value of implicitly acknowledging multiple Native national identities. At these times, "tribe"-derived words pretend to be specifically demonstrative, but really are not.

The next two examples come from a *New York Times* story about President Clinton's visit to an Oglala Sioux reservation.

> The tribes need a Marshall Plan, like the one that rebuilt Europe, Mr. Archambault said.
> *New York Times*, July 8, 1999

> But the tribes also say he [Clinton] has deserted them on other issues.
> *New York Times*, July 8, 1999

Although Archambault is identified elsewhere in the story as a "councilman of the Standing Rock Reservation," and although representatives from more than one hundred different tribes were present for Clinton's visit, Archambault's tribe and the other tribes in attendance that day are but a fraction of the tribes semantically described as such. In the second sentence, although specifiable American Indians have apparently shared with the reporter their own political reactions to Clinton's visit and his presidency overall, the tribes to which those sources belong were not the sum of the tribes alleged here to feel somewhat betrayed by him. The tribes who were perceived to have been betrayed are not quite countable, within this sentence or within the paragraph or within the story's context; nor do any journalistic mechanisms of attribution reassure readers that the sources who are mentioned were intending to speak on behalf of all Indigenous American people.

Reproduced below are several paragraphs of political background included toward the end of the 1,200-word story; in them, readers may observe varying degrees of interchangeability and nuance attached to collective referents like "tribes."

> Mr. Clinton has been given credit for holding a tribal summit several years back at the White House. Indian leaders also praise the President for protecting tribal sovereignty in siding with Indians and helping to block efforts in Congress to curb the power of Indian nations to govern themselves.
>
> But the tribes also say he has deserted them on other issues. In 1995, Congress took aim at the Bureau of Indian Affairs, passing a spending bill that cut all Bureau operations by 25 percent. The cuts were later rescinded by about half, and that measure was signed by Mr. Clinton—much to the chagrin of Indians who depend on the annual budget, of just over $1.2 billion, for many of their operations and jobs.
>
> Also, Indians fault him for not doing a better job of cleaning up the mess over trust funds, owned by perhaps as many as 500,000 individual Indians and held in trust by the Government. The documents showing how much money is managed in these funds are missing, lost or stolen, and the Indians have filed the biggest class-action suit ever by tribes to try and clean it up. A trial is under way. In the course of the trial, two Clinton Cabinet members have been held in civil contempt for not producing records in a timely way for the court case.
>
> *New York Times*, July 8, 1999

The amazing ability of "tribe(s)" to simultaneously suggest finite and non-finite reference is like one reason for the popularity of this family of words among journalists covering Indian Country.

"Tribe" as Insufficient Attribution

At times a "tribe"-based word seems to have been adopted because the reporter hesitated to make a lengthy list of numerous tribes involved in an activity (perhaps a class-action lawsuit or intertribal summit). But sometimes this pan-tribal "Indianization" may occur from a reporter's lack of specific knowledge, both about the established Indian preference for tribal identification and perhaps about the exact names of tribes involved in a news event, or of the exact tribal identification of individual news sources. Most dangerous, it seems, were instances in which "tribe(s)" or "tribal" was used when attributing sources of information. The term is far too vague to succeed in granting credibility to the source.

As an example of the dangers here, consider the following example. Among the stories selected for the study, three from the *Los Angeles Times* cover a weekend of casino negotiations: but only once in all three is the name of an individual Indian negotiator and the name of a specific Indian tribe mentioned. All other information from American Indians involved in the negotiations is said to come from "tribes" or "the Indians." When used as attributions, these terms effectively deindividuate and delegitimize the source—lending strength to complaints that mainstream media tend to perpetuate the notion that tribal cultures despite their rich variety are somehow monolithic. To illustrate, let us contrast the attribution of informational sources in four sentences, and the nuanced levels of credibility implied:

> But Mark Macarro, a spokesman for the tribes and a Pechanga tribal leader, said at the end of a day of closed-door talks that negotiations would resume today.
> *Los Angeles Times*, Sept. 1, 1999

> "All I can say is that the governor has transmitted a proposed tribal-state gaming compact to the tribes," Hilary McLean, a [governor's office] spokeswoman, acknowledged Saturday.
> *Los Angeles Times*, August 29, 1999

The individuation of attribution in those two sentences would seem to confer a more substantial credibility on the sources than these two that follow:

> However, one tribal representative described the proposal as "insulting" because it falls far short of what voters approved in Proposition 5.
> *Los Angeles Times*, August 31, 1999

> Several tribes also disliked provisions that would require them to pay more taxes to the state.
> *Los Angeles Times*, Sept. 1, 1999

"NATION(S)": SO, WHAT IS WRONG WITH SOVEREIGNTY?

We have seen that—in spite of and perhaps also because of their vagueness— "tribe"-derived words enjoyed heavy usage by the journalists who wrote the items selected for the study. This family of words accomplishes a semantic tip of the hat to Indian nationhood without requiring—of either writer or reader—any real understanding of local and national aspects of Indian nationhood. In fact, as can be seen from further evidence, journalists find the semantic resonances of Indigenous sovereignty to be more irritating than intriguing.

The evidence is in their silence. Which of the available, acceptable words did the reporters and their newspapers *not* use to describe Indian tribes?

Two words are quite noticeably absent, or virtually so, from the collective terms that emerged in the articles studied: "nation" and "sovereign." Although these two words are commonly used in American Indian media, daily speech, and interviews, non-Indian reporters in the *Los Angeles Times* and *New York Times* strongly avoided them. The word "nation," in reference to American Indians, occurred only once, in a reporter's voice, in the 11,889 words of journalistic prose about Indians covered in the study. The descriptor "sovereign" also appeared only once in a reporter's voice, and the noun "sovereignty" not at all. [9]

The two isolated utterances of "nation" and "sovereign" were these:

Clinton was greeted by Harold Salway, president of the Oglala Lakota nation.
Los Angeles Times, July 8, 1999

For all their wants, the Goshutes are a sovereign tribe.
New York Times, April 18, 1999

Remember: We are looking at the work of some of the nation's most skilled journalists on behalf of some of the nation's most elite media consumers. It is possible that these elite reporters were honestly unaware of the concept and workings of sovereignty. And yet, to a veteran journalist, ignorance is no excuse. A more likely explanation for this phrase-avoidance may have been that these highly skilled reporters were actually very aware—but leery of opening the conceptual Pandora's box of Native sovereignty within the physical confines of their carefully composed news stories. Dropped into otherwise impeccably clear sentences, certain words could provoke questions from readers (and editors). Although those questions might be of a purely technical nature—What does sovereignty mean? So, what powers does an American Indian nation have?—it is quite likely these veteran reporters, themselves, did not know the exact answers.

True, the needed explanations are available quite readily via Internet browser. But the writing task of announcing and defining those unfamiliar legalities for a completely unschooled audience—imagine this, mid-paragraph! mid-story!—must seem daunting, indeed.

And so, we hear a silence. It happens to be a silence that rhetorically disempowers, because both "sovereign" and "nation" are words of independence and political might. It is an incredibly large silence, when we pause to think about it. How is it that two of the best newspapers in our country—especially in numerous stories about intergovernmental negotiations—manage to avoid portraying the Indian nations in our midst?

One enabling lexical mechanism, as we saw above, is the word "tribe." Alert readers of the excerpts given earlier may have already observed that that word seems to have provided the margin of daring for the one reportorial utterance of the word "sovereign":

> For all their wants, the Goshutes are a sovereign tribe.
> *New York Times*, April 18, 1999

Here, the all-explanatory word "tribe" again permits a brief tip of the hat to Indian nationhood. It is but a flicker of acknowledgment; nowhere in the story does the reporter explain the legalities of Goshute sovereignty. [10] His skillful (although perhaps even unconscious) choice of the word "tribe," at a critical juncture, glosses the informational deficit. Consider how the informational "hole" in the story would have become glaring with the adoption of the more precise word:

> For all their wants, the Goshutes are a sovereign nation.

In this hypothetical substitute, the semantic impact of the sentence resides in the word "nation," and as a result readers would expect whatever sentences followed to provide explanation and substantiation of that focal subject. Also exhibited in the hypothetical example is a collocation of words that never occurred in the actual coverage ("sovereign" and "nation").

Discomfort with "Sovereign Nations"?

In the two lonely instances in which reporters in the articles studied ventured to use either "nation" or "sovereign," the sentences appear in print in oddly disparaging ways. It is as though these reporters ritually have acknowledged Indian sovereignty—while sending their readers a nod and a wink.

> For all their wants, the Goshutes are a sovereign tribe.
> *New York Times*, April 18, 1999

> The White House presented the day as a "nation-to-nation" visit, in which the president of the United States met the president of the Oglala Lakota nation."[11]
> *Los Angeles Times*, July 8, 1999

The first sentence illogically contrasts the Goshute nation's lack of wealth with its status as sovereign. Those two facts are unconnected in international law and in history. The second sentence employs the word "nation" only after prefacing it with the high authority of the U.S. presidency and placing the phrase "nation-to-nation" within in direct quotes. It seems most likely that this journalist's use of the phrase was prompted by a White House press release. Certainly the use of direct quotes around a three-word fragment, as here, is another highly unusual journalistic practice.

Newspaper style guides warn against using fragmentary direct quotes in this way; it is known that placing quotation marks around brief phrases injects bias by implying reportorial skepticism. (That is, in the present example it sounds almost as though the reporter wrote "a *so-called* 'nation-to-nation' visit.") Even beginning classes of college journalism students are made aware of this danger. The effect in the reader's perception occurs regardless of the reporter's intent and regardless of surrounding material. In this report of the meeting between the U.S. president and the president of the Oglala Nation, some communicative need or aversion induced both the writer and the newspaper's editors to override or forget basic journalistic protocol. The simplest, most obvious explanation would be discomfort in this newsroom with the idea that Indian nations exist.

CONCLUSION

Results of the analysis of fourteen news articles containing coverage of Indigenous Americans by two nationally respected newspapers indicate that reporters and their editors relied heavily on a limited array of collective terms to refer to groups (large, small, or indeterminate) of Indigenous people. Although the most frequently used terms—"Native Americans," "American Indians," "the Indians," "tribes"—are widely accepted as correct and respectful, the manner in which they were adopted in reportage of specific events reveals evidence of bias or outright racism—presumably careless, rather than intentional—to a degree that is now seldom seen in discourse referring to other recognized ethnic groups in the Unites States (African Americans, Hispanics/Latinos, Asians).

The method used for the analysis, involving broad-based and statistically randomized linguistic study (corpus linguistics), has provided important, reinforcing and generalizing evidence to support long-standing criticisms from mass media scholars and American Indians that U.S. news coverage ignores political and legal realities of American Indian sovereignty. In these randomly chosen articles from two elite U.S. newspapers, American Indians were generally portrayed as a single racial group (presumably expecting and receiving special privileges) rather than as members of discrete sovereign nations expecting U.S. adherence to treaty law. This dangerous bias is amplified each week as reporters regularly fail to provide historical and legal context for treaty disputes and regularly fail to write about American Indian tribes and nations in a manner that indicates that they have sovereign status.

This failure on the part of two excellent U.S. newspapers to present American Indian identities and legalities clearly—and as a natural part of Americana—can only deepen the persistent ignorance and confusion of the public. It quite understandably fosters many vague, unstated (mis)impressions among a confused non-Native readership—beliefs such as "If you say you're American Indian, you can go to college for free" and "American Indians want tax exemptions and other special rights based on their racial/ethnic identity."

The good news is that the linguistic problems identified here, once noted and understood, are relatively simple to address at newspaper copy desks and even by reporters in the field. Practicing journalists could find themselves better able to produce stories that are more inviting and respectful of all communities, simply by remaining aware of two or three markers in syntax. Copy desks, as well, could greatly open up the tone of the newspaper stories for diverse readers by adding a few more grammatical scans to the dozens of potential problems they already search for.

DISCUSSION QUESTIONS

1. There are pros and cons associated with each of the naming choices available to journalists writing about Indigenous peoples. Briefly summarize these for each referent term discussed in this chapter, and come up with some pros and cons of your own.
2. As a journalist, how would you make your naming choices in each sentence? How would you choose to let the context—of history, story topic, and grammatical clause — influence your decision?
3. What are the implications of using "tribe" versus "nation" in news stories about American Indians? Explain.
4. Do you think that the statistical results about word frequency in the articles studied would have been different if the stories had been drawn from American Indian news sources and newspapers? Why or why not? How could you examine this question?
5. Using Nexis-Lexis, scan American newspaper coverage today to examine journalistic naming choices in coverage of American Indian people and issues. Do you find any possible trends of change since the article 's data were collected in the early 2000s? Do you see indicators of other possible writing patterns in this coverage?

NOTES

1. See Keever, Martindale, and Weston 1997; Weston 1996; Lewis 1995; Giago 1991.

2. The likely paraphrase that used "American Indian" was a descriptor stating source identification: "But Ron Andrade, an American Indian tribal specialist for the U.S. Census Bureau" (*Los Angeles Times*, April 19, 1999).

3. Why the newspapers differed in this respect is not clear, as both papers' stylebooks explicitly permitted either, and as our sampled stories were published over the course of a year by multiple reporters at both papers. Apparently each

newsroom (or copy desk)—either formally or informally—had determined an in-house hierarchy of preference.

4. In fact, "Native American" may qualify as "more politically correct" only among non-Natives. Among Indigenous Americans there is ongoing disagreement over the dubious distinctions between "Indian" and "Native American"; one area of consensus, however, is that tribal names are preferable to either.

5. Ishi was the last living member of the Yahi tribe. After he surrendered to white authorities, he was housed from 1911 through 1916 at the University of California at San Francisco as a living anthropology exhibit. At his death an effort was made to arrange cremation according to what had been learned of his heritage; but his brain, recovered in autopsy and sent to the Smithsonian Institution, was not reunited with the ashes in California until 2000.

6. Nowhere in the casino coverage, however, is there indication that American Indians were seeking a race-based waiver to some (hypothetically possible) California law requiring that all businesses be unionized.

7. Although quantifying modifiers such as age or group size can enhance individuation within coverage of a specific minority group, the corpus of news items analyzed here exhibited a disturbing pattern of only applying numeric modifiers to people of color. For example, this hypothetical sentence would have been unlikely to appear:

> The government violated its duty to safeguard trust accounts for more than 300,000 white people, a federal judge ruled today.

8. The evidenced journalistic comfort with the word "tribe" in coverage of American Indians is especially interesting given the negative reputation the word gained among copy editors and media diversity advisors in the early 1990s. When genocides were being covered in central Africa among the Tutsis and Hutus, world media coverage commonly referred to these two peoples as "tribes." A brief time later, when genocides erupted in what became Bosnia and Herzegovina, world media commonly referred to the Croatians, Serbs, and Albanians as "ethnic groups." This disparity in labeling was so consistent and so apparently racist that conferences, articles, and stylebook chiefs began issuing prohibitions against almost all uses of the word "tribe." Cautionary guidelines like the one still published in the CIIJ *Newswatch* stylebook (2002) were common knowledge among U.S. journalists in the late 1990s:

> "tribe": Avoid. Use "nation" or "ethnic group" most of the time, except for specific entities like a "tribal council" on a reservation. Within the U.S. Native Americans prefer "nation" because their people have signed treaties with the U.S. that recognize them as nations. Some Native Americans prefer their national affiliation instead of using generic term Native American, e.g., Navajo, Hopi, Cherokee. In Africa, avoid referring to different ethnic groups as tribes. Hutu and Tutsi are ethnic groups, just like Serbs, Croats, and Muslims in the former Yugoslavia.

In this context we can view the marked popularity of the "tribe" word in the corpus analyzed in the present study as even more noteworthy than it would be, otherwise.

9. I use the word "nations" here to designate the self-organized groupings of Indigenous Americans prior to colonization. Today, some tribes are officially recognized by the U.S. federal government as nations; others are not. This added nuance has made "tribes" an even more useful term to reporters (who are not allowed to use footnotes and would otherwise have to pause midparagraph to explain this legal inconsistency). Given the absence of information about Indian national sovereignty in this coverage, however, we cannot assume that this particular fine line of distinction troubled the minds of reporters.

10. Both words appeared three times in total; twice in direct and indirect quotation. For example:

> Indian leaders also praise the president for protecting tribal sovereignty in siding with Indians and helping to block efforts in Congress to curb the power of Indian nations to govern themselves.
>
> The *New York Times*, July 8, 1999

> The White House presented the day as a "nation-to-nation" visit, in which the president of the United States met the president of the Oglala Lakota nation.
>
> *Los Angeles Times*, July 8, 1999

11. This sentence appears midway through a story about a plan to store nuclear waste on the Goshute reservation in Utah. Tribal members had voted to approve the plan; the Utah state governor had vowed to block it. This lengthy story, like many others in the corpus chosen for study, presented a natural need and opportunity for a few background paragraphs about U.S. Indian nations as sovereign entities. But no such attempts at explanation appeared in this story, or, for that matter, anywhere in the corpus.

6

Smoke Signals as Equipment for Living

JENNIFER MENESS

Smoke Signals offers Native people equipment for living, from their simple desire to see themselves in the media, to a way to fill the loneliness experienced in an urban environment. This chapter explores ways in which the film Smoke Signals *uses Native humor, in-group jokes, and recognizable universal characters to fill the void and create a connection with Native viewers through familiar scenes of "home" on the reservation and universally recognizable characters. Resolution of the characters' problems and conflicts may offer viewers symbolic closure for their own experiences.*

> It's a good day to be Indigenous!
> Randy Peonne, DJ for KREZ Radio, voice of the Coeur
> d'Alene Indian Reservation, in *Smoke Signals*

Smoke Signals premiered in 1998 in Park City, Utah, at the Sundance Film Festival.[1] Based on Sherman Alexie's book *The Lone Ranger and Tonto Fist Fight in Heaven*, the screenplay was written by Alexie and co-produced with Chris Eyre. Accolades garnered by the film at its premiere include the Audience Award for Dramatic Films, the Filmmakers Trophy, a nomination for the Grand Jury Prize, and a special showing and reception hosted by Robert Redford. *Smoke Signals* was the first film written, directed, and co-produced by American Indians to achieve such success. It features an almost exclusively Native cast, including American Indian actors in lead roles.

Through distribution by Miramax and Shadowcaster Entertainment, *Smoke Signals* soon reached Native and non-Native audiences. Mark Gill, president of Miramax Los Angeles explained, "*Smoke Signals* hit a human chord, which was very specific in its telling but was universally understandable to a broad audience. . . . *Smoke Signals* demonstrated that contemporary Native American stories could appeal to mainstream audiences."[2] Amanda Cobb, author of *This Is What It Means to Say "Smoke Signals": Native American Cultural*

Sovereignty, remarked that "when placed in the context of the long and colonizing history of American Indians and film, [*Smoke Signals*] is an achievement because it exists at all."[3]

Hollywood has a long history of white people telling their versions of Native stories. They often use non-Native actors to portray Native people in stereotypical roles or use the voice and perspective of a non-Native character to tell the story. *Dances with Wolves* (1990), for example, was a story about a white Civil War hero, played by Kevin Costner, who "went Native" in the Western frontier. *Thunderheart* (1992), a story based on the incident at Oglala in South Dakota in 1973, relied on Val Kilmer's character, a half-Native FBI agent referred to as the "Washington Redskin," to awaken his "Indianness" and save the day. And *Windtalkers* (2002), a historically factual movie about how the Navajo Code Talkers helped the U.S. Marines gain an advantage in World War II, starred Nicholas Cage with Native actors again taking a supporting "Tonto" role. Lou Diamond Phillips, an ethnically ambiguous actor of Filipino, Japanese, and Hawaiian descent, has been frequently cast to play Native roles in several movies including *Young Guns* (1988) and *Shadow of the Wolf* (1992).

Alexie reports that he went through a lot to get *Smoke Signals* made the way he wanted. He explained to Mary Elizabeth Williams, who interviewed him about the process: "I had a lot of bullshit meetings with white producers and actors and executives, if that's what you mean. It seems that every white person in Hollywood has a pet Indian project. It's something that's very appealing to white liberals."[4]

Alexie described meetings in which it was suggested that Lou Diamond Phillips play the lead, to which Alexie responded, "He's a good actor, I like him a lot, but he's not Indian. . . . As soon as somebody said anything about casting, or about casting whites, the meeting was over."[5] Alexie's successful stand against Hollywood's attempt to control his film was the first step toward reclaiming our stories, our voice, our cultures, and our people from mainstream exploitation. Alexie took this all-or-nothing approach with Hollywood because, as he put it, "I have a lucrative literary career, I made a lot of money from my writing. I'm one of the most critically acclaimed authors in America. I don't need to do this."[6]

Smoke Signals was a major triumph in Indian Country because for the first time Native people were telling Native stories from our own perspective. Beverly Singer, author of *Wiping the War Paint off the Lens: Native American Film and Video,* explains that being self-determined as an Indian is deeply connected to telling our own stories and writing our own literature. "It is part of a social movement I call 'cultural sovereignty,'" Singer explained, "which involves trusting in the older ways and adapting them to our lives in the present."[7] Film and video revive storytelling and restore our foundation by helping Natives reconnect with relationships, traditions, beliefs, and feelings. Singer goes on to write that "oral tradition is fundamental to understanding Native film and video and how we experience truth, impart knowledge, share information, and laugh. Traditional American Indian storytelling practices and oral histories are a key source of our recovery of our authentic identity."[8]

THE COLLECTIVE "NATIVE AMERICAN"

As Native people, we know that there are many cultural differences among the tribes and nations and that we are not all the same. Customs, language, traditions, spiritual beliefs, food, clothing, dwellings, social structures, and physical features vary among tribes and geographical regions. The United States government has generally grouped all of these diverse tribes and nations together and structured policy that treats us all as one people. Although individually we maintain rich cultures and distinct tribal identities, we became the generic, collective "Native American" through these shared experiences as a result of U.S. policy.

In 1870, residential schools were designed for cultural genocide under Captain Richard H. Pratt's doctrine of "Kill the Indian, save the man." Children were taken away from their families and placed in residential schools, many of which were run by churches, in an attempt to strip away the children's heritage and break the their spirit so that they could be "civilized" and made "acceptable" in white society. The schools were overrun with diseases, and the children suffered under horrific conditions. Punishments included starvation, forced labor, sexual abuse, and torture, which resulted in the deaths of nearly half of the children who attended. The traumatized survivors of these schools often suffered from alcoholism and substance abuse, and many committed suicide. Damage caused by these boarding schools contributes to the continuing social disintegration in Native communities, because the results of the trauma were passed down to successive generations through spousal and child abuse and through neglect. The last residential school operating under this doctrine closed in 1989. Broken treaties, loss of rights, forced assimilation, and psychological trauma continued through government policies, including the Termination and Relocation Acts of the late 1940s to the early 1960s. The struggle to maintain what is left of our cultures and rights continues to this day.

In 1924 Native people were "granted" U.S. citizenship through the Indian Citizenship Act in another attempt to assimilate Native people. The civil rights movement of the 1960s made great strides toward equality for minorities, but Native people still are subjected to governmental and corporate discrimination to the present day. Institutionalized racism is perpetuated throughout mainstream American culture. Derogatory misrepresentation by Hollywood and dehumanizing sports team names (such as the Braves and the Redskins) and mascots create damaging stereotypes. Use of Native words such as "squaw," an Algonquian derogatory slang term for the vagina, improperly used to mean "woman," and commercial use of tribal names (such as the Jeep Cherokee) demonstrate a complete lack of respect and consideration. Blatant disrespect is shown for our spiritual leaders by using their names or likeness to market products against which they spoke passionately, such as Crazy Horse Malt Liquor. These are but a few examples of how mainstream culture continues to mock and degrade our existence, a reality that until *Smoke Signals* was mirrored in the movies.

Shared conditions, experiences, and situations create a collective consciousness. As cultures continually grew, changed and adapted, a "pan-Indian" culture emerged. Self-recognition as collective Native Americans gave rise to intertribal traditions such as powwows.[9] Powwows are social gatherings that allow Native peoples to come together and to celebrate culture through song, dance, storytelling, and traditional foods. Fry bread, for instance, is a traditional comfort food and staple of powwow cuisine; most tribes prepare some variation of this fried or baked dough staple. More than half of all Native people now live in urban areas, and many cannot return to their reservations as often as they would like. Attending powwows and celebrations cultivates a bond among members of the Native community and acts as a support system for displaced individuals and families by creating a substitute tribe or extended family. Just seeing other people of one's own race helps one feel a cultural connection and at least temporarily soothes the longing for "home."

AN ANALYSIS: PERSONAL USES FOR MEDIA
AS EQUIPMENT FOR LIVING

It is this pan-Indian collectiveness and the desire to connect with our own race that establishes *Smoke Signals* as equipment for living for Native people. Analysis of significant scenes reveals how familiar snapshots of reservation life invite us in to share the story of our "cousins."[10] Significant scenes from the movie may offer viewers symbolic satisfaction or closure as a means of coping with situations in real life.

Alexie explained, "The story line is a variation of the odyssey theme. In this instance, rather than focusing on a warrior/father struggling to return to his home, the plot turns on a warrior/son struggling to physically and emotionally find an alcoholic father who fled his home and died in self-exile."[11]

Alexie's summary of the film's story line echoes literary theorist and philosopher Kenneth Burke's suggestion of using anecdote as a method for literary criticism; it was Burke who introduced the theory of "literature as equipment for living."[12] Barry Brummett applied Burke's theory of equipment for living as a way to analyze media.[13] A second relevant premise is that of uses and gratifications theory,[14] which considers how people find personal uses for the collective messages in the media. Applying these two theoretical approaches in tandem, I demonstrate how the movie *Smoke Signals* becomes equipment for living specifically for Native people.

An ancient Lakota proverb tells us, "The longest journey a man will make is from his head to his heart." Burke posits that "proverbs are strategies for dealing with situations. Insofar as situations are typical and recurrent in a given social structure, people develop names for them and strategies for handling them."[15] The Lakota proverb symbolically parallels the genre of *Smoke Signals* (a road trip), as well as the characters' personal, psychological, and spiritual journeys to reconcile the realities and perceptions that exist in their minds with the truth and feelings in their hearts. The characters and audience share a universal human quest for personal resolution.

A SYNOPSIS OF *SMOKE SIGNALS*

Set on the Coeur d'Alene Reservation in Idaho, *Smoke Signals* opens with a view of a remote intersection on the reservation, where Lester Falls Apart's van has been broken down since 1972. Left right where it broke down, it became a scouting location for Lester, the weatherman and traffic reporter for the tribal radio station KREZ. He comments on traffic—"A big truck just went by . . . now it's gone"—as well as on cloud formations, local gossip, and who he saw arguing in what passing car.

On "white people's independence day," July 4, 1976, a house fire rages after a party. Baby Thomas Builds-the-Fire is thrown from the second story window of his parents' burning house. The baby is caught safely by Arnold Joseph and delivered into the arms of Thomas's grandmother. Thomas's parents are killed in the fire. Victor, Arnold's infant son, also is saved from the same house fire. It is through this event that the connection between Victor and Thomas is forged. Eighteen years later, Victor has grown up to be a handsome athlete with long, flowing hair. Thomas has been raised by his grandmother and, under the influence of the movie *Dances with Wolves*, has grown into an eccentric storyteller and wears his hair in two braids.

Ten years earlier, Arnold had abandoned Victor and his wife, Arlene, and neither has heard from him since the day he left. Arlene receives a call from Suzy Song, Arnold's neighbor in Phoenix, Arizona, who informs her that Arnold has passed away: someone should come pick up his personal effects. Through flashbacks, we see Victor and Thomas as children who have very different memories of Arnold Joseph. Thomas has glorified memories of Arnold as a father figure winning fry bread eating contests and taking him out for breakfast at Denny's. But Victor resents Arnold's relationship with Thomas and remembers Arnold as a drunk, abusive father who often beat him and his mother. Arlene doesn't have enough money to send Victor to Phoenix, but Thomas offers to pay for the trip on the condition that Victor take him along. They embark on the journey via a Greyhound bus, on which they experience racism, explore their expectations of Indianness, and discover differences in their relationships with and memories of Arnold.

Later in the story, after the men arrive in Phoenix, Suzy reveals that Arnold had accidentally started the house fire that killed Thomas's parents by shooting off fireworks while he was drunk. Arnold's guilt and regret over starting the fire and killing Thomas's parents contributed to his descent into alcoholism and the abuse that tore his family apart. It is not until Suzy reveals Arnold's secret that Victor finally begins to understand the underlying cause of Arnold's drinking and abusive behavior. After learning this truth, Victor is able to forgive his father, understand Arnold's relationship with Thomas, and reconcile the missing pieces of his own life. Through understanding and forgiveness Victor completes the symbolic journey from his head to his heart.

UNDERSTANDING NATIVE HUMOR

Alexie was born with hydrocephalus that left him with severe complications, including an enlarged skull and seizures due to surgeries to correct this condition. Often teased and ridiculed as a result, from childhood he learned the value of humor as a way to deflect abuse from other children and also as a means of personal empowerment. "Humor is self-defense on the rez," he claims. "You make people laugh and you disarm them. You sort of sneak up on them. You can say controversial or rowdy things and they'll listen or laugh."[16] Using humor as self-defense, Alexie honed his wit.

Native people have a very different form of humor from mainstream culture. *Smoke Signals* was written for everyone to enjoy, and the film is successful in engaging the non-Native audience in what Roger Welsch, author of *Enter Laughing: But Beware the Es-Ex Factor,* discusses as the esoteric-exoteric concept: "The idea that some things are appropriate for insiders to say, but inappropriate for outsiders, is a common cultural distinction."[17] Some inclusionary examples of es-ex material are the use of in-group language and a form of teasing or acceptance, "when standard insults against one group are, in a humorous way, turned back toward a member of the usually offending group."[18] Welsch, who is non-Native, uses the example of being told by an American Indian friend that he was a "credit to his race." Welsch explains, "What this friend was doing was essentially honoring me by insulting me just as so many of his kinsmen have been insulted. He knew that I understood the remark said seriously by a white man was a foolish insult. And he knew that I would like nothing more than to be included in the insulted group—his."[19]

Throughout *Smoke Signals* Alexie makes Native es-ex jokes and shares them inclusively with non-Native audience members. Jokes that reference Custer, Columbus, the Catholic Church, broken treaties, and oppression are commonplace in Native humor. Cobb explains: "The political subtext succeeds because it is never overtly political. For non-Native viewers, *Smoke Signals* is guilt free."[20] Joking about what would otherwise be sensitive topics becomes a way to defuse the tension as well as a way of remembering a shared past. Symbolic use of humor and sharing "in-group" humor becomes equipment for living because it satisfies the human need to feel connected.

An example of historical humor in the film occurs when Thomas says, "and then Columbus moves into the neighborhood, driving down all the property values." Another example can be found in dialogue between Victor and his mother, during which she asks him to promise to return from Phoenix. Victor promises to return, then asks, "You want me to sign a paper or something?" His mother replies, "No way. You know how Indians feel about signing papers."

In one of Thomas's stories, Arnold is arrested at a protest against the Vietnam War, for assaulting a private in the National Guard. Thomas tells us, "First they charged him with attempted murder, but they plea-bargained that down to assault with a deadly weapon, and then they plea-bargained that down to being an Indian in the Twentieth Century, for which he got two years at Walla Walla." Through teasing that merely being Indian is in itself a crime, the penalty for which is incarceration, Alexie gives a nod to the perception of Native people as subhuman and to the fact that, like other minorities, Native people are not always treated fairly by the judicial system.

Although many Native people have embraced Christianity, and many of them are Catholic, there exists among many American Indians a deeply rooted love-hate relationship with the church, such that jokes about religion are not off-limits. In one instance, Thomas brags to Suzy that Victor's mother makes the best fry bread in the whole world and that they use it for Communion on the reservation. Thomas exaggerates that "Arlene Joseph makes some Jesus fry bread, fry bread that can walk across water, fry bread risin' from the dead." Another example emerges in Arnold's story about a two-on-two basketball game that he and twelve-year-old Victor played against two Jesuits. Arnold says, "By the way they were playin' I could've swore they had seven of the twelve apostles on their side because every time I tried to shoot the ball, there was a storm of locusts come flyin' in an' blind me. . . . We were up against the Son and the Father and these two were gonna need the Holy Ghost to beat us." Other forms of humor are self-depreciating or make jabs at oppressors. As the game continues, Victor makes the winning basket, and Arnold proclaims, "It was the Indians versus the Christians that day, and for at least one day, the Indians won!"

Woven throughout the film are subtle explanations and insights into the culture that help non-Native people become part of the in-group experience of the movie. For example, Thomas and Victor meet two female cousins driving down the road in a car that only runs backward. The women ask if the men want a ride, and then ask what they are going to trade for it. A Native person would be familiar with the system of exchanges; however, to cue the non-Native audience in on this custom, one of the women reminds the men,

"We're Indians, remember—we barter." In another example, Thomas is talking to Suzy and Victor about Arlene's fry bread when he says, "A good piece of fry bread could turn any meal into a feast." The characters having the discussion and the Native audience would already know this, but making the statement tells the non-Native audience about the cultural significance and importance of fry bread.

NDN KARZ

While some of the "in" jokes and references may not be understood on the same level by non-Native audiences, they are presented in the film in a way that their humor on any level can be shared. Alexie describes the two women in the car driving backward as an in-joke: "It's one of those moments that I think everybody can find amusing, but non-Indian audiences are going to say, 'OK, this is funny, but what the hell's going on?' Because there is no explanation for it. Indian audiences are really going to laugh, however, because they're going to completely understand it. I call those kinds of things Indian trapdoors, because an Indian will walk over them and fall in, but a non-Indian will keep on walking."[21]

To understand the full ramifications of this particular "trap door," one must completely appreciate an "NDN Kar." Julie Tharp, author of *Fine Ponies: Cars in American Indian Film and Literature,* explains that "for the Average American, the car is inseparable from individual freedom, an icon of social, sexual, and geographical mobility . . . you are what you drive."[22] For American society, a car is a class-based statement: the newer the car, the better the make and model, the greater image of success. The automobile as an expression of culture in American Indian film and literature differs radically from this American ideal. According to Tharp, "Automobiles serve, in much Native literature and film, as expressions of characters' differences from and relationships to the larger culture."[23]

Reservation Indians are among the poorest of the poor, and by the time they can afford a vehicle, it is generally a beater in poor condition. Reservations generally do not require cars to be registered or even to have license plates and may not even require the driver to be licensed. Tharp states that reservations allow "any variety of impoverished transportation imaginable."[24] Whatever the condition of the car, it offers some sense of freedom, mobility, and escape.

NDN Karz are an integral part of reservation life. They may have any number of repurposed parts. For example, there may be a flashlight duct-taped into one of the wells where a headlight used to be, or a sheet of clear plastic may be taped up to create a back window, or a mirror from a broken cosmetic compact might be taped to what's left of the rear-view mirror. Quarter panels of all different colors and homemade spray paint jobs may complement homemade wooden bumpers held in place with old belts. There are even stories of people driving on the rims because they couldn't afford tires. The best NDN Karz have dented hoods from substituting for drums at the 49s.[25] NDN Karz are also known as rez rides, war ponies, or painted ponies, and these cars are sometimes raffled off at powwows or traded for other items. These vehicles are so loved in Indian Country that stories about them are shared and songs are even written in their honor. Because of sporadic breakdowns and their awkward appearance, NDN Karz are often compared to the Trickster, a character in traditional stories. Tricksters are often likeable and good-hearted, but their mischievous characters complicate situations or change the natural course of events.

The song "NDN Kars" by Keith Secola has been universally accepted as the American Indian pop anthem.[26] In discussing the song, Tharp writes that "the dilapidated condition of the car does not seem troubling; in fact, it contributes to the feeling of freedom—no responsibility for material possessions."[27] These cars become symbolic equipment for living as representations of freedom, the Trickster, or the companionship of a somewhat trusty sidekick.

SIGNIFICANT SCENES AS EQUIPMENT FOR LIVING

As in other depressed communities, alcohol consumption is a problem on many reservations. Philip May, author of *The Epidemiology of Alcohol Abuse among American Indians: The Mythical and Real Properties*, comments that "at least two problem drinking patterns are common among subgroups or 'peer clusters' in many tribal communities. One is a chronic alcoholic drinking pattern . . . called 'anxiety drinking.' The other is the 'recreational' pattern."[28] Anxiety drinkers are more typical of the chronic alcoholic; they may be unemployed, downwardly mobile, and socially marginal. They drink alone or with other buddies. Recreational drinkers are usually between the ages of 15 and 35, and they drink sporadically, on special occasions, at parties, and on weekends. Their pattern of drinking is comparable to the drinking habits of college fraternities.[29]

May continues: "the flamboyant drinking styles that are very common in a number of Indian peer clusters (recreational and anxiety drinkers) emphasize abusive drinking and high blood alcohol levels. Further, heavy drinking peer groups among many tribes encourage, or do not discourage, the frequent mixing of alcohol impairment, risky behavior, and risky environments. Driving while intoxicated, sleeping outside in the winter, aggression, and other unsafe practices are examples of this element."[30] Suicides, homicides, and accidents resulting in death are committed more frequently under the influence of alcohol. Aggression, confrontation, and violence are intensified by alcohol and sometimes result in permanent physical loss of teeth, eyes, and limbs.

We return to a significant scene in the movie, set on the Fourth of July eight years after the fire that killed Thomas's parents. Eight-year-old Victor and

Arnold seem to be sharing a father-son bonding moment as they ride home from the trading post in Arnold's truck. Victor looks up at Arnold with deep admiration and adoration. Arnold is drinking bottles of beer as he drives, and the mood becomes uncertain as Arnold says he feels independent and hints at making himself disappear. Because Independence Day marks the anniversary of the house fire that killed Thomas's parents, Arnold's guilt is welling up inwardly. When they arrive home, Arnold asks Victor to hand him his beer, but Victor accidentally drops the bottle and beer spills all over the floor of the truck. In anger, Arnold hits Victor in the face with his fist. As Victor weeps, Arnold tells him, "Quit cryin'. I didn't hit you that hard."

Later that night we see the Fourth of July party at Arnold and Arlene's house, and they are both drunk. Arnold calls Victor to come dance with him and Arlene. He then asks Victor, "Who is your favorite Indian?"—to which Victor several times defiantly replies, "Nobody," angering Arnold.

The next morning, Arlene and Arnold are lying passed out in bed when Arlene is awakened by a repeated banging noise. Looking out her bedroom window, she sees Victor repeatedly smashing full beer bottles against the tailgate of Arnold's pickup truck. Because Victor cannot physically confront his father or articulate his feelings, he takes out his frustration and anger toward his father, the drinking, and the abuse by hitting the truck, a symbolic representation of Arnold. At that moment, Arlene understands how much their drinking hurts Victor. She turns around, kicks the bed where Arnold is sleeping, and yells "We ain't doin' this no more! No more! We're done with it!"

Stephen Young, author of *Movies as Equipment for Living: A Developmental Analysis of the Importance of Film in Everyday Life,* writes, "It is likely that different movies have different functions for different viewers, and the commonly cited functions of movies probably have many manifestations."[31] A Native person watching *Smoke Signals* may be reminded of similar parties where someone ended up passed out in an unusual place. From a different perspective, the scene may be remindful of being at one of those parties as a child, recalling the disgust, anger, and neglect that kids feel when they see their parents intoxicated. It may also bring back related memories of sexual abuse, which although not addressed in the movie, sometimes occurs at drunken parties. Sexual assault and abuse happen to children, adolescents, and adults after everyone else has passed out and there is no one coherent enough to hear the victims or stop the offenders. The perpetrators are usually extended family or community members, and their actions are not discussed or prosecuted, in order to "keep the peace." Viewers with no personal frame of reference for such experiences may merely see the party in the movie as an event in the unfolding story.

Viewing such party scenes could be used as equipment for living from several perspectives or from a combination of experience and perspective. Young relates that a person "might view a particular film at just the right time and find [his or] her perspective on life altered."[32] Watching these scenes with memories of attending similar parties, one could see from a sober perspective how children react to being at such a party and seeing their parents drunk. This scene may open the viewer's eyes and cause regrets about what similar events in real life may be doing to the viewer's own children by placing them in such a harmful environment. From the perspective of remembering such parties as a child, the viewer may be able to resolve uncomfortable feelings symbolically through watching young Victor take out his aggression and frustration over his parents' drinking by smashing bottles of beer against his father's truck. Adult viewers might then be equipped with a new understanding that could lead to a change in their behavior.

Continuing the sequence, in the next scene, later the same day, young Victor is watching TV when his parents enter the living room, arguing. Arnold is rummaging through Arlene's purse, looking for money to buy booze. Arlene attempts to wrestle the purse away from Arnold, yelling, "It's over, no more drinkin'! Did you hear me? No more!" Arnold yells, "Let go!" and backhands her across the face so hard that her feet fly off the floor and her whole body falls like a rag doll. Epitomizing the strength and will in Native women, she stands up and faces Arnold. "Hit me again! Come on!" Victor stands up in protest to his father's actions, symbolically ready to defend his mother. Arnold glares at him and then storms out of the room.

Unfortunately, spousal abuse is not uncommon in reservation life. *Women's Health Weekly* discusses a study based in southwestern Oklahoma in which 312 Native American women, from twenty-nine different tribes, who were patients of a clinic for low-income pregnant women and women of child-bearing age, were asked to fill out a questionnaire relating to their experiences of assault by a partner. (About three-fifths, 59 percent, of the women had non-Native partners.) The study found that "thirty-nine percent of the women questioned had been severely assaulted by a partner at some point in their life. This included being kicked, bitten, or hit with a fist, being choked, or being hit with an object. One in five of the women reported that they had been 'beaten up' and almost one in nine had been threatened with a knife or a gun."[33]

In the next scene, Arnold is leaving the house with a small suitcase and his hat. Arlene throws all his clothes out the door behind him, and they scatter on the lawn. She yells, "If you leave now, don't you ever come back! You hear me? Don't you ever come back!" Arnold gets in his truck, slams it into reverse, and angrily backs out of the driveway. Young Victor runs after him, yelling, "Don't leave, Dad! Don't leave, Dad!" He runs down the road after the truck, catches on to the tailgate, and swings into the truck's bed. Arnold stops the truck, gets out, lifts Victor out of the back and hugs him tightly. "Oh, Papa!" Victor sobs. Arnold puts Victor down on the road. Arlene pulls Victor away and hugs him while Arnold speeds off in the truck. That is the last time Victor and Arlene see Arnold.

An abused woman may fantasize about standing up to her abuser. She may even fantasize about leaving him, or about throwing him out. Watching that sequence in *Smoke Signals* as equipment for living, she can symbolically live the fantasy. Abused women often stay with their abusers, but watching Arlene stand up to Arnold could be symbolically satisfying and may encourage a woman to take a stand in her own situation. A woman who is a survivor of abuse may watch that sequence and relate to her own escape from an abusive situation. She may recognize a past version of herself in that situation and realize how far she has come. A woman who has been abandoned may find symbolic closure in Arlene's actions. A man who is abusive may see throughout that sequence how much pain he causes, and perhaps because of it he will someday walk away from an abusive situation before the violence escalates and he inflicts severe physical harm or commits murder.

Watching Arnold leave Victor is heart-wrenching. The scene is Alexie's way of "exploring the feeling of abandonment" and his belief that fathers are missing in every ethnic community. He points out that "brown artists—African American, Chicano, Indian, and so on—write about fathers who physically leave and don't come back. White artists deal with fathers who leave emotionally, who sit in the chair in the living room but are gone. It's a theme that resonates. The actual physical presence of the father varies with ethnicity . . . my father did leave to drink but he always came back."[34]

Expanding on this theme, the scene could be symbolically interpreted as abandonment in other areas of the viewer's life. Young states that people value film for its ability to "facilitate emotional connections to their lives even if they [are] not sure what to do with these connections."[35] They may describe the feelings created by the films as identifying, relating, understanding, or emphasizing.

Perhaps the most humorous and well-known scene in the movie takes place between Victor and Thomas on the bus to Phoenix. Within this exchange, as the characters explore media stereotypes of American Indians, we see how they affect the characters' identities.

> Victor: Why can't you have a normal conversation? You're always tryin' to sound like some damn medicine man or something. I mean, how many times have you seen *Dances with Wolves*? A hundred, two hundred? Aw, geez. You have seen it that many times, haven't you? Don't you even know how to be a real Indian?
>
> Thomas: I guess not.
>
> Victor: Well, shit, no wonder, geez. I guess I'll have to teach you then, enit?
> *(Thomas gives a wide grin and nods his head enthusiastically.)*

> First of all, quit grinnin' like an idiot. Indians ain't supposed to smile like that. Get stoic.
>
> You gotta look mean, or people won't respect you. White people will run all over you if you don't look mean. You gotta look like a warrior. You gotta look like you just came back from killing a buffalo.
>
> Thomas: But our tribe never hunted buffalo. We were fishermen.
>
> Victor: What? You want to look like you just came back from catching a fish? This ain't *Dances with Salmon*, you know. Thomas, you gotta look like a warrior.
>
> And second, you gotta know how to use your hair. You gotta free it. An Indian man ain't nothing without his hair.[36]

In this sequence, Victor derides Thomas for internalizing a stereotypical medicine man role from repeatedly watching *Dances with Wolves*. In fact, Victor attempts to make Thomas exchange the medicine man stereotype for his own internalized stoic warrior stereotype. According to Young, "The viewing of a film multiple times over a period of years becomes a central ingredient in how a person makes sense out of an aspect of their experience and identity."[37] Cobb adds to the argument, writing that "unfortunately for Native Americans, fictional representations of Indians from a past century have become a litmus for 'authenticity' of contemporary Indian identity. . . . it also illustrates the true insidiousness of Hollywood images of Indians—these images are often internalized by the very people they objectify."[38] We understand how the character of Thomas has internalized the medicine man stereotype from *Dances with Wolves* to create his identity. But through this same process, the pan-Indian culture has embraced and internalized the characters of Thomas and Victor and used them to shape and define their own Native identities.

Later in the film, Thomas comments to Suzy about a Western playing on TV, "You know the only thing more pathetic than Indians on TV . . . is Indians watching Indians on TV." This could be an influence from the warrior lesson on the bus, and Thomas is finally rejecting his own internalization of Indians portrayed in mass media. It could be that all that exists in the media are stereotypes, and Indians learning to be Indians from watching TV is indeed "pathetic." Or perhaps Alexie is instructing Native people to reject the internalization of his own characters. Eyre discussed this phenomenon: "I grew up watching all the movies with Indians in them, and I love them . . . we loved just to see ourselves on screen. We were starved for our own image."[39]

It was interesting to observe the influence of the movie *Smoke Signals* on pan-Indian culture and how we learned to be "more Indian" through the characters. After the movie, I noticed an increase of exaggerated "Indian" cadence in conversation with Native people that mimicked the characters in *Smoke Signals*. In Indian Country, internalization of the characters was evident as people imitated Thomas and Victor's mannerisms and speech patterns. Some spoke with more stories and analogies like seer/storyteller Thomas; others acted more like the hardened, bad-ass Victor. The expression "Enit?" became so popular in Indian Country that I remember hearing it used to replace a similar regional or tribal expression. At times I would call this adopted expression to another Native friend's attention by teasing, "You're Mohawk, don't you say 'unh?' [with a rise in the palate], or I'd gently remind a Navajo friend that the Navajo word is "na?"

As Stephen Young suggests,

> One of the issues that should be important to audience research is the self-other distinction. In regard to film viewing, audience members are conceived of as possessing a sense of self that engages and interacts with a film, an externalized "other" or "object," yet when film becomes equipment for living, this symbolic object is taken into the self and takes part in altering the self, at least in minor ways. As viewers apply their interpretations, they are necessarily looking to symbols located in the world outside of themselves to find relevance for their own experience.[40]

Native people living in urban areas do not always have the opportunity to feel connected through an intertribal community. S. Elizabeth Bird writes, "Indian people do believe media representations are important, both for their sense of personal identity and literally as mediators, filtering relationships between themselves and others."[41] The pan-Indian community can be very small. These actors were community members long before they made it to Hollywood, and they continue to be part of the community after their success. Knowing these actors on any level, meeting them at a powwow, watching them play hockey, or seeing them speak at other events personalizes the movie-viewing experience. It can also blur the lines drawn between a Native actor playing a Native role and an Indian being his authentic self.

After Victor and Thomas dialogue about stereotypes, in the next scene we see Thomas emerging from a rest stop, transformed, long hair flowing in the wind behind him, stone cold look on his face, wearing a Fry Bread Power t-shirt. The tension is broken when he puts on his glasses and flashes his toothy smile, and we see that while he may have adopted the warrior look on the outside to please Victor, it hasn't changed who Thomas really is.

As the two get back on the bus, they find that their seats are now occupied by two white men, one wearing a white cowboy hat and the other a gruff-looking fellow wearing a ball cap that reads My Gun Cleaning Hat. Thomas points out politely that they are in his and Victor's seats. After a rude reply from the man, Victor tries to be the warrior and backs Thomas, which results in a stare down. The gruff-looking white man replies, "These are our seats now, and there ain't a damn thing you can do about it. So why don't you and

Super Injun there find yourself someplace else to have a powwow. Okay?" The displacement of Victor and Thomas by white men who have claimed their seats indicates that Native people are still marginalized. The displacement also symbolizes governmental and corporate injunctures of tribal lands. As Victor and Thomas retreat to empty seats at the back of the bus, the following exchange takes place:

Thomas: Geez, Victor, I guess your warrior look doesn't work every time.

Victor: Shut up, Thomas!

Thomas: Man, the cowboys always win!

Victor: The cowboys don't always win!

Thomas: Yeah, they do. The cowboys always win. Look at Tom Mix. What about John Wayne? Man, he was about the toughest cowboy of them all, enit?

Victor: You know in all those movies, you never saw John Wayne's teeth. Not once. I think there is something wrong when you don't see a guy's teeth.
(Victor taps on the seat and begins singing in the "49" style.)
John Wayne's teeth, hey-ya
John Wayne's teeth, hey-ya
Hey ya, hey ya hey

Thomas: (Thomas joins in, both are singing)
John Wayne's teeth, hey-ya
John Wayne's teeth hey-ya
Hey ya, hey ya hey
Are they false, are they real?
Are they plastic, are they steel?
Hey ya, hey ya hey
Whoop!

"Counting coup" in battle traditionally means that it is more honorable and takes more bravery and courage to humiliate an enemy than to kill him. Cobb comments that "Ironically, this is one of the most self-determining moments of the film. Victor sits at the back of the bus in defeat, but he does not do so silently. Instead of just moving to the back of the bus and chalking up another one for the cowboys, Victor uses humor to count coup in this 'battle.'"[42] This "defeat" may be another instance that contributes to Victor and Thomas's experience of what Desjarlait calls Historical Trauma Response (HRT): "Descendants of people who have suffered genocide not only identify with the past, but also emotionally re-experience it in the present. Thus, as a result of their loss as protectors and providers, Indian men in succeeding generations were affected with emotional pain, anger, and powerlessness."[43]

The after-effects of HRT seriously impact the entire culture by affecting the physical, emotional, mental, and social well-being of individuals, which also affects their families.

In symbolically besting the white men by making fun of the ultimate cowboy, John Wayne, Victor and Thomas are able to keep their pride and dignity. Their making up a 49 song and singing it loudly annoys the other people on the bus and makes them uncomfortable. But through this act Victor and Thomas prove that "there is more than one way to win."[44] This solution, as equipment for living, offers the use of traditional humor and symbolically counting coup as coping mechanisms. By making fun of and thereby "one-upping" an enemy, one can still win symbolically.

CONCLUSION

As Native people, we desire to see ourselves on-screen. Our insecurities about ourselves as a people and even our identities will continue to be influenced by our use of the media. Edward Buscombe, author of *Injuns! Native Americans in the Movies,* writes encouragingly, "These modest beginnings show that an Indian cinema is possible. Digital technology will make independent filmmaking cheaper." But he also warns that "access to distribution networks will still be difficult."[45]

He continues: "Indian films will never change Hollywood on its own ground. We won't get alterNative westerns, in which the Indians win, because if Indians make films it seems unlikely that they would want to make westerns. They have their own stories."[46] Sharing stories satisfies a hunger of spirit, and feeding this hunger is necessary for our survival as Native people.

DISCUSSION QUESTIONS

1. Uses and gratifications theory posits that people use media for personal purposes and that they receive some satisfaction or gratification from the media they choose. It has been demonstrated that mass media shape attitudes and teach us about societal expectations. From your own experience, how have movies, scenes from movies, television shows, or songs contributed to shaping personal identity? In what way do you use media for gratification? For example, songs can bring back memories and affect mood, television shows may remind you of familiar times and places, and characters may remind you of people you know or once knew.

2. *Smoke Signals* uses in-group humor and jokes with cultural references to create familiarity and bond with the Native audience. What are some patterns of in-group humor, and how is it used to build a bond among participants? For example, think about the difference in the humor when the group

is all men or all women. What types of jokes are shared that the "other" group would not understand because of their lack of in-group knowledge? Discuss other examples. What other purpose does in-group humor serve?

3. NDN Karz play a significant role in Native culture, as do automobiles in mainstream culture. In what way is your vehicle a reflection of who you are? Have you modified your vehicle in any way to make it unique? Does it have a name? What attachment, if any, do you have to your car? What does your vehicle symbolize? What role does it play in your life?

4. Think about what you know about Native people. How were those attitudes and opinions formed? Where did those ideas originate? Think about what mainstream culture has taught the general public about Native people. Discuss ways in which media influence mainstream formation of opinions, values, and attitudes. How can media be used to create a more realistic portrayal of Native people?

5. Alexie comments that it is imperative for Native people to be cast in Native roles, to make the characters believable. Reflect on how many Native people you have seen in Native roles, either on television or in movies, and discuss the difference their cultural life experience makes to the characters they play.

NOTES

1. *Smoke Signals,* motion picture produced by Chris Eyre and Alexie Sherman, Directed by Chris Eyre (Plummer Ida.: Shadowcatcher Entertainment; Seattle: Welb Film Pursuits; distributed by Miramax Films, New York and Los Angeles, 1998). All citations of the film in this chapter refer to this edition.

2. Quoted in Aleiss 2005, 159.

3. Cobb 2003, 206.

4. Quoted in Williams 1998.

5. Quoted in Williams 1998.

6. Quoted in Williams 1998.

7. Singer 2001, 2.

8. Singer 2001, 3.

9. A powwow is a pan-Indian gathering that celebrates life. Alcohol is not allowed on the powwow grounds, and an arena director makes sure that no one is intoxicated at the event. Powwows are family gatherings, and children are encouraged to participate in the dances. Traditional songs and social dances are shared, as well as honor songs for veterans and other causes, occasions, and accomplishments such as birthdays and graduations. Other honoring events, such as a "give-away," may take place. A person may show appreciation for an honor by presenting blankets full of gifts to significant people as well as to dancers, singers, and the general community. A powwow can be either traditional, where most songs are "intertribals" and everyone is invited to dance, or a competition, where

singers and dancers compete for cash and prizes for song and dance categories broken down by dance style and age. There is always food at a powwow, including pan-Indian favorites: fry bread, Indian tacos (taco fixings on top of fry bread instead of a tortilla or shell), and other traditional foods that vary by nation and region. In the Southwest mutton might be traditional fare, but in the North selections may include wild rice and venison stew or fried fish.

10. "Cousin" is a way Native people may address each other, whether they are actually related or not.

11. Quoted in West and West 1998, 29.

12. Burke 1941, 296–297.

13. Brummett 1984, 161–178.

14. Uses and gratifications theory says that people use media to fulfill needs and that those needs motivate media use. The theory also assumes that people have an active role in their use and choice of media. The theory was first assembled in Jay Blumer and Elihu Katz's *The Uses of Mass Communication: Current Perspectives on Gratifications Research* (Beverly Hills, Calif.: Sage Publications, 1974).

15. Burke 1941, 296–297.

16. Quoted in Grassian 2005, 2.

17. Welsch 1996, 64–65.

18. Welsch 1996, 64–65.

19. Welsch 1996, 64–65.

20. Cobb 2003, 213.

21. Quoted in West and West 1998, 29.

22. Tharp 2007, 79.

23. Tharp 2007, 79.

24. Tharp 2007, 79.

25. A 49 is a social gathering that takes place after a powwow and usually includes alcohol and "snagging" which means trying to meet members of the opposite sex. The name 49 comes from a story about 50 warriors who went into battle, but only 49 returned. The 49 returning warriors honored their fallen brother by singing songs in memory and celebration of his life. Songs for 49s have a different drumbeat than powwow songs, similar to the hard/soft, hard/soft cadence of a heartbeat. Many 49 songs exist as part of the culture, and new songs are made up all the time. Because the songs follow a specific call/response pattern, it is easy to sing along. In *Smoke Signals*, "John Wayne's Teeth" and the "Basketball Song" are examples of spontaneous 49 songs.

26. Secola 1987.

27. Tharp 2007, 90.

28. May 1994, 127.

29. May 1994, 128.

30. May 1994, 129–130.

31. Young 2000, 452.

32. Young 2000, 452.

33. "Domestic Violence: Low-income Native American Women Suffer High Rates of Domestic Abuse," *Women's Health Weekly,* June 10, 2004, 51.

34. Quoted in West and West 1998, 30.

35. Young 2000, 459.

36. Long hair is valued among most tribes. Traditions include the belief that hair is a gift from Creator and that it is an extension of the heart and only to be cut as a sign of mourning. An in-group joke among Native men is that the length of one's hair corresponds to the length of one's penis.

37. Young 2000, 460–461.

38. Cobb 2003, 216.

39. Quoted in Cobb 2003, 216.-

40. Young 2000, 454.

41. Bird 2001, 109.

42. Cobb 2003, 215.

43. Desjarlait 2001, 12.

44. Cobb 2003, 215.

45. Buscombe 2006, 150.

46. Buscombe 2006, 150.

7

The "Fighting Whites" Phenomenon

An Interpretive Analysis of Media Coverage of an American Indian Mascot Issue

LYNN KLYDE-SILVERSTEIN

When a group of intramural basketball players at the University of Northern Colorado took the name Fightin' Whites to protest the use of American Indian mascots, the team became an international media sensation. The short-lived notoriety surrounding the Fightin' Whites provides an exceptional opportunity to examine the issues at the forefront of the mascot controversy and to examine the stories that mainstream media outlets create about American Indians through their coverage.

MASCOTS AS MARKERS OF DIFFERENCE

Images like that of the Cleveland Indians' Chief Wahoo, with his hooked nose and grinning buck teeth, have been a part of the sports landscape since the beginning of the twentieth century.[1] This chapter examines one group's opposition to an American Indian mascot and, more important, what the media's coverage of that opposition reveals about attitudes toward American Indians in the mainstream press and its readership. College mascots like the University of Illinois's Chief Illiniwek and Florida State University's Chief Osceola who lead their teams onto the football field each week in the fall have been surrounded by controversy since the 1990s. Opposition to the use of American Indians as mascots actually began in the late 1960s, although the issue received little attention in the mainstream press until the late 1980s, when an Illinois graduate student, Charlene Teeters, grabbed the spotlight with her protests against Chief Illiniwek.[2]

There exists a growing field of research on the mascot issue itself. Several researchers have concluded that the use of American Indians as mascots misuses religious symbols, stereotypes all Native tribes by erasing their many differences, and misrepresents the United States' past by casting Natives as aggressive warriors. In their analysis of Florida State's Osceola, King and

Springwood say that the mascot "draws on the Euro-American knowledge of Native American cultures, misconceptions that paint them as savage warriors removed from the mores of civilization and constantly eager for combat."[3] Others have written that American Indian mascots misuse sacred objects, actions, and symbols like drums, feathers, and dances and, in doing so, dehumanize all American Indians.[4]

Other researchers have examined how the media have dealt with the mascot controversy. Rosenstein found that after protests surrounded the 1995 baseball World Series, in which the Cleveland Indians took on the Atlanta Braves, many reporters and editors became more open to the issues surrounding American Indian mascots.[5] Since then, some media outlets, including the *Lincoln* (Neb.) *Journal Star,* the *Oregonian* (Portland), the *Minneapolis Star Tribune,* the *St. Cloud* (Minn.) *Times,* the *Portland* (Me.) *Press Herald,* and the *Kansas City Star,* have taken a more active approach to the issue, refusing to publish nicknames and logos they deem racist or derogatory.[6] Nevertheless, the media have received their share of blame for the perpetuation of stereotypes about American Indians.

A growing body of research exists on the media's coverage of American Indians in general. Weston concluded that two myths about American Indians have survived since the seventeenth century: the "good" Indian or "noble savage," and the "bad" Indian.[7] Whereas the "good" Indian was admired for his wholesomeness, dignified manner, and closeness to nature, the "bad" Indian needed to be civilized out of his warring ways.[8] These stereotypes prevailed in newspaper coverage through most of the twentieth century.[9] At the same time, Indians were not quoted in the press; this meant they had no voice.

The activism of the 1960s and 1970s marked a turning point in the coverage of American Indians in the mainstream press. Not only were there more stories about American Indians, but Indians also were beginning to have a voice—some were quoted extensively, and others had become journalists themselves. The 1980s and 1990s saw still more coverage of American Indian issues, but the old stereotypes of "good" and "bad" Indians persisted.[10]

Several researchers have concluded that the media are in part to blame for the perpetuation of stereotypes about American Indians.[11] American Indian Movement veteran Dennis J. Banks goes so far as to say that sports journalists "engage in institutionalized racism" when they cover teams with Indian mascots as though these are nothing special.[12] According to Coleman, unless Indians continue to educate journalists, the mainstream media will never truly get past the stereotypes that still find their way into coverage.[13]

INTRODUCING THE FIGHTIN' WHITES

The story of the Fightin' Whites begins in Eaton, Colorado, a small town about six miles north of Greeley, home to the University of Northern Colorado

Every thang's gonna
be all white!!!

A "Fighting Whites" logo.
Courtesy of Charles Cuny.

(UNC). In 2000 a group of activists led by UNC doctoral student Dan Ninham, a member of the Oneida tribe, began pressing Eaton High School to drop its mascot, which many consider racist. The mascot features a caricature of an American Indian with a misshapen nose, an eagle feather, and a loincloth. Ninham and Francie Murry, a member of the Cherokee Nation who was then an associate professor at UNC, started a group called Coloradoans against Ethnic Stereotyping in Colorado Schools (CAESCS). The group presented its case to the Eaton School Board, which decided not to drop the mascot and refused subsequent invitations to meet with the activists.

The Fightin' Whites came into existence when a group of students and staff members at UNC signed up to play intramural basketball under the name Native Pride. Scott VanLoo, director of the university's Hispanic cultural center, came up with the alternative name Fightin' Whites. VanLoo, who is of Lebanese and Dutch descent, said he was frustrated by the fact that the Eaton School Board had dismissed the activists' pleas so easily.

VanLoo took a satirical approach, retooling Eaton's Fightin' Reds mascot to fit the Fightin' Whites. He added a clip art image of a white man with slicked-back hair and a necktie, and the mascot was born. Although he invited several media outlets to the team's first game, VanLoo said, no one showed up. The first article about the team ran on Wednesday, March 6, 2002, on page 2 of UNC's student newspaper, the *Mirror*. Four days later, a story ran in the local paper, the *Greeley Tribune*, also on page 2. During the next two weeks, the Fightin' Whites became an international phenomenon, with coverage by such media outlets as the *New York Times*, the *Los Angeles Times*, the *San Francisco Chronicle*, the *Toledo* (Ohio) *Blade*, CNN, the *Today Show*, and National Public Radio's *All Things Considered*. Jay Leno joked about the team during his monologue on the *Tonight Show*. Team members appeared on the Fox Network's *Best Damn Sports Show Period*, and Rush Limbaugh mentioned the story. Team member Solomon Little Owl, UNC's director of Native American Student Services, received hundreds of calls and e-mails from media outlets as far away as Canada, Japan, England, and Australia. He said he talked to at least fifty radio stations.[14] Outlets such as NBC News, Fox Sports, and CNN visited the Native American Student Services Center, a small house in the middle of UNC's campus. Demand for articles about the team crashed the *Greeley Tribune's* website on March 13.[15] So many people wanted to purchase t-shirts featuring the Fightin' Whites logo that the team set up a nonprofit company and began selling merchandise online. The company was so successful that in January 2003 the team presented a check for $100,000 to UNC to help fund minority scholarships.[16]

SELECTING MATERIAL FOR AN INTERPRETIVE ANALYSIS

An interpretive analysis was undertaken of coverage of the Fightin' Whites episode in four newspapers that serve the Greeley and Eaton communities. The *Mirror,* which is produced by students at UNC, is published three days a week during the fall and spring semesters. In 2000 the *Denver Post* and the *Rocky Mountain News* were owned by the Denver Newspaper Agency and published under a joint operating agreement. (The *Rocky Mountain News* ceased publication in 2009.) In 2000 the *Post* was published Sunday through Friday, and the *News* was published Monday through Saturday. Each paper employed its own editorial staff. The *Greeley Tribune* (now *The Tribune*), which covers Eaton as well as Greeley, is published seven days a week.

About a year before the Fightin' Whites came into being, the *Tribune* published an award-winning series of articles on the issues surrounding the Eaton Reds mascot. Around that time, the *Tribune's* editorial board discussed the option of not running racially charged nicknames and logos, but the issue was voted down.[17] In January 2002, just weeks before the Fightin' Whites made their splash, the *Tribune* published an editorial calling for Eaton to change its mascot.[18]

For analysis, issues of the four newspapers were examined for a one-month period, from March 6, 2002 through April 6, 2002, beginning with the day the first Fightin' Whites story ran in the *Mirror.* In total, eighty-two references to the Fightin' Whites were identified: twenty-five bylined articles, one brief, two wire stories, seven columns, one editorial, forty-three letters and calls,[19] one front-page teaser, and two stand-alone graphics. Twenty-eight of the stories ran ten paragraphs or longer.

ANALYSIS: THE STORIES BEHIND THE STORY

Interpretive analysis involves in-depth examination of texts in an attempt to identify themes that explain particular phenomena. Analysis of the material on the Fightin' Whites phenomenon selected from the four area newspapers identified five themes, or stories, about American Indians:

1. American Indians were not treated as a single homogeneous group but rather were discussed as members of individual tribes with distinct histories.
2. American Indians made their own news and spoke for themselves.
3. Despite their gains, American Indians were not allowed to frame the issue themselves.
4. Some readers and some reporters trivialized the issue of American Indian mascots.
5. Because whites usually occupy a position of power, many of them did not understand the mascot issue.

Theme 1. No Longer One-Dimensional

Unlike in the past, in the coverage that was analyzed, American Indians were not regarded collectively as one monolithic group but rather were discussed as members of individual tribes with distinct histories. This was quite evident in the *Denver Post*'s coverage, which put the issue in its proper context. On Sunday, March 31, 2002, the paper published a package of three articles on the controversy. The articles not only ran on Sunday, the day of the paper's largest circulation, but they also began on the front page of the "Denver and the West" section.[20] The package's lead article, which ran to thirty-four paragraphs, discussed the efforts of CAESCS—the activists who had taken a hand in the Eaton mascot activism—to rid Colorado schools of Indian logos and nicknames.[21] It was CAESCS's intervention in the Eaton controversy that had eventually led to the creation of the Fightin' Whites.

The *Post* article not only outlined the steps taken by members of CAESCS, it also recognized that the movement to end the use of American Indian mascots was thirty years old. Perhaps most importantly, the article pointed out the irony of Indian mascots created by non-Indians and provided a comment on the topic from CAESCS co-founder Francie Murry: "Many Indian mascots, Murry said, were conceived by Anglos for mostly white schools and don't reflect history or contemporary Native Americans."[22] The article went on the describe the Savages, mascot of Lamar High School, located not far from the site of the 1864 Sand Creek Massacre, in which U.S. soldiers killed about 150 Cheyenne and Arapahoe people, mostly women, children, and elders. The article was supplemented with a graphic illustrating seven American Indian logos from Colorado high schools, including those of Lamar and Eaton.

The second article in the package discussed how the principal of Arapahoe High School, located just south of Denver in Littleton, had taken the time to form ties with the tribe whose name the school had adopted, the Northern Arapahoe of the Wind River Indian Reservation in Wyoming. An Arapahoe artist had redesigned the school's mascot, a warrior in a headdress, in a rendition with dignity and without caricature, and the gymnasium was renamed for a tribal elder. The school also removed the Indian logo from the gym floor so that no one would walk upon it.[23]

The third story of the package discussed schools with American Indian mascots in towns whose citizenship consisted of American Indian majorities. The author mentioned three such schools: Red Mesa High School (the Redskins) in Teec Nos Pos, Arizona, with a population that is 99 percent Navajo; Shiprock High School (the Chieftains)in Shiprock, New Mexico, on the Navajo Reservation; and Round Rock Elementary School (the Braves) in Round Rock, Arizona, part of the Red Mesa district. The article explained that many Indians do not care about the mascot issue, but several sources articulated a more likely rationale: these mascots were viewed as acceptable because they were chosen by American Indians themselves, for schools they attended. As a senior from Red Mesa High School put it, "If white people do it, it's not OK."[24]

This series of articles was only one example of how the area newspapers did not treat American Indians as one-dimensional, but tried to convey tribal and individual identities and opinions.

The *Post* package was not the only extensive journalistic effort to cover the mascot issue in context. Less than a week after the Fightin' Whites story broke, the *Rocky Mountain News* published an eighteen-paragraph article on the issue. This article, which ran on the front page of the "Greater Denver" section, described the Eaton mascot controversy from the perspective of a former teacher in the Eaton School District. The teacher, an Anglo, and her husband, a Crow, were embarrassed at school events where American Indian caricatures were prevalent.[25]

The *Tribune* in Greeley also published columns on the issue, two in agreement with the activists and one opposed. Several other newspapers also featured stories about a complaint filed against Eaton with the U.S. Department of Education's Office of Civil Rights.[26] Several also wrote about the UNC faculty senate's vote to urge the university's athletic department not to play teams with racist mascots or names. The *Mirror*'s story on this issue quoted two sources from the University of North Dakota, which at that time played against UNC teams in the same athletic conference.[27] The *Mirror* coverage also quoted a senior associate to the president at USD, as well as a representative from the school's Native American Media Center.[28] In-depth coverage such as this helped put the story of the Fightin' Whites in context for readers.

Research has generally shown that the press has historically tended to view all American Indians as a single, monolithic group. Coverage of the Fightin' Whites, however, did not do this. The *Denver Post*, the *Rocky Mountain News,* and the *Greeley Tribune* almost always identified sources by their tribal heritage, rather than simply calling them "American Indians" or "Native Americans." All of the papers reviewed for analysis, except the *Mirror,* mentioned athletes' backgrounds on first or second reference. For instance, the *Tribune*'s first story on the Fightin' Whites identified team member Ryan White as a Mohawk and his teammate Charles Cuny as an Oglala Dakota; the *Denver Post* coverage identified the tribal heritage of one team member and four activists; and the *Rocky Mountain News* identified team member Brooks Wade as a Choctaw from the Oklahoma Band.[29]

Identification of individuals by tribal affiliation contradicts previous research in two ways: it acknowledges that American Indians are not a single homogeneous group, and it lets readers know that Indian culture is alive and well in the twenty-first century.

Theme 2. Allowing Indians to Speak for Themselves

Analysis of media coverage of the Fightin' Whites also reveals recognition in the press that American Indians made their own news and were able to speak for themselves. According to research, this is a growing trend. Weston has described a change dating from the late 1980s, when mascot protestors were spoken for by non-Native activists, to the early 1990s, when Native activists began to be treated as legitimate leaders who spoke for themselves. This change helped legitimize the American Indians' cause.[30] That this trend continued can be seen in the case of the Fightin' Whites, as all of the newspapers examined for analysis featured quotes from American Indian team members and activists in every story.

In fact, the newspapers may have gone too far in quoting Solomon Little Owl, who was often described incorrectly as the founder of the Fightin' Whites. Little Owl, a Crow and director of Native American Student Services at UNC, had the most noticeably Indian name of the team's players, who also included Ryan White, a Mohawk; Brooks Wade, a Choctaw; and team founder Charles Cuny, an Oglala Lakota. Often left out of the limelight was Scott VanLoo, the director of UNC's Hispanic cultural center. Although often quoted, he was also often not given credit by newspapers for being the creator of the team's name and logo. It could be that Little Owl was used as a source so often because of his role as director of Native American Student Services, or because he was a professional on the staff whereas Cuny was a student. However, there is no ignoring the impact his name created in print.

Ultimately the abundant use of American Indian sources in the news coverage that was analyzed for the study showed that reporters and editors were interested in allowing Indians to speak for themselves.

Theme 3. Who Frames the Issue? Who Has the Power?

Although they made their own news, American Indians were not allowed to frame the issue themselves. The issue was galvanized by the way in which the Fightin' Whites were described in all four newspapers surveyed. Even though the team's shirts clearly read "Fightin' Whites," all four newspapers, from the outset, miscalled the team the "Fightin' Whities." The *Mirror's* student reporter got the team's name wrong in first story written about the team, which ran March 6, and it is quite likely that the three other papers simply repeated the mistake as they found it.[31] By the next story, however, on March 15, the *Mirror* had corrected its error, and further issues contained no more references to "Fightin' Whities." The March 15 story included an informational graphic that explained the mistake: "The Fightin' Whites intramural basketball team reiterated Thursday that the name of the team is Fightin' Whites, not Fightin' Whities."[32] The *Tribune* and the *Post* were not so quick to change.

The *Tribune* continued to refer to the team as the "Fightin' Whities" for another two weeks after *Mirror's* correction. A front-page graphic in the *Tribune* on March 29 at last stated that the team members wanted to be referred to as the "Fightin' Whites" because of the negative connotation of "Whities."[33] In that day's story, as well as in all subsequent stories, the *Tribune* correctly called the team the Fightin' Whites.

The *Post* never stopped using the name Fightin' Whities. In several stories the reporter stated that the team's name had evolved from Native Pride to the Fightin' Whites to the "more in-your-face Fightin' Whities."[34] The *Rocky Mountain News* continued to use "Whities" in several stories and, like the *Post,* included in its coverage a sentence inaccurately describing the evolution of the name: "But the nickname has evolved to the more-barbed 'The Fightin' Whities.'"[35] In all, the *Tribune,* the *Post,* and the *News* ran eleven main headlines, two subheads, five jump headlines, and eleven leads containing the word "Whities." Given that many people read no more than headlines and leads, these statistics represent a troubling degree of misrepresentation.

Many readers probably assumed that the name of the team was in fact "Fightin' Whities," which has a very different connotation from "Fightin' Whites." Although "Whites" might be seen as derogatory, it does not carry the overtly negative overtones of "Whitie." That the *Denver Post,* which is read by people throughout the state of Colorado and beyond, continued to call the team by the wrong name for an entire month is especially problematic, because many readers would have known next to nothing of the background story of the Eaton High School Reds and CAESCS, the group that had initiated the call for Eaton High School to change its mascot. In fact, the only way most readers outside Weld County ordinarily find out about the area is from the *Post* and the *News.*

That the *Mirror's* prompt and prominent correction of its initial misspelling of the team's name was not followed quickly and consistently by other area newspapers that covered the story in depth poses the question of just who was creating the story as it unfolded. That the two area newspapers with wider circulation that carried the story, the *Post* and the *News,* persisted in reproducing the misspelling and embellished it with comments suggesting that it had been intentional on the part of the team, makes abundantly clear that for some, at least, the power of the story overrode the interests and stated preferences of the team members themselves, whose aim had been to point up a difficult issue, not create an "in your face" reaction to it.

Theme 4. Trivializing the Issue, and the Indian

Some readers, and some reporters as well, made fun of the issue, belittling the idea that Indian-themed sports and school mascots could truly cause harm. The *Rocky Mountain News* and the *Greeley Tribune* both reported on a Denver radio station's attempt to change the name of Eaton's mascot to the "Eaton Beavers." The station had even commissioned t-shirts, complete with a picture of a beaver reclining on its back. A March 14 *Tribune* story devoted seven paragraphs to this stunt, and a *News* story devoted one paragraph to it.[36] One *Tribune* caller referred to the mascot issue as "namby-pamby," and another called it "trivial."[37] After a story about the dangers of obesity appeared in the *Post,* several readers wrote in to say that the common sports nickname "Huskies" is worse than names like "Redskins" and "Savages," because obesity is so unhealthy.[38] Several readers obliquely compared Indians to animals, asking why animal rights activists did not similarly protest the use of animal nicknames and images for mascots. Even columnists got in on the act. Ed Quillen of the *Post,* a former newspaper editor, wrote that "hardly anyone takes this mascot stuff seriously."[39] He compared the Reds to other possibly derogatory nicknames, such as the Demons (anti-Christian), Wizards (referring to the Ku Klux Klan), and Trojans (sexual overtones). In his weekly column Mike Peters of the *Tribune* devoted two paragraphs to the issue, joking that the Eaton School Board had started the controversy to "brighten people's lives" during the winter months. He called the controversy a "fun issue" and then quipped that Eaton's real mascot should become the "Fightin' Green Artichoke . . . as long as we don't offend vegetarians."[40]

Trivialization of the mascot issue is nothing new for American Indian activists, who have been told again and again that they should stick to the "important" issues instead of focusing on sports logos. A guest columnist in the *Tribune* indeed wrote that activists should focus on "societal wrongs" instead of wasting their time on mascots.[41] The writer failed to mention what any of those "societal wrongs" might be.

When the researcher Laurel Davis interviewed activists working to end the use of racist mascots, she found that when the activists did work on the "important" issues, these did not garner anywhere near the media attention that mascot controversies did.[42] Charles Cuny, founder of the team that became the Fightin' Whites, echoed those sentiments, explaining that most American Indians are in fact more interested in issues like improved health care, tribal treaties, and mineral rights. But airing the issues about Indian-themed mascots can open a path toward dialogue about those more significant concerns.[43]

Theme 5. Whites Just Don't Get It—How Could They?

Because most whites occupy positions of power without even realizing it, many have not understood the issue of American Indian mascots and its ramifications. This theme was evident in readers' letters and phone calls to the area newspapers that covered the Fightin' Whites story, as well as in two staff-written columns. To be fair, several letters and phone calls to the editor showed that white readers understood the sarcasm in the Fightin' Whites' choice of their team name, and many sympathized with the cause. Many other letters and calls, however, showed just how difficult it is to get a minority point across to members of a majority. Fourteen letter-writers or callers made the general point that as they were not offended by the Fightin' Whites' team name and mascot, so Indians should not be offended by the Reds mascot and other mascots with Indian attributes. Several of these correspondents compared the Eaton Reds to other mascots named for human ethnic groups, like the Notre Dame Fighting Irish and the Minnesota Vikings. A small sampling of the calls and letters is worth presenting here:

> It doesn't offend me because I recognize that mascots are caricatures of real life—exaggerations meant to represent courage and strength of a school.[44]

> Years from now, when white guys like me are studied in history because we have long been relegated to the scrap heap of modern culture, I'll be proud my heritage is remembered.[45]

> News flash, I'm proud to be white—Italian and Norwegian to be exact.[46]

> There's nothing wrong with being an Indian any more than there's something wrong with being an Irishman.[47]

> Maybe they should look at it as a compliment to their race.[48]

> I would be highly honored by Fightin' Welshman.[49]

> Thank you so much for considering white people worthy enough to be a mascot of an athletic team.[50]

> I'm glad that they finally have a team that represents us. They need more of them.[51]

Several white people actually canceled their orders for t-shirts when it was announced that the clothing would now include the phrase "Fighting the use of Native American stereotypes."[52]

That some white people felt proud to be represented by the caricature of the Fightin' Whites shows how difficult it is for minorities to make the majority understand their issues. In a column about this problem in the *Rocky Mountain News* Roger Hernandez wrote that it is impossible to insult white people with words like "gringo," "honky" and "whitie" because regardless of the intended slur, whites remain part of the dominant culture.[53] Sportswriter Ross Maak of the *Greeley Tribune* took a similar tack when he wrote that although white stereotypes do exist in the sports world, they do not offend people the way the Eaton Reds mascot offends.

William Hilliard, editor of the *Oregonian,* discussed this idea in his explanation of why his paper stopped using racially charged nicknames and logos. Hilliard, who is African American, at first did not see the harm in American Indian mascots. Now, though, he likens the use of American Indian nicknames in sports to his son's being pulled over by highway police just for being black. Both of these issues, he says, are difficult for white people to understand because whites are rarely, if ever, exposed to real prejudice.

CONCLUSION: ROADBLOCKS TO UNDERSTANDING MEDIATED MASCOTS

The analysis reported here revealed five themes, or stories, about American Indians that emerged from area newspapers' coverage of the Fightin' Whites phenomenon. These stories can tell us something about how both the mainstream media and mainstream Americans view American Indians.

Theme 1 involved the important evidence that in this instance American Indians were not regarded together as one generalized group of people but rather were discussed as members of individual tribes with distinct histories. This stance shows an improvement in attitude over evidence discussed in much of the existing literature, which concludes that the use of American Indian mascots reinforces the false idea that Indians are a homogeneous group. When American Indians are discussed as Crow, Lakota, or Oneida, they occupy equal footing with Europeans described as French, German, and Italian. When American Indian issues are put in their proper context, readers may learn something more about them than what mascots tell them—that Indians wear feathers and carry spears. This is the beginning of nonbiased coverage.

Theme 2 relates to how American Indians made their own news and spoke for themselves. This growing trend, which began in the late twentieth century, is another way in which readers can learn that American Indians are more than logos, with ideas and stories independent of the stereotypes perpetuated by the use of mascots. Coverage of this nature helps make Indians seem like more than mascots; instead, it makes them look like ordinary Americans.

Theme 3 focused on the fact that despite their gains, American Indians were not allowed to frame the Fightin' Whites issue themselves. The mainstream media in the local area made the Fightin' Whites into the Fightin'

Whities. A newspaper with statewide readership continued to use the incorrect name throughout its coverage, and a local paper took two weeks to correct the mistake. What does this say about how the press views American Indians, if newspapers will not take the stated and published wishes of the newsmakers into account? This case is particularly troubling for two reasons. First, several of the stories which used the word "Whities" in headlines and copy were accompanied by photographs that clearly showed the team's shirts, which carried the logo "Go Fightin' Whites." This shows that journalists were either not paying attention or did not care. Whichever the case, something was definitely wrong. Second, the word "Whities" is much more negative in tone than "Whites." In changing the team's name, the newspapers attributed a confrontational tone to the Fightin' Whites' cause—never intended by the team—that could not have been stripped away easily, despite the corrections run in the UNC *Mirror* and the *Greeley Tribune*. In sticking with the name "Fightin' Whities" for an entire month, the *Denver Post* invested the team and its cause with a hostile dimension that probably affected the manner in which readers reacted to the issue.

Theme 4 focused on how readers and reporters trivialized the issue of American Indian mascots. Combined with research indicating that the use of American Indian mascots dehumanizes American Indians, this levity is quite troubling. It is not surprising, however, when one considers that newspapers themselves trivialized the mascot issue by not allowing the activists the courtesy of maintaining the spelling of their own team's name. More important, however, is that in trivializing the issue of mascots, the newspapers also trivialized American Indians in general, as well as the activists involved in particular. Through trivialization, newspapers created a picture of American Indians as unimportant to mainstream American life.

Theme 5 illustrated how whites, who are usually in a position of majority and power, have trouble understanding how ethnic or racial nicknames and mascots can cause harm. That many people do not even realize that they occupy positions of power makes it more difficult for whites to understand the problem. The issue of power undergirds each of the other four themes as well. American Indians gain power when they are treated as equals, not as a homogeneous group, and they gain power when they can speak for themselves, report their own news. Just as it seems like they are gaining equality, however, American Indians lose that power when they are not allowed to frame their own issues in the public eye. They lose that power when they and their stories are trivialized. They lose that power when their pleas for change are ignored by whites who hold even more power.

More than a quarter of a century ago, Berkhofer wrote that whites were able to classify all American Indians into a stereotype because they had the power to do so.[54] The present study indicates that not much has changed. As long as American Indians lack the power to lend or deny their names to schools and athletic teams on terms they find acceptable, create the related logos, and frame the related news, their issues will be ignored until people like the Fightin' Whites grab the headlines for a few weeks. This not only places a burden on activists, it also creates a double standard.

Rosenstein noted that American Indians face a perplexing conundrum: the media refuse to acknowledge their issues unless they are "newsworthy," yet Indian-related mascots and team names remain in the news every day.[55] Because few newspapers have chosen to refuse them, logos like the Cleveland Indians' Chief Wahoo and the Eaton Reds' mascot, as well as names like the National Football League's Washington Redskins, are considered acceptable for inclusion in the sports section each and every day. To make the opposite view heard, by contrast, activists must create a newsworthy event like naming their team the Fightin' Whites. This double standard indicates that American Indians still lack the power to make their issues heard by the majority. The news media can help distribute that power equally by continuing to perfect its coverage of American Indian issues.

DISCUSSION QUESTIONS

1. How have sports mascots helped perpetuate stereotypes about American Indians?
2. In what ways did the media's coverage of the Fightin' Whites basketball team help perpetuate stereotypes?
3. In what ways did the media's coverage of the Fightin' Whites basketball team change the way in which American Indians were covered?
4. Are there any schools in your area that use American Indian nicknames and mascots? If so, has there been any discussion about changing these names and mascots?
5. Should schools be allowed to use American Indian nicknames and mascots? Why, or why not? Is there a difference between public and private schools' using these names? If so, what is that difference? What about schools with mostly Native populations?

NOTES

1. For an extended analysis of the legal battles over the use of Indians as mascots see chapter 11 in this book, "A Shifting Wind? Media Stereotyping of American Indians and the Law."
2. Rosenstein 2001.
3. King and Springwood, 2000.
4. Davis 1993; Hawes 2001; Banks 1993.
5. Rosenstein 2001.

6. Rutledge 2003.

7. Weston 1996.

8. Native women suffered from severe negative stereotyping as well. See chapter 8, this volume, "The 'S'-Word: Texts and Media Coverage Related to the Movement to Eradicate 'Squaw,'" by Stacey J. T. Hust and Debra Merskin.

9. Weston 1996.

10. Weston 1996.

11. Weston 1996; Banks 1993; Hilliard 1992, 20–21.

12. Banks 1993.

13. Coleman 1992.

14. Solomon Little Owl, interview by author, Greeley, Colo., February 2, 2003.

15. Julio Ochoa, "Fightin' Whities Gain National Attention," *Greeley Tribune,* March 13, 2002, A1.

16. Fightin' Whites merchandise is still for sale at http://www.cafepress.com/ fightinwhite (accessed July 12, 2011), and the money continues to go toward the Fighting Whites Scholarship Fund Inc.

17. Chris Cobler, interview by author via e-mail, March 19, 2003.

18. "Change Moves Us Forward and Unifies All," *Greeley Tribune,* January 27, 2002, A6.

19. The *Greeley Tribune* was the only paper to publish calls. They ran on the editorial page with callers' first names only.

20. In December 2002, paid circulation for the weekday *Denver Post* was 305,060; Sunday circulation was 789,137. "End of Deep Subscription Discounts Fuels Circulation Drop at Denver Dailies," *Newspapers and Technology,* December 2002, 1B–4B.

21. Coleman Cornelius, "Group Targeting All Colo. Indian Mascots," *Denver Post,* March 31, 2002, 1B–4B.

22. Cornelius, "Group Targeting All Colo. Indian Mascots," B4.

23. Coleman Cornelius. "School Fostered Ties with Tribe," *Denver Post,* March 31, 2002, B4.

24. Electra Draper, "Redskins Not an Issue at Ariz. Indian School," *Denver Post,* March 31, B4.

25. Joe Garner, "'Whities' Mascot Is about Education, Not Retaliation," *Rocky Mountain News,* March 12, 2002, 4A.

26. Julio Ochoa, "Protest Filed in Mascot Dispute," *Greeley Tribune,* March 28, 2002, A1. Coleman Cornelius, "School Fostered Ties with Tribe," *Denver Post,* March 31, 2002, 1B. Alecia Gallegos and Josh Opitz, "School Faces Complaint," *Mirror,* March 29, 2002, 12.

27. USD's mascot has likewise been the subject of protest and discussion in recent years. The North Dakota Board of Education voted in 2009 to end the use of the Fighting Sioux mascot to comply with National Collegiate Athletic Association rules barring the use of "hostile and abusive" mascots and logos. Under the stipulations of a settlement with the NCAA, UND had until October. 1, 2009, to

obtain the permission of two Sioux tribes in the state to continue using the mascot, which features a Native American wearing feathers.

28. Alecia Gallegos, "Faculty: UNC Must Adhere to Diversity," *The Mirror*, 1.

29. Julio Ochoa, "Team Picks White Man Mascot to Make Point," *Greeley Tribune*, March 10, 2002, 2A. Coleman Cornelius, "'Whities' Fightin' for a Cause," *Denver Post*, March 17, 2002, 1B. Michael BeDan, "International Eye Drawn to 'Fightin' Whities,'" *Rocky Mountain News*, March 15, 12A.

30. Weston, 1996.

31. Alecia Gallegos, "Basketball Leads to Controversy," *Mirror*, March 6, 2002, 2.

32. Alecia Gallegos, "Team Defies U.S. Racism," *Mirror*, March 15, 2002, 1.

33. "What's in a Name?" *Greeley Tribune*, March 29, 2002, A1.

34. Coleman Cornelius, "Town Fights Mascot's Stereotype with Humor," *Denver Post*, March 12, 2002, 1B–3B.

35. Garner, "Whities' Mascot Is about Education," 4A.

36. Julio Ochoa, "T-Shirts in Demand," *Greeley Tribune*, March 14, 2002, 1A. BeDan, "International Eye Drawn to 'Fightin' Whities,'" 12A.

37. Allison, "What's Implied about Me?" *Greeley Tribune*, March 16, 2002, 36. Chris, "We Might Have Listened," *Greeley Tribune*, March 18 2002, A8.

38. E. J. Michal, "Of Mascots and Mass," *Denver Post*, April 5, 2002, 8B.

39. Ed Quillen, "A Refreshing Twist on the Mascot Wars," *Denver Post*, March 17, 2002, 6E.

40. Quillen, "A Refreshing Twist," 6E.

41. Wayne Brown, "Fighting Whities Should Worry about Societal Problems," *Greeley Tribune*, March 27, 2002, A8.

42. Davis 1993.

43. Garner, "Whities' Mascot Is about Education," 4A.

44. Robert James, "Fightin' Silliness," *Denver Post*, March 20, 2002, 10B.

45. Jon Vogt, "Conservative White Guy Proud to Have His Race Immortalized in Team Mascot," *Rocky Mountain News*, March 22, 2002, 45A.

46. Natalie, "Proud to Be White," *Greeley Tribune*, March 18, 2002, A8.

47. Stan, "More Power to Them," *Greeley Tribune*, March 21, 2002, A10.

48. Mary, "Spend Money on Education," *Greeley Tribune*, March 3, 2002, A10.

49. York M. Nix, "Team Mascots Are Used to Honor American Indians," *Greeley Tribune*, March 21, 2002, A6.

50. Julie, "Good Enough to Be a Mascot," *Greeley Tribune*, March 8, 2002, A8.

51. Anthony, "A Representative Team," *Greeley Tribune*, March 18, 2002, A8.

52. Anne Cumming, "Fightin' Whities Find Way to Handle T-shirt Craze," *Greeley Tribune*, March 20, 2002, A1.

53. Roger Hernandez, "Mascot Furor Underscores America's Triple Standard," *Rocky Mountain News*, March 28, 2002, 64A.

54. Berkhofer 1978.

55. Rosenstein 2001, 254.

8

The "S"-Word

Activist Texts and Media Coverage Related to the Movement to Eradicate "Squaw"

STACEY J. T. HUST AND DEBRA MERSKIN

The word "squaw," often referred to by American Indian women as the "S"-word, appears in more than 119,000 place-names within the United States. In recent years American Indian activists have led a movement to eradicate the term "squaw" from U.S. place-names. This chapter argues that the offensive term, which some say refers to women's genitalia, subordinates American Indians and humiliates American Indian women. Renaming places and improving media representation of the issue could allow American Indians to re-create their ethnicity within a modern and historical context.

> There are so many stereotypes about us that we begin to believe that crap ourselves. When people know there's discrimination, and they can feel it, they've got to internalize some of that eventually. They've got to. So we've got to learn!
>
> Wilma Mankiller, Chief, Cherokee Nation, 1985–1995

A CONTESTED IDEA IN PUBLIC SPACES

In 2001 Oregon legislators passed Senate Bill 488, which required the renaming of all places that used the term "squaw."[1] The legislation resulted from two years of lobbying by members of the Confederated Tribes of the Warm Springs Reservation. American Indian activists, including those who had faced defeat in other Pacific Northwest states, including Idaho, considered passage of the Oregon law to be a success. On January 1, 2005, in Curry County, Oregon, Squaw Valley Road became Cedar Valley Road. This was not the property owner's idea. It was not the idea of the county commissioners. It was the law. A headline in the *New York Times* emphasized the controversial aspects of the issue: "Renaming 'squaw' sites proves touchy in Oregon."[2]

Oregon has the greatest number of "squaw" place-names, so its commit-
ment to change seemed a step in the right direction. Yet in his review of the
legislation, Mark Monmonier, who has written a definitive work on inappropriate place-names, commented that the Oregon legislation was "little more
than a toothless attempt at moralizing and buck passing."[3] Furthermore, the
renaming process was fraught with conflict and disagreements about appropriate replacements for offending place-names. In fact, by 2006, only four
Oregon "squaw" places had been officially renamed.[4]

The word "squaw," often referred to by American Indian women as the
"S"-word, is in more than 119,000 place-names within the United States. In
September 2007 the U.S. Board of Geographic Names approved removal
of the word "squaw" from eight places in Northern Idaho, three within the
Coeur d'Alene Reservation and five outside the reservation, but part of the
tribe's traditional lands.[5] The impetus for the name change came directly from
tribal members who found the term offensive. Many argue that it is a derogatory word that refers to an American Indian woman's genitalia. Not everyone sees the change as positive or necessary. Some opponents to the Idaho
name change argued "the colorful history of the Wild West should not be
plowed under simply to be polite.[6] The headline for that day's coverage, in the
Spokesman-Review (Spokane), read "Tribe Wants 'Squaw' off Map."

Idaho State Representative Dick Harwood (R–St. Maries) opposed the
change with an argument remarkably similar to those who advocate the
maintenance of racist sports team mascots: "It was an honor. It's how you use
the word, not what the word means."[7] But to many American Indian people,
renaming is not just a matter of politeness; it is an effort to reclaim Indigenous
identity and decolonize the landscape. For example, in the St. Joe National
Forest, the tribe proposed renaming Squaw Creek as Chimeash Creek; the
name roughly translates to "young woman of good character." A Judith Basin
(Montana) County commissioner downplayed the issue: "When these things
were named a hundred years ago, they didn't mean to offend anybody. . . .
And it's a waste of time. Everybody's still going to call it 'Squaw Coulee.'"[8]
Yet, even if its use is no longer consciously connected to its etymology, as the
editor of the *Navaho Times* pointed out, "The most offensive term used to address American Indian women is 'squaw.'"[9]

Some argue that the slow process of renaming "squaw" places and the lack
of genuine support from state legislators has occurred because the necessary
changes would be too expensive. Others assert that it alters historical accuracy. Still others fault disagreements over replacement names. As this chapter shows, many American Indian activists believe that retention of offensive
names, now that the issue has been identified, serves to further subordinate
American Indians and to humiliate American Indian women. American Indian life was altered dramatically when Europeans colonized American land.
Remnants of that colonization appear today to remind American Indians that

they are historical peoples whose sovereign nations happen to lie within the boundaries of the present-day United States. Offensive language in place-names transmits a constructed ethnicity of American Indians that is both rooted in the past and implies inferiority to white culture.

Beginning in the early 2000s a group of American Indian activists have worked to eradicate "squaw" from place-names, media, and popular culture. The events of this movement can best be understood as a process of community empowerment. Activists are trying to regain control over the language and images that define who they are as American Indians.[10] In a struggle to recapture their identity and bring it into modern times, American Indian women and men are trying to redefine their ethnicity by first naming the appropriate terms. Elites, in this case the colonizers, often control the stories of a minority group.[11] The "S"-word social movement is instead founded upon the stories and voices of American Indian women. These voices are found most often in the texts produced to disseminate the movement's messages. Given that this social movement is geared toward changing majority opinions, it is also important to understand how successful American Indian activists have been in disseminating their arguments to a wider population.

This chapter has three goals: (1) to explore the term "squaw" as an element of discourse that frames a version of Indigenous femaleness consistent with the historical colonial construct of stereotypes of American Indians in general as animalistic, savage, and subhuman, (2) to describe themes present in texts used in 2003 to convey activists' arguments for banning the word "squaw," and (3) to discuss the presence of these themes in newspaper coverage of the debate. The theoretical emphasis of this chapter is "representational ethics"; that is, "who has the right to represent others and under what circumstances?"[12] It is written, in the same spirit as d'Errico's essay on hyphenated Americans, as a "provocation toward the deconstruction of definitions which have trapped Indigenous Peoples in the dreams of others."[13] As early as 1990, the American Indian Mental Health Association of Minnesota wrote in its position statement: "We are in agreement that using images of American Indians as mascots, symbols, caricatures, and namesakes for non-Indian sports teams, businesses, and other organizations is damaging to the self-identity, self-concept, and self-esteem of our people."[14] We argue that words and names can have the same affect.

Thus the intention of this chapter is to explore the problematic nature of the word "squaw," to hear voices and messages that American Indians produced to convince others to eradicate the word, and finally to determine whether media coverage has included their arguments in coverage of the debate. In the media these representations not only reinforce dehumanizing and limiting views of the capabilities of American Indian women but also result in "structural exclusions and cultural imagining [that] leave[s] minority members vulnerable to a system of violence," symbolically and actually.[15]

THE "S"-WORD: PUBLIC DISCOURSE AND
THE REALITY OF A STEREOTYPE

Drawing on Butler, Nagel asserts that "the performative construction of real-ity rests heavily on discursive acts, i.e., on the power of naming and speech to define reality."[16] A deconstructive approach takes its examples from the past, recognizing that "squaw" is still with us: "Deconstruction is thus an attempt not simply to reverse certain categories but to displace, dislocate, or to shift (if ever so slightly and slowly) a historical structure and the logical system that has served as a convenient excuse for it."[17]

By describing the persistence, pervasiveness, and perpetuation of "squaw" in public discourse, this chapter extends Schroeder and Borgerson's model of a representational ethics of images[18] to include words and draws from Del-gado and Stefancic's critical race theory[19] to explore the following questions: How is the word "squaw" characterized in the contemporary popular imag-ination? What are the implications of this stereotype for American Indian women? We argue that the persistent use of the stereotypical "squaw" is far from harmless. Rather, we claim that messages conveyed through the author-ity of mass media (broadly defined to include print and broadcast journalism, advertising, and photojournalism) and popular culture rigidify and perpetu-ate the stereotype in American imagination, reifying the hierarchical position of dominant Euro-American culture by controlling access to resources and power. "Although it has yet to rival 'nigger' in out-loud offensiveness, 'squaw' clearly upstages 'Negro' as the thorniest issue in applied toponymy."[20]

In 2008 a Google search of the term "squaw" yielded more than 4.8 million "hits." Some of these were discussions of the word, its etymology, and ap-propriateness (or lack thereof), but most were links for resorts, casinos, and landforms. The word elicited a mixture of revulsion, pity, claiming, desire, and nostalgia.

The etymology of "squaw" is complex, contested, and extensively interro-gated in both scholarly and popular literature.[21] To summarize, it appears to be one among a number of Eastern Algonquian words appropriated by En-glish and French explorers during the early contact period in American his-tory. Around 1634 the term begins to show up in historical documents and literature from the English colonies along the Atlantic seaboard. Some say the word meant "young woman" (Massachusett), others say "woman," or "an Indian woman or wife."[22]

The *Oxford English Dictionary*,[23] at its first level of definition, only says that squaw is "a North American Indian woman or wife." But the entry also indi-cates this use is rare. Sanders points out that the term "squaw . . . turned into a slur on the tongues of White settlers, who used it to refer derisively to Indian women in general or a part of their anatomy in particular."[24] This is evident in an excerpt from Welcker's *Tales of the Wild and Woolly West* (1890): "By way of expressing their utter contempt for him they called him a 'squaw.'"[25] According to Stubben and Sokolow, "squaw" is a synonym for "prostitute," "harlot," "hussy," and "floozy."[26] In the Algonquian and Mohawk languages, the word means "vagina" or "female genitalia." It has myriad meanings or may not exist at all in hundreds of other American Indian languages. According to Mihesuah, "the 'squaw' is the dirty, subservient, and abused tribal female who is also haggard, violent, and eager to torture tribal captives."[27] Neutrality exists only in the minds of the bestowers:

> That curious concept of "squaw," the enslaved, demeaned, voiceless child bearer, existed and exists only in the mind of the non-Native American and is probably a French corruption of the Iroquois word *otsiskwa* meaning "female sexual parts," a word almost clinical both denotatively and connotatively. The corruption suggests nothing about the Native American's attitude toward women; it does indicate the *wa-sichu's* [non-Native's] view of Native American women in particular if not all women in general.[28]

Regardless of its ancient origins, "squaw" has come to signify something quite different from its original meaning. In an appearance on nationwide television in 1992, on the *Oprah Winfrey Show*, the notable American Indian activist Suzan Harjo set the public conscience straight on this inflammatory and racist word: "The word 'squaw' is an [Algonquian] Indian word meaning vagina, and that'll give you an idea of what the French and British fur trappers were calling all Indian women, and I hope no one ever uses that term again."[29]

STICKS AND STONES

> Olivia Wallulatum finds it hard to even look at the sign, a marker for the Squaw River. It reminds her of all the names she was called as a girl. And she wants something done about it. She wants the name changed.[30]

Naming or renaming of landforms, erasing what Indigenous people of an area have called a place, is a form of colonization. Watner and McElroy call it the "hegemonic project," when "Native names for flora, fauna, insects, mountains, valleys, [and] birds were effaced and replaced by the nouns and taxonomies of the conquerors."[31] Thus, relabeling someone or something in the language of the oppressor not only appropriates the person, place, or thing but also transfers power for the oversight, management, and control of what has been renamed.[32] Giving or taking away land, giving and taking away names, are both forms of colonization.

In the Christian faith, at the moment when God gave Adam the power to name the animals, the animals no longer belonged to themselves. Once categorized as members of groups, they were no longer individuals. Similarly, using a single label drawn from their own worldview (in which "the Indies" referred to islands off the subcontinent of India), colonists named Native American peoples collectively as "Indians." More names of this type were applied by European settlers to particular tribes, and decisions about what words are or are not odious came from the European perspective. Akin to recent controversies over the degree of offensiveness in the adoption of American Indian names and images for sports team mascots and nicknames, such as the Atlanta Braves or the Washington Redskins,[33] the debate about which Indigenous words adopted for mainstream usage are problematic depends upon the eyes and ears of the beholder. In the absence of the opportunity for self-definition by Native sources, words and names, regardless of ancestry, have been assigned to peaks, mountains, roads, creeks, and buttes. In 2001 in Maine the use of "squaw" was prohibited under all circumstances. Yet it took a formal complaint to make the small town of Stockton Springs, near the Penobscot Nation, to change place-names and road signs. A particular challenge was the Squaw Point Home Owners Association (its name ultimately became Defence Point).[34] According to Donna Loring, the Penobscot Nation's representative in the state legislature, "It is not about political correctness. It is about human decency. Many of you don't understand when living, feeling, breathing, Native people tell you they are dehumanized by the use of the word."[35]

The problem with racist names for landforms attracted widespread public and government attention in the 1990s when American Indian activists organized and lobbied governments to force change on the grounds that, from their point of view, the words were derogatory. Unlike other racial and ethnic groups who have the numbers and political clout to change stereotypical representations about themselves, American Indians are often invisible, or are viewed as one-dimensional. As Marubbio notes, "They are America's racial Other and alter ego: rejected in order to justify the violent treatment of them as part of progress and civilization, yet also desired for the freedom, land, and innocent state they represent."[36] Some scholars argue that the term per se may not be the most problematic issue, but rather that it is particularly objectionable because, as Monmonier puts it, it "seems more deeply rooted in the white majority's often-brutal treatment of indigenous North Americans."[37] He also points out that the term came to attention "from relative obscurity."[38] Both content and context matter:

> We've been degraded for 500 years and to the general public they're walking around thinking that they did something great by naming a creek or a river Squaw. It stings a little. It'd be like if a shopping mall [was] called Holocaust Mall. We're not angry, we know what it means. But we have to educate the general public first.[39]

THEMES IN THE ACTIVISTS' ARGUMENTS, 2003

In October 2003 an Internet search conducted for any text that included the terms "squaw," "Native American," and "grassroots," in order to identify articles representing members of the social movement to eradicate the "S"-word, produced 29 unique texts. Of these, 25 texts addressed the issue directly; and four that dealt with the issue indirectly were dropped from consideration. The final sample of 25 texts chosen for the analysis described here included personal writings, academic reports, and newsletter and newspaper articles. The guiding methodology relied upon close readings of these texts and upon inductive tenets of qualitative content analysis.

With few exceptions, the authors of the texts were American Indians. Almost all of the authors identified their community membership within their byline. They represented various communities, such as the Cherokee, the Shoshone-Bannock, the Cheyenne, and the Hodulgee Muscogee. The majority of the authors were members of the social movement to ban "squaw." It should be noted that the majority of the articles were persuasive and reflected the sentiments of the social movement's members. The texts, overall, would be considered items of media advocacy, rather than traditional informative news writing. Most of the authors and sources were identified as activists. Additionally, the texts often used calls to action as a rhetorical strategy. For instance, J. Wickham stated at the end of his text, "Let's send a powerful message against a shameful history of bigotry and ethnic hatred and erase the words 'squaw' from all Colorado communities and natural landmarks."[40] Interestingly, the texts often gave an impression of militancy. Many of the texts first mentioned opinions of their opposition, and then countered them. And much of the writing conjured images of the battlefield, as authors used words such as "struggle," "battle," and "fight."

It was difficult to prove who the audiences were for these texts. Many of the texts were produced in American Indian venues that would primarily be viewed by American Indians, but certainly much of the writing indicates that the authors were also trying to convince members of the mainstream majority. The authors, it seems, assumed that their audience would be ignorant of the fight over the "S"-word and would need both historical and modern-day contexts. Many of the texts assumed audience members would be hostile toward the change, for the authors persistently wrote persuasive essays and editorials. Five themes emerged in the activists' arguments.

Theme 1. "Squaw, Squaw, Squaw, Slut, Slut, Slut"

Tim Giago asserts that to most American Indian women the word "squaw" is synonymous with the word "slut."[41] Like most other authors in our sample who wrote about this topic, he offered a possible definition of the "S"-word as a foundation for his argument. In part, the movement's members have had to redefine the word as derogatory and insulting because modern-day language experts ignore its meaning. Suzan Harjo argued that English dictionaries have helped blur the accurate definition of the word. Also, they "cleaned it up, defining it as an Indian wife or woman, or as a jocular reference for any kind of wife."[42]

For many authors, the definition they stated in their articles set the tone for their subsequent debate of the issue. Many defined "squaw" as derogatory and insulting. When discussing the historical roots of the word, the authors often referred to specific communities—such as the Iroquois, Mohawk, and Algonquians—whose language provides similar words or words germane to "squaw." In most instances these references were used to provide legitimacy to the argument that historically, across communities, "squaw" referred to a woman's vagina. Other authors allowed their sources to articulate the implications of the word "squaw." Harjo quoted a former sportswoman from St. Bonaventure University to explicate her point. The university's mascot for female athletes had been a squaw. The sportswoman stated: "We were so proud to be Squaws. Then a Seneca chief and clan mothers came over from the reservation and asked us to stop using the name, because it meant vagina. We almost died of embarrassment. Of course, we stopped using it immediately."[43]

Authors also readily cited historians, national activists, and scholars when they set the boundaries for their arguments, which also served to add credibility to their definitions.

The authors did not just define "squaw" in an American Indian context, however. They also cited dictionary and thesaurus definitions of "squaw" as a means to justify that the argument was relevant to a non-Native audience. For instance, "Pitter" Glinda Ladd Seabaugh wrote: "The *Thesaurus of Slang* identifies the term Squaw as a synonym for prostitute, harlot, hussy and floozy. The Dictionary identifies this word as one that is used to offend Native females."[44]

In contrast, some authors did not agree that "squaw" in its original form was offensive or derogatory. These authors also defined the term, but primarily as a word that meant the "totality of being female." Many of these authors argued that colonizers had usurped the power of this word and manipulated it to mean whatever they wanted it to. "Early European fur-traders shortened the word to "squaw" and its usage implied the crudest sexual connotations," according to Brenda Norrell.[45] The fact that colonizers had clouded the word's meaning left some authors blaming the colonizers for the proposed present-day ban. Marge Bruchac, who opposes banning the term, stated, "If we banned everything the Europeans misused, we would be left with nothing."[46]

Theme 2. Still a Colonized People

Even though the authors differed in the techniques they used to define the "S"-word, they typically agreed that its modern usage is an extension of the abuse that Indigenous peoples suffered with colonization. Bruchac acknowledges that "although the European invasion is only a small part of our long history, it has proved to be the most difficult challenge of all."[47] In fact, when defining the word the authors typically point to the misappropriation and colonization of Native languages as part of the problem. As activist Bruce Two Eagles explained, "The word squaw is a European bastardization of 'otsikwaw,' a Mohawk insult referring to the female genitalia."[48] A resident near Arizona's Squaw Lake told reporter Brenda Norrell that the word was a "French corruption of an Iroquoian epithet for vagina."[49]

The colonization of American Indian culture and American Indian language is at the root of the social movement to ban the word "S"-word. Many activists argued that there was no need to agree on a historical definition of the word, because the colonizers' use was so hurtful that the true meaning can never be reclaimed. Giago remarked that "it doesn't matter what the word 'squaw' means. It is how the word transformed its meaning from the early settler days. Any white man married to or living with an Indian woman was known as a 'Squawman.' When white men went looking for sex they went 'squaw hunting.'"[50] Many authors, among them Wickham, came to similar conclusions, arguing that "squaw" was "a reflection of the past practice of selling Indian women to white men for a life of slavery and servitude."[51]

Other tribal members were trying to reclaim the Native word's original meaning: "The 'Institute for the Advancement of Aboriginal Women' in Edmonton, Alberta has reclaimed 'esquao,' the northern linguistic equivalent of 'squaw'—and declared that it will no longer be tolerated as an insult, but will instead be recognized as a term of honor and respect."[52] The reclaiming of the native word signifies recognition of the colonization, and by extension the codification, of the American Indian image by European colonizers. Yet, it also indicates that they will regain control over the language that is used to define their identity.

Theme 3. Reclaiming Identity: "Together We Stand, Divided We Fall"

Many of the activists in the articles that were analyzed likened their struggle over the "S"-word to the larger Civil Rights Movement and to other battles over language such as the "N"-word for African Americans. They explained that "squaw" is comparable to other terms that have already been recognized by the American public as being racist and unacceptable in place or business names. "In 1967, 143 place names containing the word nigger were changed to Negro by order of the U.S. Board on Geographic Names," Seabaugh reported.[53] Chavers likewise pointed out that in 1967 the word "Jap," which was present in 26 place-names, was also outlawed.[54]

To argue their positions, activists also relied on some of the powerful language first adopted by the Civil Rights Movement. "Together we stand, divided we fall," stated Gloria Muñoz in an article for the *Sho-Ban News*.[55] In one article, a North Carolina school board's decision to keep a 25-foot-tall warrior statue on its lawn was likened to the racist policy decisions of Bull Conner and Lester Maddox of the 1960s.[56] In addition, two authors likened the historical plight of Native Americans to the Jewish Holocaust.

The activists also argued that American Indians are no different from other minorities living in America. Many stated that the indecencies they suffer through the use of such stereotypical images and words as "squaw" and "redskin" would not be tolerated if targeted toward a different minority group. "Images such as Little Black Sambo, Fu Man Chu and the Frito Bandito have all but been exiled from popular expression," stated the authors of the Native American Journalists Association's 2003 "Reading Red Report."[57] Many stated that American Indians are not treated the same as other minority groups because they are ignored and kept out of conversation. Two Eagles told a reporter that American Indians are almost never mentioned in debates about civil rights: "We're the invisible culture . . . created by the wars against the Indians."[58] Other authors pointed out that few mainstream journalists or government officials actually ask American Indians what they think about issues.

In fact, part of the movement's goal is to have members of the dominant society include more American Indians in their decision-making processes. Covering the rally to change place-names in Idaho, Edmo-Suppah reported that "Louise E. Dixey, a rally organizer and Shoshone-Bannock, called on legislators to get diversity training and for the governor to appoint Native women to commissions."[59] In this manner, Dixey was arguing for popular participation in that the participation would give more control to American Indian women who previously were not included in the decision-making process. As Majid Rahnema states, popular participation should enable grassroots populations to regenerate their life spaces.[60] In this way, Native women will become more empowered and more able to define their identity.

Theme 4. "Out with Squaw, In with Respect"

Research indicates many hunting and gathering societies were based on gender equality.[61] Many American Indian communities were structured with women and men each holding important roles. "They were simply regarded as different," Bowker states. "Both sexes were valued for the contributions they made to their society, and their roles were regarded as complementary rather than competitive."[62] When Europeans colonized what is now the United States, they brought with them a society based on patriarchal ideals. Mihesuah has argued that these patriarchal ideologies "still affect Native women's positions within their tribes and the respect given to them by men."[63] Wilma Mankiller, chief of the Cherokee Nation 1985–1995, stated that "our tribe and others which were matriarchal have become assimilated and have adopted the cultural value of the larger society, and, in so doing, we've adopted sexism."[64]

Some researchers have cited the use of the word "squaw" as an example of how the dominant society continues to belittle American Indian women and perpetuates sexism. Klein and Ackerman point out that the term "squaw" assumes that a woman has no social input and no respect: "She is an inferior to her husband and necessary only for her labor and for her sexual and reproductive duties."[65]

Some feminist scholars believe that derogatory use of the word "squaw" began as a means of sexualizing Native women. This theme was also present in the articles analyzed in the study reported here. Two of these articles, predominantly focused on violence against women of color, stated that the use of "squaw" was another means, both historically and currently, to sexually violate American Indian women. Chavers has remarked that the word also has a very restricted meaning, in that it identifies only American Indian women.[66] Historical evidence shows that American Indian women were killed by Europeans so that their tribes would be prevented from reproducing.[67] "Not only were they killed," according to Andrea Smith in *The Color of Violence Against Women* (2000), "but they were routinely raped and sexually mutilated as colonizers tried, both symbolically and literally, to control Native women's reproductive capacities."[68]

Even though some activists mention that all women should be concerned over use of the word "squaw," the issue has not been framed as part of the wider women's movement that began in the 1970s. In fact, Edmo-Suppah has specifically argued that the issue should not be framed as part of the larger women's movement.[69] Even so, some activists do point out that this is primarily a women's issue: "Unfortunately, racial justice organizing has generally focused on racism as it affects men and has often ignored the forms of racism and sexism that women of color face."[70] Despite this disagreement, almost all of the authors of articles analyzed in the present study articulated a need to involve Indian women in the conversation about eradicating the "S"-word.

This theme was significantly related to the authors' continued discussion of empowerment. Many of the articles in the analysis discussed this theme in terms that implied what Michael Papa and his colleagues have termed a "discursive consciousness," a state of mind that "reflects a conscious awareness of one's domination by ideological systems."[71] The activist authors made many references in their articles to their own sense of being dominated. For example, Giago states: "It is so easy for white men to sit back and speculate— or I should say, expectorate—over the name squaw without asking an Indian woman how she feels about it."[72]

Theme 5. "I Is for Indian"

Much research has focused on the effects of stereotypical images on children and their ethnic or racial identity.[73] Scholars have pointed out that few children of the majority learn about American Indians as modern-day peoples. Rather, children often only know that "I is for Indian," and that Indians wear head-dresses and are typically men. Native children cannot help but absorb the message behind this stereotyping. Growing up without positive images of one's ethnicity can drastically alter a child's self-perception.[74] Bowker states, "According to American Indian writer Darcy McNickle, the treatment of the Indian from the time of the European colonization to the present day has resulted in the loss of Indian ethnic, tribal, and self-identity."[75] By extension, the remnants of colonization still present today have resulted in the creation of an imagined ethnicity and the loss of a true American Indian identity.

Thus it is not surprising that one of the most prevalent themes in the texts that were analyzed was the psychological effects that stereotypes and fractured racial identity can have on children. The foundation of this argument is that children and adults begin to view themselves as the dominant society views them.[76] Pewewardy reports that studies have shown that the demeaning images present in the media and in place-names lower the self-esteem of many Indian young people.[77] He has observed, too, that these negative images not only influence Native American children's perceptions of themselves but also non-Native children's attitudes toward American Indians.[78] Thus, these negative images, which cause unhealthy and undemocratic feelings toward self and family, may contribute to behavioral problems that continue to plague the American Indian population.[79] It has been claimed that American Indian youth are paying the price of this alienation with some of the highest high school dropout rates in the United States and some of the highest incidences of suicide.[80] Stereotyping children, says Norrell, "keeps them down on a daily basis so they feel like they can't rise up and achieve very much."[81]

Many activists related the renaming of places directly to an increase in their children's self-esteem. For instance, an Indian activist told a reporter about changing the names of places in Arizona: "If we can get this changed, the youths will have a lot more pride in themselves. They have no self-esteem. They have no pride in who they are."[82] In fact, many activists mentioned that they were involved in this fight because they wanted to make the world a better place for their children and grandchildren. "Maybe one day," reflected Two Eagles, "when I'm long gone and my granddaughter has children, there won't be any more shame to [being] an Indian."[83] Not only do they want to empower themselves, but they want their children to be empowered as well.

PREVALENT THEMES IN NEWS COVERAGE
OF THE "S"-WORD DEBATE

The Lexis-Nexis Academic database was used to search for articles that included the term "squaw" in the headlines that were published in major United States newspapers from November 2003 through May 2008. The original search netted 243 articles, but the majority was not relevant to the current project, and some were duplicates. Many of the articles not included in the analysis referenced an actual location (e.g., Squaw Peak) but did not discuss the debate to change the place-name. To prioritize news coverage of the debate, the analysis excluded editorials, opinion pieces, or letters to the editor. Thus, 35 news articles published in U.S. newspapers during the time period were included in this analysis. The analysis of the 25 activists' texts from 2003, discussed at length above, informed the investigation of the media coverage.

The articles published in major U.S. newspapers came from Maine, Oregon, Utah, Washington, and Wisconsin. The Associated Press and United Press International also published stories about debated place-names in Arizona, Idaho, Iowa, and Oklahoma. These locations are not surprising given that those states contain a high proportion of "squaw" place-names.[84]

Overall, the activists were at least partly successful in promoting their arguments to journalists covering the policy discussions related to eradicating the term "squaw," as the news articles included some of the arguments that the activists put forth in 2003. The majority of the articles were news accounts of policy decisions related to changing place-names, and the most common themes included defining the term "squaw" and discussing alternative place-names that would honor American Indians. Slightly more than one-third of the articles mentioned racism against American Indians, and seven articles mentioned other racist terms and colonization. Very few, however, mentioned the American Indian activists or recognized the role they played in the debate.

Offensive "Squaw" Names

Nearly one-half of all the news articles analyzed (46%) mentioned that "squaw" was an offensive term. Most of these mentioned that the term was generally offensive, with phrasing such as "offensive 'squaw' names." The articles that did specify exactly whom the term offended primarily mentioned American Indians. Only two articles mentioned that the term was "considered offensive by many." Most of the newspaper articles also tried to define the term "squaw" while still acknowledging the controversy surrounding the accurate definition.

Alternative Place-Names: Balancing Honor and Pronunciation

The primary focus of many of the news articles was the process of renaming places. Once the journalists identified that "squaw" was a derogatory term, the articles quickly moved on to identify what would happen if the place-name was changed. This included references to American Indians involved in the renaming process, responses from non-Indians, and discussions about proposed name changes.

An illustrative example of this type is the news coverage regarding Washington State's Squaw Creek, which highlighted the disagreement about alternative names. One article stated that the Coeur D'Alene tribe had suggested the name Awtskin Creek, which uses the phonetic spelling of the word in their language for "lookout," in reference to a specific historical battle relevant to members of the Coeur d'Alene American Indian community. Other local residents wanted the name Jack Pine Creek, after a type of tree that grows in the area.

The news coverage highlighted the non-Native sources' personal stake in the renaming process. "If names must be changed," one resident said, "at least have the kindness to consider the wishes of those who have lived here for over 100 years."[85] Another article on the same topic also reported that "area residents say that if the spot must be renamed, they should pick the name." Residents also questioned why the Coeur d'Alene American Indians had become involved in a debate about Washington state place-names, when they are an "Idaho tribe."[86]

In response, the Coeur d'Alene tribal chairman, Chief J. Allen, acknowledged that members of his community understood residents' concerns about nonresidents renaming their land. "We know exactly what it's like to live in these and other places," he said, "and then have others come into the country . . . and apply random and arbitrary place names to one's familiar places." He then reaffirmed that Awtskin Creek was an appropriate alternative for Squaw Creek.[87]

Conflict also arose about new possibilities proposed by tribes for renaming another Squaw Creek, this one in the state of Oregon, which had passed legislation in 2001 to remove "squaw" from place-names. One reporter wrote that "around the Warm Springs reservation and the nearby town of Sisters, three years of pointed debate among local tribal leaders has produced 42 alternatives to Squaw Creek in three native languages." Many of these proposed alternatives, he remarked, were difficult for English speakers "and even some Indians" to pronounce.[88]

In both Arizona and Maine, legislators and residents tried to reinstate the "squaw" place-name even after it had been banned and names had been changed. In 2004, Republicans in the Arizona House of Representatives tried to gain control of the state's naming board in an attempt to restore the name Squaw Peak to Piestewa Peak, which had been recently renamed in honor of U.S. Army Specialist Lori Piestewa (1979–2003), a Hopi, the first Native American woman to die in combat.[89] In 2006, leaders in Piscataquis County in Maine asked the state to allow "squaw" to be restored in all places previously named so. The county had replaced all instances of "Squaw" with "Moose" in place-names when the governor had required the change in 2000.[90] Neither of the articles covering these proposals to "bring back the word 'squaw'" included the opinion of an American Indian.

Although these articles did cover the existing debates about alternatives for place-names that used "squaw," the uneven reportage further highlights the differences between Native and non-Native concerns. Many of these articles, such as those discussing Squaw Creek in Washington state, included the perspective of a number of non-Native sources, but only one American Indian, typically a tribal chairperson or a solo activist, spoke for the views of all Native interests in the issue. And articles rarely rebutted or corrected residents' claims. For example, even though a couple of articles cited residents who said the Idaho-based Coeur d'Alene tribe should not be involved in renaming Washington's Squaw Creek, the articles rarely mentioned that the Coeur d'Alene tribe once spanned much of what is now known as the Pacific Northwest. Overall, the coverage implies that the comfort and needs of other stakeholders are equally, if not more, important than those of American Indians, despite the comparatively recent arrival of non-Natives into formerly Native territories. Perhaps the most blatant example of this comes with discussion of difficulties in pronouncing proposed new American Indian place-names, which clearly prioritizes the needs of the non-Indian majority and implies an exotic "otherness" in American Indian history and cultures.

According to articles about Washington's Squaw Creek, the renaming process had in fact stalled due to disagreements about the alternative name for the creek. News coverage of the renaming process for Oregon's Squaw Creek indicates that many places have still not been renamed despite a 2005 deadline, because alternative names have not been found. One Associated Press headline reads, "Tribes, Government Want 'Squaw' Names Changed—but That's No Simple Task."[91] The article later states that in 2005, according to the U.S. Geographic Names Board, less than eight percent of all "squaw" place-names had formally been renamed.

It's the Right Thing to Do

Although specific identification of "squaw" as a racist term was not prominent in the news coverage that was analyzed, a few articles did mention the racism that accompanies such language and connected it to similar terms that have already been removed from place-names. For instance, Karyn Seamann cited Alderman Peter McKeever during her coverage of renaming Squaw Bay: "If this [name] hurts someone in my community, I see no reason at all not to change it. I care what a Native American woman feels when she hears it ought to be done simply because it's the right thing to do."[92] This type of quote was extremely rare in the coverage.

Other journalists pointed out that the United States has been committed to renaming all places that have included racist terms. An article in the *Sunday Oregonian* for October 2, 2005, states: "Wholesale name changes aren't new. The national board has twice required changes, for the pejorative forms of Negro and Japanese, in 1963 and 1974, respectively."[93] This type of coverage indicates that American Indian activists in the articles that were analyzed had successfully linked their arguments with those of the larger Civil Rights Movement.

CONCLUSIONS: REPRESENTATIONAL ETHICS AND MEDIATED TRUTHS

"Stereotyping is an ethical concern," insists Norma Peone, a member of the Coeur d'Alene tribal council, "and raises the question 'who has the right to represent others and under what circumstances?'"[94] The effort to answer this question is termed "representational ethics." This ethical stance expects that "represented identities profess to express something true or essential about those represented." A representational ethics of images requires inquiry into and an understanding of "not only the implications or consequences of representational conventions—customary ways of depicting products, people, and identities . . . but also emphasizes the ethical context from which such representational conventions emerge."[95] Beyond images, words are also representational because language is never neutral, and the selection of particular words and phrases articulates an individual's and a society's beliefs as a form of disclosure. Thus language is ideological and dialogic—we speak out of bounded systems of constructed knowledge, and every utterance is a "two-sided act."[96]

Schroeder and Borgerson's "represented identities" involve not only attention to implications and consequences of "representational conventions—customary ways of depicting products, people and identities," but also "the ethical context from which such representational conventions emerge."[97] Over time, representational conventions become a kind of "visual truth" or "authentic knowledge derived by seeing."[98] These practices construct and maintain particular types or categories that, left unchallenged, endure and have "the weight of established facts" behind them.[99] Ordinarily created through the eyes of those in societal positions of power, these representational practices "affect some people's morally significant perceptions of and interactions with people, and if they contribute to those perceptions or interactions going seriously wrong, these activities have a bearing on fundamental ethical questions."[100] Thus, if media representations cater to the interests of dominant society in maintaining suppression of one group for the gain of another, they are unethical.

Embedding racist and sexist stereotypes in brands, labels, landforms, and media images and words is an exercise in power. Stereotypes, as hegemonic tools, reduce individuals to a single, monolithic, one-dimensional type that appears, and is presented as, natural and normal, as "regimes of truth"[101] as they fit into ideological patterns of representations that serve, among other functions, to establish "in-group categorizations of out-groups."[102] This expression is written on the bodies, minds, and hearts of Indian and non-Indian people. King writes, "The racist and sexist stereotypes given voice through 'squaw,' no less than the official inscription of the term on the landscape, render embodied Indigenous women invisible, overshadowed by the iconic insistence of the trope."[103] Freire convincingly argues that an oppressive situation is one "in which 'A' objectively exploits 'B' or hinders his pursuit of self-affirmation as a responsible person."[104]

The American Indian authors established the meaning of "squaw" using linguistic devices or anecdotes that typically tied the offense to colonization. Once they defined the terms of the debate, they detailed the plethora of places and media texts that use "squaw." In an attempt to persuade readers, the activists likened their cause to other civil rights movements, especially that of the 1960s. Interestingly, the activists did not connect their cause to the larger women's movement. Embodying what Papa and his coauthors called "discursive consciousness," the activists acknowledged that while "squaw" impedes women's equality, it dominates and stereotypes the entire race. Thus, these activists argued, such stereotyping will affect their children's and grandchildren's self-esteem.

It is evident that the American Indian activists involved in this debate feel deeply and strongly about eradicating the word "squaw" from place-names and popular media representations. These findings suggest they view this language as remnants of colonization and as reminders of their oppression. The American Indian activists involved argued their ethnic identity has been manipulated and controlled by the oppressors, and reclaiming the word "squaw" is one step toward regaining the power over their representation.

The analysis that was undertaken of news coverage over this debate indicates that these American Indian activists successfully communicated their belief that "squaw" is a derogatory term. They were also successful in linking the term to colonization and, in a few instances, to racism. However, much of the coverage focused on the differences between American Indians and non-Indians and portrayed the renaming process as a debate that prioritized non-Indian opinions and arguments. This framing of the renaming process contributes to an already difficult task. A *New York Times* article on December 11, 2004, reads: "It's a problem familiar to Indians and government officials in several states where attempts to outlaw 'squaw' have been caught in a thicket of bureaucratic, historical and linguistic snares."[105]

Renaming place-names and changing media representation will allow American Indians to re-create their ethnicity within a modern and historical context. Furthermore, according to the texts analyzed, these actions are needed to permit them to help their children own a positive ethnic identity that is crucial to their success as a people.

What is or is not problematic should always be considered from the perspective of those represented. Place-names are changing, slowly, as indicated by Oregon and Idaho's legislation. Arizona's renaming of Squaw Peak in 2008, as Piestewa Peak in honor of Lori Piestewa, though strongly contested, has held.[106] As a media effect, stereotyping is an ethical problem. As Valerie Fast Horse, council member of the Washington, Idaho, and Montana Coeur d'Alene Tribe, pointed out, "They should translate the names into English and see how fast they get changed."[107]

Ultimately, racist and sexist stereotypes, while primarily impacting the lives of those (mis)represented, also influence others as well. As Stubben and Sokolow remind us, "The term squaw is not only derogatory toward Native American women, it is derogatory toward all women."[108]

DISCUSSION QUESTIONS

1. Are there any places named Squaw where you live? If so, have there been any efforts by legislators and/or activists to change them?
2. Do you see the use of "squaw" in a place or landform name as problematic? Why or why not?
3. Can you think of a name that would be offensive based on your family's history?
4. Do media organizations have a responsibility to represent individuals fairly?
5. How might communities go about finding alternative names that do not use "Squaw"? Who should be involved in the process of deciding what names are most suitable?

NOTES

Epigraph: Mihesuah 2003, 102.

1. State of Oregon, "Bill Prohibiting Use of Term," 2001, accessed July 8, 2008, http://www.leg.state.or.us/brown/pr5_31.htm.

2. Eli Sanders, "Renaming 'Squaw' Sites Proves Touchy in Oregon," *New York Times,* December 11, 2004, A12.

3. Monmonier 2006, 55.

4. Monmonier 2006, 55.

5. U.S. Geological Survey, Accessed August 4, 2008. http://geonames.usgs.gov/pls/gnispublic/f?p=136:2:9523706043659525594::NO.

6. James Hagengruber, "Tribe Wants 'Squaw' off Map," *Spokesman-Review* (Spokane), October 6, 2006, accessed July 1, 2008, http://www.spokesmanreview.com/idaho/story.asp?ID=153172&page=all.

7. Quoted in Hagengruber, "Tribe Wants 'Squaw' off Map."

8. Cody McDonald, quoted in Marisol Bello, "Pressure Mounts to Drop 'Squaw' from Place Names." *USA Today,* April 30, 2008, 1A.

9. Tom Arviso, Jr., "Watch your Language," n.d., Society of Professional Journalists, *Diversity Toolbox,* accessed May 10, 2007. http://www.spj.org/dtb7.asp.

10. Melkote and Steeves 2001; Papa, Singhal, and Papa 1999.

11. Melkote and Steeves 2001.

12. Johnston 2000, 73.

13. Peter d'Errico, "Native American Indian Studies—A Note on Names," 2005, accessed July 15, 2011, http://www.umass.edu/legal/derrico/name.html.

14. Quoted in Cornel Pewewardy, "From La Belle Savage to the Noble Savage: The Deculturalization of Indian Mascots in American Culture," 1999, accessed September 23, 2003, http://www.hanksville.org/sand/stereotypes/pewewardy.html.

15. Perry 2002.

16. Joane Nagel, "Ethnicity and Sexuality," 2000, *Annual Review of Sociology* 26: 107–133.

17. Michael Vannoy Adams, "Deconstructive Philosophy and Imaginal Psychology: Comparative Perspectives on Jacques Derrida and James Hillman," In *Jungian Criticism,* edited by Richard P Sugg (Evanston, Ill.: Northwestern University Press, 1992), 235. 18 Schroeder and Borgerson 2005.

19. Delgado and Stefancic 2001.

20. Monmonier 2006, 52.

21. Cecil Adams, "Is 'Squaw' an Obscene Insult?" *The Straight Dope,* March 17, 2000, accessed May 10, 2008, http://www.straightdope.com/columns/000317 .html; Allen 1986; Bello, "Pressure Mounts to Drop 'Squaw' From Place Names"; Bird 1999; Rukmini Callimachi, "Tribes, Gov't, Want 'Squaw' Name Changed," Associated Press, April 1, 2005, accessed July 15, 2011, http://www.bigbigforums. com/news-information/469522-tribes-govt-want-ßsquaw-names-changed.html; King 2003; Mihesuah 2003.

22. Tom Jonas, "The Controversy over the Word 'Squaw,'" 2003, accessed April 10, 2008, www.tomjonas.com/squawpeak/squaw.htm.

23. *Oxford English Dictionary,* 2nd ed., 1989, "squaw, n.ª," accessed August 1, 2008, http://o-dictionary.oed.com.janus.uoregon.edu/cgi/entry/50235256?single=1& query_type=word&queryword=squaw&first=1&max_to_show=10.

24. Sanders, "Renaming Squaw Sites."

25. Cited in the *Oxford English Dictionary* at "squaw."

26. Stubben and Sokolow 2005, 89.

27. Mihesuah 2003, 102.

28. Sanders and Peek, 1973, 184.

29. Quoted in Adams, "Is 'Squaw' an Obscene Insult?"

30. Callimachi, "Tribes, Gov't, Want 'Squaw' Name Changed."

31. Watner and McElroy 2004, 26.32. Freire 1970; King 2003; Merskin 2001.

33. Emert 2003.

34. Toensing 2007.

35. Paul Carrier, "House Says Take 'Squaw' off the Map." *Portland* (Ore.) *Press Herald,* March 16, 2000, accessed August 7, 2008, http://www.tahtonka.com/ squawstories.html.

36. Marubbio, 2006, 4.

37. Monmonier 2006, 3.

38. Monmonier 2006, 52.

39. Jonthan Buffalo, 1In "Fawn Stubben: Heritage Hero," by Todd Norden, *Gold-finch 18*, no. 1 (1996):=5–7.

40. J. Wickham, "Respect Indians by Erasing Offensive Names," *Rocky Mountain News* (Denver), May 2000, 50A.

41. Tim Giago, "Walk up to Any Indian Woman and Call Her a Squaw," *San Diego Union-Tribune,* May 2, 2003, B9.

42. Suzan Shown Harjo, "Respect Native Women: Stop Using the S-word," *Indian Country Today,* February 28, 2001. In *America Is Indian Country: Opinions and Perspectives from Indian Country Today,* edited by Tim Johnson, 2005. Golden, Colo.: Fulcrum), 170–172.43. Harjo, "Respect Native Women."

44. "Pitter" Glinda Ladd Seabaugh, "Squaw," n.d., accessed November 15, 2003, http://happytrails_2.tripod.com/sitebuildercontent/sitebuilderfiles/ squaw2.htm.

45. Brenda Norrell, "Arizona Loves Squaw Peak Name," *Indian Country Today,* August 1988, C.

46. Marge Bruchac, "Reclaiming the Word 'Squaw' in the Name of the Ancestors," November, 1999, accessed November 10, 2003, http://www.nativeweb.org/pages/legal/squaw.html.

47. Bruchac, "Reclaiming the word "Squaw."

48. Quoted in Margaret Williams, "An All-American Hero: Activist in Training Bruce Two Eagles," 2003, accessed July 3, 2011, http://www.main.nc.us/wncceib/BruceTwoEagMTXP.htm.

49. Muriel Charwood-Litzau, quoted in Norrell, "Arizona Loves Squaw Peak Name."

50. Giago, "Walk up to Any Indian Woman."

51. Wickham, "Respect Indians by Erasing Offensive Names."

52. Quoted in Bruchac 1999.

53. Seabaugh, "Squaw."

54. Dean Chavers, "Doing Away with the 'S' Word," *Indian Country Today,* March 10–17, 16:37.

55. Quoted in Lori Edmo-Suppah, "Proposed Bill to Rid 'Squaw' from Place Names," *Sho-Ban News,* May 25, 2001, 1.

56. Marty Nathan and Monroe Gilmour. "A Victory (of Sorts) at Erwin High School," Greensboro Justice Fund, n.d., p. 6, accessed November 2003, http://www.gjf.org/NL6.html.

57. Briggs and Lewerenz 2003.

58. Quoted in Williams, "All-American Hero."

59. Edmo-Suppah, "Proposed Bill to Rid 'Squaw' from Place Names."

60. Rahnema, 2010.

61. Kessler 1996; Smits 2007.

62. Bowker 1993, 36.

63. Mihesuah 2003, 42.

64. Quoted in Mihesuah 2003, 42. 65. Klein and Ackerman 1995.

66. Chavers, "Doing Away with the 'S' Word."

67. Mihesuah 2003.

68. Andrea Smith 2000, 151–152.

69. Edmo-Suppah, "Proposed Bill to Rid 'Squaw' from Place Names."

70. Andrea Smith 2000, 44.

71. Papa, Singhal, and Papa 1999.

72. Giago, "Walk up to Any Indian Woman."

73. Bowker 1993.

74. Bowker 1993.

75. Bowker 1993, 65.

76. Bowker 1993.

77. Pewewardy, "From La Belle Savage to the Noble Savage."

78. Cornel Pewewardy, "Why Educators Can't Ignore Indian Mascots," 1998, accessed September 23, 2003,

http://www.aistm.org/cornelconclusion.htm.

79. Bowker 1993.

80. Briggs and Lewerenz 2003.

81. Norrell, "Arizona Loves Squaw Peak Name."

82. Norrell, "Arizona Loves Squaw Peak Name."

83. Quoted in Williams, "All American Hero."

84. Monmonier 2006.

85. B. John Craig, "Squaw Creek Decision on Hold: Commission Split on Name Change." *Spokesman-Review* (Seattle), September 12, 2007, B.

86. A. Richard Roesler, "Tribe, Town Can't See Eye to Eye," *Spokesman-Review* (Spokane), July 1, 2007.

87. Quoted in Roesler, "Tribe, Town Can't See Eye to Eye."

88. Sanders, "Renaming 'Squaw' Sites."

89. Associated Press.

90. Diana Bowley, "Piscataquis County Leaders Want 'Squaw' Names Restored." *Bangor Daily News*, September 8, 2006.

91. Associated Press.

92. Seamann 2005.

93. Callimachi, "Tribes, Gov't, Want 'Squaw' Name Changed."

94. Quoted in Johnston 2000, 73.

95. Schroeder and Borgerson 2005, 580.

96. Johnston 2000, drawing on Voleshinov 1973.

97. Schroeder and Borgerson 2005, 580

98. Newton 2000, 8.

99. Gordon 1995, 203.

100. Walker 1997, 179.

101. Coombe 1997, 190.

102. Ramirez-Berg 1990, 294.

103. King 2003, 12.

104. Freire 1970, 40.

105. *New York Times,* 2004.

106. Sanders, "Renaming 'Squaw' Sites."

107. "For a Fallen Soldier, a Very High Honor," *Washington Post,* May 25, 2008, B02; Dyer 1993, 98.

108. Stubben and Sokolow 2005, 89.

Part III

Mediated Images and Social Expectations

9

Buying into Racism

American Indian Product Icons in the American Marketplace

VICTORIA E. SANCHEZ

In the United States, stereotypical images of American Indians are so pervasive and interwoven into the fabric of daily life that many hardly notice them; yet they are a significant factor in how the American dominant culture perceives American Indian cultures. Historical and contemporary use of American Indian symbols in advertising and branding contributes to stereotypes and prejudices and may adversely impact American Indian people.

AMERICAN INDIANS AND THE THREATS OF ADVERTISING

A review of the existing scholarly literature reveals that little has been published regarding American-based advertising media and American Indian cultures. J. Steele discusses the use of African American and American Indian images in early advertising as a means of dehumanizing Indians to defuse racial tensions. In addition, Green explores moral issues surrounding images of American Indians in advertising, which tend to fall into three broad categories of stereotypes: the noble savage, the civilizable savage, and the bloodthirsty savage. Merskin examines the semiotics of how American Indian product symbols function as signs laden with meanings based on deep-seated stereotypes. Advertising and the use of American Indian mascots and team names has been the topic of debate and activism for a number of years. Pewewardy and Staurowsky urge discontinuation of use of American Indian images as sports team mascots, exploring issues of miseducation and implications to the self-esteem of American Indian youth.[1]

This chapter proceeds in three parts: an outline of historical and contemporary use of American Indian symbols in advertising and branding; an examination of how product symbols contribute to stereotypes and prejudices; and discussion of how such use may adversely impact American Indian people.

Impacts discussed include both ethnostress and the phenomena that Steele and Aaronson term stereotype threat.[2]

HISTORICAL AND CONTEMPORARY
ADVERTISEMENTS AND IMAGES

American Indian images are commonly used as icons to identify and advertise products. The use of American Indian images in advertising is not a modern phenomenon. Although new instances continue to appear, the practice of appropriating ethnic imagery, particularly that of American Indians and African Americans, was established in the late nineteenth century. At this same time, warfare and legislation against American Indians sought to resolve the "Indian problem" in the United States.[3] Advertising images used today are essentially similar to early ones, containing Indian characters in caricature (often using the image of a comely maiden or a brave warrior in feathered headdress), and playing upon such stereotypes as stoicism, connection to nature, spirituality, bravery, and strength.

Today many of the Native images used for marketing convey a romanticized ideal, often a nineteenth-century or a pre- European contact ideal of the noble savage. Green has identified three categories of stereotypical imagery that continue to portray American Indians in advertising contexts: the stoic noble savage, the civilizable savage (capable of redemption and education), and the fierce, bloodthirsty savage.[4] Green's categories echo the dichotomy between noble savage and savage Indian that have influenced notions of the Indian since first contact.[5]

The practice of sporting teams with American Indian imagery and use of the noble savage and savage Indian images in advertising began in the latter half of the nineteenth century, as America worked to be done with the "Indian problem."[6] Ironically, the nobility of American Indians—this supposedly dying race—was to be honored and preserved even as American Indians and tribal nations were forcibly annihilated and removed from their homelands. For example, the United States Treasury minted the first Indian Head penny in the same year as the slaughter of nearly three hundred Lakota men, women, and children during the 1890 Massacre at Wounded Knee, South Dakota, by the United States Army. At about the same time, Wild West shows played to large audiences and reenacted the defeat and the taming of wild Indians in a contained and controlled theatrical setting. These forces served to link the notion of authenticity of Indians with the past, diffuse the sense of direct threat to white civilization, and minimize or eliminate consideration of American Indians within the contemporary.[7]

Within this trend, advertisements for common products that appropriated American Indian cultural images began to appear in the American marketplace. Early advertisements focused on characteristics of racial and ethnic

Contemporary examples of products commonly available in the U.S. market that use American Indian product icons or names. Photograph by Victoria Sanchez.

minority groups, depicting individuals in demeaning postures and carica-tures that reinforced the assumption of minorities as outsiders or others be-yond the American mainstream. As a result, nineteenth-century trade cards, which merchants handed out to attract potential customers, remain to this day the most graphic examples of racial and ethnic stereotypes being used as marketing tools.[8] These depictions fulfilled the two basic ingredients of preju-dice—denigration, and gross overgeneralization—and frequently drew upon images of American Indians.[9] Advertising stereotypes, both historic and con-temporary, reinforce prejudice by constructing American Indians as outside the mainstream of the dominant American culture. In addition, this action reaffirms and helps mainstream American culture to define itself by clearly showing that it could not possibly belong to the out-culture. Characteristi-cally, American Indians, as outside the mainstream, were portrayed as essen-tially homogeneous and lacking in variability.[10]

American Indians became in the nineteenth century a romanticized ab-straction with an exotic appeal suitable for use by the fledgling advertising industry.[11] One common trend was to portray American Indian people as a vegetable people, as in an image of the corned Indian on an 1886 Diamond Lawnmowers trade card discussed by Jeffrey Steele:

> Merging deeply rooted images of oral gratification, masculine sexual-ity, and racialized iconography, this [motif] represents the American

Indian as a consumable product, as food. In the face of white imperialism, this card suggests, Indian cultures (like the products appropriated from them) could be absorbed at will.[12]

The Argo Corn Starch corn maiden is an example of this motif that is still with us today.

American Indians were portrayed in ways that suggested an alien status. American Indian advertising motifs typically included American Indian imagery in outdoor settings. Images that focused on native attire, such as beads, feathers, and fringed buckskins, with references to specific treaties or Indian wars, again fixed the image of the Indian in a bygone context and created a people that were frozen outside the mainstream.[13]

In the twenty-first century, American Indian product imagery still typically employs the exoticized stereotype, usually fixed in an eighteenth-century image of an American Indian, or of Indian wars that occurred in that time frame. The Land O'Lakes product line is a prime example of such imagery and represents perhaps the most pervasive use of the Native American female logos. The Land O'Lakes website explains the history of the packaging design:

> The now-famous Indian maiden was also created during the search for a brand name and trademark [in 1924]. Because the regions of Minnesota and Wisconsin were the legendary land of Hiawatha and Minnehaha, the idea of an Indian maiden took form. In 1928, Land O'Lakes received a painting of an Indian maiden facing the viewer and holding a butter carton. Lakes, pines, flowers and grazing cows decorated the background. That painting inspired a new design for the butter carton, and remained until the spring of 1939, when it was simplified and modernized by Jess Betlach, a nationally recognized illustrator. Fifty years later, with only minor changes, his design continues to capture the goodness and quality of Land O'Lakes products.[14]

More often, product imagery employs an American Indian male archetype. Money House Blessing Air Freshener promises the protection of the warrior in a full-feathered headdress. Tecumseh engines employ a profile of an American Indian Chief in a war bonnet and promise the strength and endurance of their namesake. Calumet Baking Powder, Big Chief Sugar, Cherikee Red Pop, Indian Head Corn Meal, Crazy Horse Malt Liquor, and other products use a very similar image of the head of an American Indian chief or warrior in a full Plains-style headdress.

Additionally, specific American Indian tribal names or individual names are used to the same effect. The Winnebago Brave recreational vehicle, Pontiac (which formerly used the warrior-head image and had a line of cars known as the Star Chief), Mohawk carpeting (which formerly used the image of an infant warrior in feathers), Chief Wenatchee Apples, and Crazy Horse Malt Liquor are examples. These appropriations can result in ironic unintentional meanings. The more recently developed Pontiac Aztec juxtaposes the Ottawa leader from the French and Indian wars and Siege of Detroit with a pre-Columbian Mexican civilization. And the historical individual Crazy Horse, the much admired Lakota Chief and warrior who adamantly opposed drinking alcohol, makes an ironic symbol for malt liquor.

THE POWER OF STEREOTYPES, PREJUDICE, AND SYMBOLIC ANNIHILATION

Today American Indians make up less than one percent of all people in the United States.[15] The United States recognizes more than five hundred American Indian tribes, speaking more than three hundred native languages, as sovereign nations.[16] Still, for many contemporary Americans, contact with American Indian individuals is extremely limited. Because of limited experiences with American Indian cultures and ignorance of the diversity within their populations, most people tend to rely heavily on the stereotypical images most frequently found in the American mass media.[17] This helps to generalize, categorize, and connect these cultures outside the mainstream to non-Native cultures.[18]

Simplistic stereotypes of American Indians are constructed by recurrent portrayals of American Indians that we have grown up seeing around us every day in the mass media, particularly in movies.[19] The dominant culture then comes to expect the real people of American Indian nations to be like the artificial and incorrectly portrayed Indians that are presented by the mass media for their consumption. Indeed, these stereotypes are often powerful enough to be self-confirming even when an individual is faced with evidence that contradicts a deeply held stereotype. In addition, one may interpret the evidence to favor the stereotype, because "in addition to facilitating access to confirmatory material, stereotypes inhibit access to stereotype 'disconfirmatory' material."[20] Meanwhile, authentic members of American Indian cultures in the twenty-first century remain almost invisible in the American public consciousness. Their voices and self-representations are overshadowed by the pervasive and monolithic images perpetuated and reinforced by the institutions of the American mass media.

This symbolic annihilation of American Indian people,[21] accomplished in large part through the mass media, has very real implications for American Indian people today. Regardless of the original impetus behind the use of Indian imagery to sell products, these practices are still in operation and the effects are still present in the twenty-first century. As in the early days of advertising with Indian imagery, a stylized reality is created that bears little resemblance to the actual lives of individuals in American Indian cultures.

Michael Gray, a member of the Blackfeet, Chippewa-Cree Indian Nation and president of G&G Advertising of Albuquerque, New Mexico, explains, "I'm sure the intention is not to be racist, but Indians are portrayed as historical figures, not live people. Even Iron Eyes Cody, in the famous anti-littering ads, really didn't deal with how Native Americans are [today]."[22]

Charlene Teeters, an American Indian activist on the issue of sporting teams that use American Indian imagery, has insisted, "Indians are people, not mascots."[23] Suzan Shown Harjo, an American Indian activist and founder of the Morning Star Institute in Washington, D.C., has spent more than a decade explaining to mainstream America that such images caricature American Indian peoples and place them in past tense, as if it were acceptable to American Indian cultures to appropriate their images, names, and identities to sell a product.[24] Green argues, "these uses of such images are not morally acceptable because they depend upon an underlying conception of Native Americans that denies to them the status of human being. By so doing, it also denies to them any moral standing and thus any claim to moral consideration and treatment."[25] Indeed, a growing number of tribal governments and Native organizations, including the National Congress of American Indians, have passed resolutions denouncing the use of Indian mascots.

Proponents of using American Indian imagery as a free and common practice argue that American Indians actually enjoy a positive stereotype as a result of this use. These caricatures and other devices used to invoke American Indian cultures, they argue, pay homage to the positive attributes of Native cultures, and thus American Indians should feel honored by such treatments. However, a stereotype remains a stereotype regardless of the possible positive connotations or the intention of its use. The position that American Indian people are honored through the appropriation and caricature of their cultural identity has long been a justification of the use of Indian mascots for sports teams. Today, a majority of people from American Indian cultures resent being told they should feel honored for the use of their identity, and countless numbers have staged nationwide demonstrations asking that the use of American Indian imagery with sporting teams and in the marketplace be stopped. "The arrogance of telling any ethnic group what is important," says one commentator, "how it should interpret insults, that all members of the community must feel exactly the same way and how it 'should' feel is mind-boggling . . . and racist."[26]

These pervasive, negative ethnocentric American Indian stereotypes contribute to an institutionalized ethnic prejudice against American Indian cultures and are commonly interwoven into the fabric of American consciousness,[27] so ubiquitous that mainstream America has simply come to find them acceptable and not insensitive. In his seminal work on prejudice, Allport described ethnic prejudice as a category resulting in "disparagement" of an ethnic "group as a whole," not necessarily based on defining attributes but often including various "nonessential" and "false" attributes such as those defined through stereotypes.[28] Prejudice results from a perceived threat to one group by a different group and is often colored by self-confirming stereotypes.[29] Stereotypes form the cognitive component; prejudice, the affective component; and discrimination, the behavioral component of group category–based responses.[30]

ETHNOSTRESS AND THE IMPACT ON AMERICAN INDIAN PEOPLE

The pervasiveness of insensitive ethnocentric stereotypical images of American Indians is a contributing factor to perpetuation of deep-seated prejudice against American Indian people and cultures. The effects of stereotyping, prejudice, and stigma contribute to a chronic experience of discrimination that may impact multiple areas of an individual's life and health. Research shows that discrimination is associated with multiple indicators of poorer physical health, including higher rates of cardiovascular disease and other disease.[31] Harrell, Hall and Taliaferro show in their research that "racism increases the volume of stress one experiences and may contribute directly to the physiological arousal that is a marker of stress-related disease."[32]

There are also significant implications for mental health issues with American Indians as a result of negative ethnocentric imagery in the mass media. The disjuncture between traditional American Indian values and identities and imposed Euro-American values and identities forces American Indian individuals into a position commonly termed as "walking in two worlds." This cultural schizophrenia "has caused untold confusion and misery as well as social and personal dysfunction among Indian people."[33] The struggle to maintain traditional American Indian identities in the modern mainstream context and the resulting sense of disempowerment is symptomatic of what Cajete refers to as ethnostress.

> Ethnostress is primarily a result of a psychological response pattern that stems from the disruption of a cultural life and belief system that one cares about deeply. . . . Its initial effects are readily visible, but its long-term effects are many and varied, usually affecting self-image and an understanding of one's place in the world.[34]

One result is a set of psychological effects similar to the hostage syndrome. Dispossessed of the right to self-representation and self-determination and faced with the prescribed notion of what an Indian should be, the individual afflicted with this syndrome experiences "a range from total rejection of the perceived controllers to an attempt to actually identify with the inaccurate perception and become the same."[35] In other words, American Indian individuals may react to the psychological stress of pervasive stereotyping in a range of ways. Some may completely reject modern, non-Indian life and strive for living as completely within Native culture as possible; for others, the reaction may be to assimilate into dominant American culture and reject Indian-ness; for others still, the confusion of ethnostress may result in internalizing the stereotype and trying to conform to the prescribed notion of Indian-ness.[36] Not measuring up to an inaccurate and prescribed identity can result in a crisis of self-identity and self-worth. It is these feelings of low self-worth that contribute to alarming rates of suicide and dropout among American Indian youth. American Indians, both young and old, have a suicide rate considerably higher than the national average. The dropout rate in states with the highest percentage of American Indian and Alaska Native students averages about 50 percent.[37]

Stereotypes produce an expectation that individuals will conform to the stereotype and may influence the way individuals are treated. In a process known as the "self-fulfilling prophecy," or "behavioral confirmation," one who holds stereotypes of others interacts with them as if they conform to the stereotype, thereby eliciting confirmatory behavior from the target. This process makes the target more predictable and controllable.[38]

The academic abilities of racial and ethnic minorities are typically targeted in these stereotypes.[39] Stereotypes involving low levels of ability or competence (such as would be suggested by many stereotypes of American Indians) also undermine an individual's performance directly when the individual is aware of the possibility of being compared to the stereotype, a condition called a stereotype threat.[40] Steele and Aronson first described stereotype threat as

> An immediate situational threat that derives from the broad dissemination of negative stereotypes about one's group—the threat of possibly being judged and treated stereotypically, or of possibly self-fulfilling such a stereotype. This threat can befall anyone with a group identity about which some negative stereotype exists, and for the person to be threatened in this way he need not even believe the stereotype. He need only know that it stands as a hypothesis about him in situations where the stereotype is relevant.[41]

Throughout a series of studies with African American and women students, Steele and Aronson demonstrated that behaviors and poor test performance in relation to white male students are not the result of gender or racial differences but are a temporary result of (often subtle) situational factors activating the stereotype threat condition.[42]

An individual's level of stereotype vulnerability increases with the depth of the sense of attachment or identification with one's group. It has long been established that children as young as five are capable of developing a strong sense of ethnic identification. Individuals who care deeply about and are proud of their group identity may also have a heightened awareness of and expectation of discrimination, a condition Pinel terms "stigma consciousness." These stigmas can induce defense mechanisms, which typically include self-handicapping behaviors, avoidance of challenge, self-suppression, and disidentification.[43] For one to be successful in any domain (school, work, etc.), one must have some degree of self-investment in that domain: it has to matter. But, if it matters, then one is susceptible to stereotype threat.[44]

Stereotype threat hampers achievement in several ways. Experienced during a performance situation, performance can be directly affected by the anxiety and feared inferiority. As a chronic condition, stereotype threat can lead to internalization of the negative stereotype and devaluing of one's self or group. Stereotype threat can also trigger disidentification, a reconceptualization of one's self and values to remove the domain as something that matters to one's self-identity. Disidentification is a protective strategy, but it can easily result in undermining motivation and performance in the domain. One's sense of belonging and/or competence in the domain can be affected. Disidentification and sense of not belonging can prompt withdrawal from the domain altogether. In a domain as important as school, the consequences can be costly.[45]

Stereotypes can also have an effect on those who interact with members of stereotyped groups. Cohen and Steele note that teachers who work across ethnic lines may become conscious that they might be perceived as treating minority students according to stereotypes. The teachers then may overcompensate, creating a self-fulfilling situation in which they may treat students in an overly positive manner, thus impeding their education.[46]

CHANGING PRACTICES

Appropriation of cultural images and symbols is a widespread and institutional practice that shapes the general public's concept of American Indians. Activism on this issue has centered largely on sporting teams (including national franchises, collegiate sports, and local school teams) that adopt American Indian imagery for mascots, as this facet of the issue may be positioned for greatest public exposure.[47] However, this practice extends to product symbols and other stereotypical representations.

Cohen and Steele recommend that in an educational setting the situational threat of stereotyping be addressed by teaching strategies that demonstrate to students that their abilities and belonging are presumed rather than doubted and that they will not be treated stereotypically. This approach mitigates the stereotype threat, encouraging minority students to trust their educators and remain invested in the academic situation.[48] Neglecting to identify and address stereotypical marketing icons such as sports team nicknames, or even

Land O'Lakes dairy products in the school cafeteria, would obviously be counterproductive to such an effort.

The American Indian Mental Health Association of Minnesota issued a position statement in 1992 specifying the negative impact of use of American Indian advertising and marketing icons and mascots and called for their elimination from schools:

> As a group of mental health providers, we are in agreement that using images of American Indians as mascots, symbols, caricatures, and namesakes for non-Indian sports teams, businesses, and other organizations is damaging to the self-identity, self-concept, and self-esteem of our people. We should like to join with others who are taking a strong stand against this practice.[49]

On April 13, 2001, the U.S. Commission on Civil Rights likewise issued a statement calling for an end to use of American Indian team names and images by non-Native schools.[50] The American Sociological Association issued a Statement on Discontinuing the Use of Native American Nicknames, Logos and Mascots in Sport on March 6, 2007.[51] Similar resolutions have been passed by a number of institutions, including tribal organizations, educational boards, professional associations such as the Modern Language Association and the National Education Association, and civil rights groups such as the NAACP and the Southern Poverty Law Center. The National Collegiate Athletic Association's Minority Opportunities and Interests Committee conducted an eighteen-month study, releasing in October 2002 the document "Report on the Use of American Indian Mascots in Intercollegiate Athletics." Among its recommendations, which were adopted in August 2003, were that member institutions with American Indian mascots "complete a self-analysis checklist to determine if the depiction of the mascot, nickname, logo, or behaviors can be viewed as offensive" and that the NCAA would continue to monitor the use of American Indian mascots by member institutions.[52] Following this study, the NCAA issued a ruling "prohibiting colleges or universities with hostile or abusive mascots, nicknames or imagery from hosting any NCAA championship competitions," effective February 1, 2006.[53]

Some sport teams have changed their names or mascots because of these initiatives. One highly contentious and high-profile example is the University of Illinois's Chief Illiniwek mascot.[54] However, most schools and teams are reluctant to break with the "tradition" of using American Indian imagery, such as the Cleveland Indians professional baseball club, the Florida State University Seminoles, and perhaps most tenaciously, the University of North Dakota Fighting Sioux.[55] One convoluted example: in 1999 the Associated Press reported that "the trustees at Indiana University of Pennsylvania voted to change the school's mascot from an Indian to a bear, although the team's nickname will remain the Indians." A follow-up report in 2002 indicated that "some students wanted to do away with the name of the replacement, a bear nicknamed Cherokee."[56] IUP is included on the list of schools affected by the NCAA ruling. An interesting counterpoint is the University of Northern Colorado intramural basketball team that has adopted the image of a clean-cut Caucasian man as its mascot in a rhetorical turnabout to fight the use of Native American stereotypes.[57]

In the early 1990s, two newspapers banned use of Indian nicknames and pictures of mascots in their coverage of the teams. The *Oregonian* (Portland) was the first, in 1992, followed by the highly controversial decision by the *Minneapolis Star Tribune* in January 1994; shortly after, the *Kansas City Star* decided no longer to run pictures of the Cleveland Indians Chief Wahoo mascot.[58] In 2002, the Native American Journalists Association urged the news media to stop using Indian mascots and nicknames; few if any additional newspapers had adopted the policy in the intervening years.[59]

Although progress has been slow in negating the use of sports mascots and American Indian imagery, there seems to be even less progress with advertising products using American Indian stereotypes, especially when compared to some marketplace responses to complaints regarding racialized exploitation from the Latino and African American communities. For example, Frito-Lay, Inc., discontinued using its "Frito Bandito" advertising theme by the early 1970s, and only the original eatery of the once-national Sambo's restaurant chain, now located in the predominantly white enclave of Santa Barbara, California, remains open. And although Aunt Jemima and Uncle Ben's product lines and logos remain on store shelves, their original slave/servant images have been updated. However, Calumet Baking Powder has used essentially the same American Indian imagery since its inception in 1889. Many newer products with similar American Indian motifs have been added to the marketplace.

In the case of American Indians, the dissenting voices of American Indian individuals and cultural groups alone are not sufficient to effect widespread change in this kind of business practice. A significant paradigm shift will be required to create change; business and communications ethicists and the general public must reconsider the use of American Indian imagery as a marketing tool and recognize the consequences of continuing such use. Several cases have emerged that have begun to bring the issue to light.

In 1992 Congress passed a bill, signed by then-President George H. W. Bush, which prohibited the use of the name Crazy Horse on alcoholic beverage products. This action was in response to suits involving the Crazy Horse family and the Hornell Brewing Company, producer of Crazy Horse Malt Liquor. The family contended that the revered Oglala Lakota warrior and spiritual leader "strongly opposed the use of liquor and encouraged his people to abstain from alcohol."[60] For this reason they viewed the use of his name and the image of a warrior in headdress representing him as especially offensive. The Supreme Court eventually overturned the law based on the Hornell Company's free speech arguments. The Stroh Brewing Company (which had owned Crazy Horse Malt Liquor before selling the product line to Hornell) formally apologized in a 2001 ceremony.[61] But federal and state suits continue to be filed against Hornell Brewing Company.

In another instance demonstrators gathered outside the Liz Claiborne corporate offices in Manhattan, New York, urging consumers to boycott J. C. Penney's distribution of Claiborne's Crazy Horse clothing line. The demonstration organizer, Bill Means (a member of the Oglala Lakota Nation), explained: "Anyone who knows anything about American history knows the name Crazy Horse. When they use that name to sell things, they offend an entire race of people."[62]

In contrast to the corporate obstinacy surrounding Crazy Horse brands and many sports teams' American Indian imagery franchises, some corporations are more attuned to cultural issues. The Binney & Smith Company, for example, owners of Crayola Crayons, have changed the name of their colors only four times in the brand's long history, the first three instances in response to teachers' requests. In 1958 the crayon color "Prussian Blue" was changed to "Midnight Blue." In 1962 the crayon color "Flesh" was changed to "Peach" in response to the Civil Rights Movement, to acknowledge that not all people are of the same skin color. In 1999 the name "Indian Red" was changed to "Chestnut" because children wrongly perceived the color to be that of Native Americans, when in fact the name had its roots in a pigment from India.[63]

CONCLUSION: MASS MEDIA, AMERICAN INDIAN CULTURES, AND CHANGE

This issue is ultimately one of representation and self-determination. The situation is perhaps most critical for young people—American Indians and non-American Indians alike. Developing minds are in the process of building the conceptual frameworks necessary for critical thinking and are not equipped to understand in depth the historical and cultural inaccuracies that have become accepted as mainstream perceptions of American Indian cultures.

Regardless of the intention behind the appropriation of American Indian images, the historical context and real implications must be acknowledged. Any appropriation of American Indian images or cultural imagery to sell a product amounts to perpetuation of institutionalized racism and is a contributing factor to insensitive stereotypes, prejudice, discrimination, and stigmatization. Despite the slow changes that are beginning to dismantle and contradict stereotypical images, significant progress is difficult. Allport's group-norm theory of prejudice postulates that those who perceive themselves as excluded often develop characteristic codes, beliefs, and groups outside the mainstream to suit their needs and that subtle pressures keep each individual's beliefs in line with the group's perceptions. He accordingly suggests that to change individual attitudes effectively it is necessary to change group norms. When new group norms are established, the resulting group dynamic will create individual attitudes conforming to that norm.[64] By their nature, the mass media are in a position to help affect such a change in attitudes and beliefs concerning American Indians.

DISCUSSION QUESTIONS

1. Generate a list of common products that use American Indian images and/or names. Had you been consciously aware of how pervasive this practice is, or of its deep history, before reading this chapter? Have you purchased any of these items? In what other ways might you be "buying into racism" without realizing it?

2. How would you describe the population of American Indians in the United States today? How do their numbers affect this issue? Do you personally know any American Indian people? Are they like the images portrayed by product icons?

3. In 1992 the Oprah Winfrey Show aired an episode featuring the American Indian activists Tim Guiago, Suzanne Harjo, and Michael Haney. As Giago noted in a 2008 commentary, "It was the first time in television history that a major talk show allowed Native Americans to discuss openly why we do not appreciate our use as mascots for sports teams," and as symbols for commercial products. Has this topic been covered since then by other major television shows? In regard to this issue, what has changed, or not changed, since then?

4. Why do companies continue to use American Indian product icons? What are they "selling" when they do so?

5. How can you contribute to ending this practice, as an individual? As a consumer? As a media consumer? As a media practitioner?

NOTES

1. J. Steele 1996; Green 1993; Merskin 2001; Pewewardy 1998; Staurowsky 1999.
2. Ethnostress: Cajete 1994. Stereotype threat: Steele and Aronson 1995.
3. J. Steele, 1996; Berkhofer, 1979.
4. Green, 1993.
5. Berkhofer, 1979.
6. J. Steele, 1996.
7. Link with past: Berkhofer 1979. See also Morgan 1986.
8. Steele 1996, 47.

9. Allport 1954.

10. Fiske 1998.

11. Jay 1987.

12. J. Steele 1996, 53–54.

13. J. Steele 1996, 53–54; Allport 1954.

14. "Land O'Lakes history," (n.d.), Land O'Lakes Company, accessed June 14, 2002, http://www.landolakes.com/ourCompany/LandOLakesHistory.cfm.

15. United States Census Bureau, "Profile of General Population and Housing Characteristics: 2010," (American Fact Finder Table), 2010 Demographic Profile Data, accessed July 16, 2011, http://factfinder2.census.gov/faces/tableservices/jsf/pages/productview.xhtml?pid=DEC_10_DP_DPDP1&prodType=table.

16. United States Department of the Interior, Bureau of Indian Affairs, accessed July 16, 2011, http://www.bia.gov/index.htm.

17. Lippmann 1922.

18. Fiske 1998.

19. Mihesuah 1996.

20. Disjksterhuis and van Knippenberg 1996.

21. Strinati 1995.

22. Lou Belmont, "Beware His 'Wall of Shame': Agency Tunes Message for Native Americans," *American Marketing Association Marketing News,* November 22, 29; Belmont, "New Mexico Ad Agency Aims to Combat Stereotypes of American Indians," *Denver Post* (2nd ed.), November 5, 1999, A32.

23. Quoted in Rosenstein 1997.

24. Suzan Harjo, in "American Indians," *The Oprah Winfrey Show: Racism in 1992,* November 1992.

25. Green 1993, 323.

26. Metz 1995, 15.

27. Berkhofer 1979; Deloria 1998; Dippie 1982; Mihesuah 1996.

28. Allport 1954.

29. Fiske 1998.

30. Fiske 1998.

31. Williams, Neighbors, and Jackson 2003.

32. Harrell, Hall, and Taliaferro 2003, 247.

33. Cajete 1994, 144.

34. Cajete 1994, 189.

35. Cajete 1994, 190.

36. Internalizing: Allport 1997. Effort to conform: Cajete 1994.

37. "Suicide Facts at a Glance," 2009, Centers for Disease Control and Prevention (CDC), National Center for Injury Prevention and Control (NCIPC), accessed July 15, 2011, http://www.cdc.gov/violenceprevention/pdf/Suicide-Data Sheet-a.pdf. John Hatch, "American Indian and Alaska Native Adult Education, and Vocational Training Programs: Historical Beginnings, Present Conditions, and Future Directions," in *Indian Nations at Risk: Listening to the People,* edited

by Patricia Cahape and Craig B. Howley (Charleston, W.Va.: ERIC, 1992). "Status Dropout Rates of 16–24-year-olds, by Race/Ethnicity: Selected Years, 1980–2008," National Center for Educational Statistics (NCES), accessed July 18, 2011, http://nces.ed.gov/fastfacts/display.asp?id=16. Susan C. Faircloth and John W. Tippeconnic III, "The Dropout/Graduation Rate Crisis among American Indian and Alaska Native Students: Failure to Respond Places the Future of Native Peoples at Risk" (Los Angeles: The Civil Rights Project/Proyecto Derechos Civiles at UCLA), accessed July 18, 2011, http://civilrightsproject.ucla.edu/research/k-12-education/school-dropouts/the-dropout-graduation-crisis-among-american-indian-and-alaska-native-students-failure-to-respond-places-the-future-of-native-peoples-at-risk/faircloth-tippeconnic-native-american-dropouts.pdf.

38. Expectation of conformity: Allport 1954. Self-fulfilling prophecy: Merton 1957. Behavioral confirmation: Snyder 1984; Hatch, "American Indian and Alaska Native Adult Education, and Vocational Training Programs." Control of target: Fiske 1998.

39. Birenbaum and Kraemer 1995.

40. Aronson 2002; C. Steele 1997; C. Steele 1998; Steele and Aronson 1995.

41. Steele and Aronson 1995, 798.

42. Steele and Aronson 1995, 798; C. Steele 1997; Aronson 2002; Spencer, Steele, and Quinn 2002.

43. Stereotype vulnerability: Aronson 2002. Identification with group: Aronson 2002; Steele and Aronson 1995, 798; C. Steele 1997. Ethnic identification in young children: Allport 1998. Stigma consciousness: Pinel 1999. Defense mechanisms: Aronson 2002.

44. C. Steele 1997.

45. C. Steele 1997.

46. Cohen and Steele 2002.

47. See Chapter 11, "A Shifting Wind? Media Stereotyping Of American Indians and the Law," for analysis and discussion of specific legal battles over the use of Indians as sports mascots and some of the public impact of such usages.

48. See Chapter 11, "A Shifting Wind?"

49. Quoted in in Pewewardy 1998.

50. U.S. Commission on Civil Rights, *Statement on the Use of Native American Images and Nicknames as Sports Symbols,* 2001, accessed June 27, 2011, http://www.usccr.gov/press/archives/2001/041601st.htm.

51. American Sociological Association, *Statement by the Council of the American Sociological Association on Discontinuing the Use of Native American Nicknames, Logos and Mascots in Sport,* 2007, accessed July 14, 2011, http://asanet.org/about/Council_Statements/use_of_native_american_nicknames_logos_and_mascots.cfm.

52. "NCAA Executive Committee Issues Guidelines for Use of Native American Mascots at Championship Events," NCAA press release, August 5, 2005, accessed July 18, 2011, http://fs.ncaa.org/Docs/PressArchive/2005/Announcements/NCAA

+Executive+Committee+Issues+Guidelines+for+Use+of+Native+American+Ma
scots+at+Championship+Events.html.

53. NCAA Minority Opportunities and Interests Committee, "Report on the Use of American Indian Mascots in Intercollegiate Athletics to the NCAA Executive Committee Subcommittee on Gender and Diversity Issues." October 2002, accessed November 1, 2002. http://www.ncaa.org/wps/wcm/connect/NCAA/ Legislation%20and%20Governance/Committees/Assoc-wide/Moic/2003/ Mascot%20Report/mascotreport.htm.

54. Brad Wolverton, "After Years of Debate, U. of Illinois Drums Out Its Controversial Mascot," *Chronicle of Higher Education,* March 2, 2007, accessed July 13, 2011, http://chronicle.com/article/After-Years-of-Debate-U-of/21707/.

55. Lindsay. Bosslett, "NCAA Treads Warily in North Dakota, Critics of Fighting Sioux Mascot Say Tournament Should Not Be Held on the Campus," *Chronicle of Higher Education* 49, November 11, 2002; *Chronicle of Higher Education,* "North Dakota's 'Fighting Sioux' Law Won't Prevent Penalties, NCAA Says," *Chronicle of Higher Education,* April 19, 2011, accessed July 14, 2011, http://chronicle.com/blogs/ticker/ north-dakotas-fighting-sioux-law-wont-prevent-penalties-ncaa-says/32279.

56. Associated Press, "IUP Votes to Keep 'Indians' Nickname, School Will Change Mascot to a Bear," *Centre Daily Times* (State College, Penna.), March 6, 1999, 4A; Associated Press, "UP Considers New Name For Mascot," *Daily Collegian* (University Park, Penna.), March 1, 2002.

57. Fighting Whites, "Official Website of the Fightin' Whites Intramural Basketball Team of the University of Northern Colorado," 2004, accessed July 14, 2011 http://www.cafepress.com/fightinwhite.

58. Tim McGuire, "Racism in Sports," speech delivered during racism and sports conference in St. Paul, Minn., November 20, 2001, accessed December 8, 2004, http://www.naja.com/pr-mcguire.html.

59. Native American Journalists Association (NAJA). "NAJA Calls upon News Media to Stop Using Mascots," 2002, accessed December 8, 2004, http://www .naja.com/pr-stopmascot.html.

60. Metz 1995, 15.

61. Bruce E. Johansen, "Crazy Horse's Estate Reaches Settlement in Malt Liquor Case," *Native Americas,* August 31, 2001, 6.

62. "Crazy Horse's Tribe Protests Brand Name," *Philadelphia Daily News,* December 12, 2000, 17.

63. The fourth change was from "Torch Red" to "Scarlet" in 2000. Crayola Crayon Chronology" Crayola, 1999, 1A, 7A, accessed 21 June 2011, http://www.cra yola.com/colorcensus/history/chronology.cfm. Jennifer Brown, "Crayola Crayons Break with 'Indian Red' Label," *Centre Daily Times* (State College, Penna.), March 1, 1999.

64. Allport 1954.

10

The Notion of Somebody Sovereign

Why Sovereignty Is Important to Tribal Nations

PAUL DEMAIN

Journalist Paul DeMain (Oneida/Ojibwe) is considered to be the dean of contemporary American Indian newsmakers, because of his broad experience and influence. In this chapter, DeMain weaves personal experiences, historical analyses, and insights from his interviews with prominent Indian leaders into an exploration of the complexities of "living" in the United States as a sovereign person.

DEFINING THE FUNDAMENTALS OF SOVEREIGNTY

It would be easy enough to cloud the issue of "What is sovereignty?" and entangle readers in particular pieces of historical litigation, court rulings, and governmental pronouncements. There exist numerous books of legalese already written. It does not take much time to locate volumes of material to be cited, quoted, and rearranged in order to present some type of academic, linear proposal for what I think is a simple, plain, fundamental idea, albeit with many tentacles. Sovereignty, in my view, is a plain principle and basic right of human beings to exist and function in society as they choose for themselves and without interference.

My position as a news editor, a radio commentator, and journalist brings me in contact with a repeating smorgasbord of issues that touch on the edges of "sovereignty" on a regular basis. Yet most people in the general public and most students of academia would be at a loss to describe it. They could not tell how it impacts them on a local or governmental level, or how it might shape their daily lives.

For Indian Country, the newsworthy issues relating to sovereignty make headlines at a regular pace. "Tulalip Claim Beach Rights," or "Protests Grow around Bear Butte Development," or maybe "Descendants of Hawaiian Royalty Meet to Discuss Self-Governance," are all examples of headlines in a 2006 issue of *News From Indian Country,* all containing important elements of sovereignty-based arguments.[1] Each one of these conflicts bears an important impact and principle for tribes wanting to exercise and maintain self-rule, self-governance, and some control over the "interference" that other governments, entities, or actions like economic development, land acquisition, or public access allege to have over Native rights.

A more recent headline from Red Lake, Minnesota, reads, "Tribal Conservation Wardens Confiscate Boat of Fisherman." It seems unlikely that the war of words the owner has unleashed, in regard to whether Minnesota should have rights to regulate use of the lake for all public citizens, will ever lead to the man's getting his boat back.

Usufructuary rights are the legal rights of using and enjoying the fruits or profits of something.[2] Religious freedom is just what it says, but without access to your own cathedral of privacy, the idea is rendered almost useless. Self-government, or attempts to be self-governing after a century of occupation and rules imposed by the biggest, allegedly most powerful government in the world, attempts at exercising jurisdiction or the remnants of sovereignty—they can even be dangerous. But what about you and me, and our understanding of what sovereignty is? Why is it that most people still don't carry a basic understanding of what it means and why it is important to tribes?

According to John Echohawk, "If you don't understand tribal sovereignty, you don't understand Indians." As a journalist, I would even propose a relationship with elements of sovereignty in the media. In my opinion sovereignty is expressed best by the freedom of being able to speak out, the freedom to record and distribute without interference. A free press is as free as its ability to convey what is necessary, available, or valued for people to consume. A radio station is as free as its license to broadcast lets it be.

In other words, there is a constant battle between factions pushed and pulled by the strings of "interference" at many levels, not all necessarily reliant on government. Some might argue that under those circumstances the Internet represents the ultimate in "free press" or free communication—a newfound sovereignty of its own kind. That is, until somebody places a filter, or pulls the plug.

Can a government enhance its sovereignty by reining in the press in places like Cuba or Iran—or even in the United States—where press workers are under new pressures and being jailed for leaking information from government sources? Or can a government enhance its sovereignty and power further by the exercise of free and open dialogue and information and the tolerance of critical dissent?

TRIBAL PERSPECTIVES ON SOVEREIGNTY

From a Google search we learn a number of valuable things, but not much about tribes and their interests, unless you look at the concept deeper. In one search we find a simple definition: "Government free of external control."[3] That definition could sum up the whole issue, if not for the notion, and perhaps fact, that most Native governments today come with many different ties to the United States government, from formation to funding.

Further searching reveals many other subtopics relating to governments subjecting, governments establishing, governments claiming, governments handing over, governments exercising, and even God being invoked in the question "What is sovereignty?" That notion (especially in our modern-day society, which has become more universal in its economic, social, and military nature, including outward exploration into the stars) might keep us mindful. Mirror, mirror on the wall: who is the truest sovereign of all?

One of the simplest terms defining sovereignty came from an Iroquois chief some years ago in response to a long of line of inquiries. He described it as something as simple as this, which I have summarized in my own words: First of all you need to have a people, a people that are distinct and related by common bonds. Second, you need to have a land base and territory, and you must know the borders of that territory in which you reside, and then you need to conduct business involving that land, and the business that is conducted within those borders is that which concerns those people, and that is the exercise of sovereignty in its simplest form.[4]

Sometime in 1993, Oren Lyons, who is connected to the same confederacy of chiefs, was recorded speaking on behalf of the Onondaga Nation of the Iroquois Six Nations Confederacy, and when asked, "What is sovereignty?" responded:

> I note that sovereignty is probably the most used and misused word as it relates to Indian Nations. Self-recognition, that's first. Self-determination, the ability to govern oneself, exercising national power in the interest of the nation and its peoples, is fundamental to sovereignty. This, along with jurisdiction over the lands and territories we live and exist on, is sovereignty. Simply put, sovereignty is that act thereof. It is a state of mind and the will of the people, no more, no less. That is sovereignty, as we understand it, sovereignty is freedom. Sovereignty, as I heard the word, is responsibility. . . . The Haudenosanee are a separate, sovereign Nation. We have our own passport, and we travel about the world independently. That is an act of sovereignty. We didn't go to the federal government and ask them, "Can we have a passport?" We issued it, and we traveled. And we continue to do so.[5]

With that contextual description, I bring the discussion back home to that closest level of understanding that I might relate to. What if there was only one human being on this earth? He would be the governor or president of his own territory; he would govern over himself with his own consent. He would engage in all activities with himself, in his own language, practicing his own faith, and living within his own territorial boundaries and body politic. This individual—call him Number 1—would be a sovereign unto him- or herself.

When relating to some of the elders I studied under in the Great Lakes region, it became apparent that some of them exercised what I would term a great deal of personal sovereignty. Old man Pipe Mustache, a Lac Courte Oreilles Ojibwe, didn't need his tribal government's permission to speak his language, conduct the ceremonies of his ancestors, or relate to the creation and environment in the way that his elders had prescribed for hundreds or thousands of years.[6] He needed no body of thought but himself to go about his business without interference. He was independent, in a cultural sense, of those intervening rules of governmental powers around him. But at each level of his existence, as is true with everybody else in a modern society, he was forced to cede elements of his personal sovereignty. He was forcibly educated in government schools. When he was employed, he paid taxes to the federal government. He had to learn English in order to conduct everyday transactions, or to comply with the rules of obtaining Social Security and the prevailing social order with rules as simple as the law that says you must wear a seat belt when riding in a car.

If he didn't follow those rules, some law enforcement, on behalf of a larger political body, would interfere with his social order and make him pay a fine. What was clear from observing elders such as Pipe Mustache or another independent traditionalist like Archy Mosay of the St. Croix Chippewa, and from reading stories you find from across Indian Country—these types of people were and are very independent of the influences of modern society and very self-sufficient. This included those who continued to move farther away in a futile attempt to avoid change and to maintain a sense of separateness from the world of events around them. Change, at times, simply moved around them, especially when they became an obstacle to that change and refused to adapt.

The Kickapoo of Wisconsin fled thousands of miles in a futile attempt to avoid interference, ending up near the border town of Eagle Pass, Texas, where they reside today.[7] Stripped of all their traditional institutions, the attempt to avoid the imposing powers of the growing United States only left them destitute and in poverty, but able to maintain a family and tribal social order that preserved traditions, language, and social "sovereignty" within their small community.

SOVEREIGNTY AND GLOBAL PERSPECTIVES

Saddam Hussein's claim in 2006, four years after the U.S. invasion of Iraq and shortly after his capture, that he was still the duly elected president of that country, may hold some symbolic truth, but in terms of exercising any governance, direct control, or influence in the decision-making processes of the

Iraqi government, that claim was totally diminished. Hussein thought of himself as the ultimate Iraqi sovereign, or was looked upon as a sovereign dictator with absolute powers. He was soon to understand that the U.S. government, after toppling the Iraqi government in a still contested military action, had, in ceremony, handed the sovereignty of the country over to another group of people who are now empowered to exercise the sovereignty of the Iraqi government and the Iraqi people, like it or not. Saddam Hussein could no longer impose, influence, or enforce any rules of law, but he certainly made statements that were intended to "interfere" with the political order of the "new Iraq." Even though he could have interfered in a roundabout way, I doubt if anyone would, or could, have considered him a "sovereign," or anything more than a nuisance waiting to be sentenced and ultimately executed for exercising his former "ultimate" power.

Here we now begin to see the proposed elements of true sovereigns: the ability to claim and assert (or interfere) with the freedoms of each level of social order, powers derived from exercising or enforcing sovereignty, laws and order, or disorder, or in some cases withdrawing the exercise of power, which is an exercise of sovereignty. You might describe it as the right to decide not to make a decision. And nations have exercised that right at times as well to achieve certain goals. Do we exercise our sovereignty by intervening, or do we exercise our sovereignty by not intervening? Either decision might tip the balance of power, but either is empowering by either action or inaction.

With only one human being, alluded to earlier as Number 1, exercising sovereignty over all the decision-making processes within his or her territory, the arrival of another human being, Number 2, means the division of, or consolidation of, sovereign powers.

Would two human beings share decision-making power within a territory, taking on joint sovereignty, or divide the territory, making each entity a true sovereign within his or her own boundaries, and hence dividing the powers to decide and control human action as the population might grow?

Most modern-day tribal governments claim inherent sovereignty from their mere existence, from the fact that their people, their government, their boundaries, and ruling conduct preceded the establishment of the United States or Canadian governments. But the mere interaction of governments is an exercise of sovereignty, just as the sharing or division of territory between two people avoids the interference of rules over each other, or implements them in a joint consensus-making process. Modern-day tribal governments point to treaties and agreements between the United States, Canadian, and other governments in defining their ability to regulate their own members within their diminished territories. They have the ability to implement local courts of law, issue license plates, banish undesirable individuals from within their boundaries, protect natural resources or confiscate the property of offenders, define who their member citizens are, levy taxes, create corporations, sue on behalf of their communities, and establish casino gaming on their lands. In some cases tribes are exercising sovereignty by allowing law enforcement officials to cross into their territories while in hot pursuit, or to present warrants for arrest and extradition to be served in the community by local tribal law enforcement and judicial officials, or by sharing in the taxation of gas and cigarettes.

Native nations at times have even been able to the get the world courts and United Nations to rule on their behalf, even though decisions are routinely ignored by the standing governments who are accused.

In one sense, Native governments are seen as a small model, or mirror, of what the federal, state, or county governments already are. The exercise of sovereignty means that tribal governments may mirror the image of local governments but are very much governments in their own style, some with powers equal to, or above the states'.

LOCAL IMPLICATIONS: THE EXERCISE OF SOVEREIGNTY

In some cases, the exercise of sovereignty is confined, and defined, by the relationship between government agencies and tribal programs. This simply means that the United States can, through influence or interference, help mold tribal policies and hold tribes accountable when they are financially dependent, or on the other hand, help them chart their own futures by legislative activism empowering tribes to become more independent. The fact is that although many historic treaties with the United States spell out many different rights, the nature of federal Indian law is such that certain powers exercised by one tribe may have been ceded to the U.S. government by another. Ultimately, the give and take that different governmental entities have with each other regarding tribal government is an element of sovereignty. Most tribes voluntarily ceded very little land title over the course of two hundred years.

There is no state within the United States, to my knowledge, that has a treaty with the federal government or with other countries, as many Native nations do. Treaties intentionally are a higher, binding type of international law that bestows upon tribes a recognition that neither states nor other local forms of government have. Treaties rarely conveyed powers upon tribes that the tribes didn't inherently possess. The treaty-making era with tribes was essentially one in which the United States either seized or sought a conveyance of some resource or jurisdictional power from the tribes.

The differences from other types of localized governments become most recognizable and confrontational when local arguments erupt over taxing, law enforcement, resources, and jurisdictional types of issues.

A recent federal ruling in northern Wisconsin (*Lac Courte Oreilles Band of Chippewa Indians v. Voigt*) by a conservative appeals court upheld the "retained usufructuary rights to hunt and fish on land ceded by them to the United States."[8] This becomes just one prime example of conflict that led to the greater exercise of governmental powers by a modern-day Native government.

I note that the right to hunt and fish had historically belonged to the Chippewa, and was not sold, traded, or ceded in any manner. Over the course of one hundred years, because of neglect of the federal treaty and trust agreement, the state was able gradually to prevent Chippewa tribal members from exercising those off-reservation rights through arrest and confiscation. This led to the modern-day filing in the courts of a lawsuit alleging that the state of Wisconsin was illegally depriving Chippewa tribal citizens from accessing their own property.

The Lake Superior Chippewa or Ojibwe, as they are also known in federally ratified treaties in the U.S. Senate, ceded millions of acres of land to the U.S. government in the 1800s, but explicitly, in plain English, written down in the treaty, retained the right to hunt and fish within the land they once owned according to their customs. Modern-day legal language might describe usufructuary as a retained easement right to access resources while selling the title to occupy the land to somebody else—a fairly simple, well-defined canon of universal property law. Also, in Germany former property owners have reserved and owned legal title to the hunting and fishing permits on pieces of land that have been sold, and title transferred to another owner for occupancy.[9] So, why can these principles not be applied to lands American Indians once owned?

Many Wisconsin state citizens had a hard time understanding the first ruling, trying to argue that, somehow, what the Chippewa saved in a treaty one hundred years ago was lost because today was a different time element than a week, or year, or century ago. Either way, the element of time did not erode the retention of certain rights and did not make a difference in this ruling. The courts basically concluded that rights not sold, conveyed, or stolen by military actions or theft remained with the proper owners in the absence of a legal taking.

More important to the Chippewa was the idea that once that right was upheld, Ojibwe citizens would not just participate in some license-free state-sponsored hunt of deer or other resource-gathering activity but, under their sovereign rights, would establish their own licensing, their own natural resources analyst and agency, their own fish and game law enforcement arm, on and off their reservations, and their own hunting and fishing seasons with bag limits that reflected their own needs.

Several other tribes have either won previous court decisions of the same magnitude or have pursued them since to the aggravation of the state of Wisconsin, which has argued that the resources within a state are the state's public property, to be regulated for the benefit of events and other activities generally of a fun and sporting or income-generating nature.

While the state attempted to find a court-forced remedy to rein in the Ojibwe, the judicial decisions upheld the tribe's self-regulatory schemes, which the state was advised to contribute to, but not interfere with.

HISTORICAL DIMENSIONS: TURNING POINTS AND CROSSROADS

However diminished modern-day tribal governments may appear to some, tribes have more recently become empowered to rebuild their institutions. The Iroquois Chief Canasatego, in council in 1744, spoke to colonial governors about the formation of the Iroquois Confederacy, one of the must formable Native governments observed by the founding fathers of the U.S government:

> Our wise forefathers established Union and Amity between the Five Nations. This has made us formidable; this has given us great Weight and Authority with our neighboring Nations. We are a powerful Confederacy; and by your observing the same methods, our Wise Fathers have taken, you will acquire such strength and power.[10]

One of those observing Canasatego's speech was none other than Benjamin Franklin, who went on to help frame a constitution of checks and balances of power based upon many of his observations of the Iroquois Confederacy. Abraham Lincoln never let the world forget that the Civil War involved an even larger issue. This he stated in a most moving way when dedicating the military cemetery at Gettysburg:

> That we here highly resolve that these dead shall not have died in vain— that this nation, under God, shall have a new birth of freedom—and that government of the people, by the people, for the people, shall not perish from the earth.[11]

The recital of responsibility for the governing powers, which Iroquois chiefs held in great reverence when placed in office, was basically the same but went like this: "A government of the People, by the People, for the People, and for those yet unborn." Lincoln may have thought that the exercise of sovereignty could not be extended far beyond those who did not already exist.

Power and strength are obviously part of the formula that defines sovereignty.

Our two individual human sovereigns, Number 1 and Number 2, unable to share or divide the powers of inherent sovereignty, might engage in what seems to be another part of the natural order. One day one of these individuals decides he wants some resource the other has, or perhaps thinks that the only way to bring about a more democratic form of government, for both sides of the world, is to impose it upon the other. While "interfering" with the pleasant or decrepit living standards of the second human being, Number 1 becomes the ultimate bully, taking what he wants, infringing upon somebody else's freedoms under the notion that the rules and regulations now imposed are "in the best interests" of the other.

Thomas Jefferson observed the nature of many governments and their exercise of control and the rule of law and then compared them with Native governments against the potential of thirteen smaller states of power, confederated under a central government. He observed (referring here to the Indians of Virginia):

> Imperfect as this species of coercion may seem, crimes are very rare amongst them; so much that were it made a question, whether no law, as among the savage Americans, or too much law, as among the civilized Europeans, submits man to the greatest evil, one who has seen both conditions of existence would pronounce it to be the last: and that the sheep are happier of themselves, than under the care of the wolves. It will be said, that great societies cannot exist without government. The savages, therefore, break them into small ones.[12]

As history shows, governments allied with each other in a confederacy or coalition, as many tribal nations did, served the purpose of building a "collective ultimate power," at least temporarily.

Perhaps most people can best relate to the issue of sovereignty by examining the United States' experience since its invasion of Iraq. In 2003 the United States (a sovereign government) invaded (and interfered with) Iraq without its permission and took control of its ability to govern itself (the loss of ultimate power). The army, the police, educational institutions, its oil fields and territory within its defined borders all came under the control of an occupying sovereign, just as the lands of many Native nations did.

The United States invaded Iraq not because of any inherent sovereignty it had—it did so because it perceived the policies of another government as threatening those of the United States, and therefore "regime change" under the guise of fighting global terrorism became the justification. "Regime change" has become the clouded legal basis for a previous policy that justified invasion, destruction, and subjugation. Called the Discovery Doctrine, it became well established in U.S. federal law in 1823 when the Supreme Court embraced the idea in *Johnson v. McIntosh:*

> While the different nations of Europe respected the right of the Natives, as occupants, they asserted the ultimate dominion to be in themselves; and claimed and exercised, as a consequence of this ultimate dominion, a power to grant the soil, while yet in possession of the Natives. All has understood these grants, to convey a title to the grantees, subject only finitely to these States.

The United States, then, have unequivocally acceded to that great and broad rule by which its civilized inhabitants now hold this country. They hold, an to the Indian right of occupancy. (For which some form of compensation was usually paid.)

No(t) one of the powers of Europe gave its full assent to this principle, more unequivocally than England. The documents upon this subject are ample and complete.

Thus, all the nations of Europe, who have acquired territory on this continent, have asserted in themselves, and have recognized in others, the exclusive right of the discoverer to appropriate the lands occupied by the Indians. Have the American States rejected or adopted this principle?

By the treaty which concluded the war of our revolution, Great Britain relinquished all claim, not only [to] the government, but to the "property and territorial rights of the United States" By this treaty, the powers of government, and the right to the soil, which had previously been in Great Britain, passed ded assert in themselves, the title by which it was acquired. They maintain, as all others have maintained, that discovery gave an exclusive right to extinguish the Indian title of occupancy, either by purchase or by conquest; and gave also a right to such a degree of sovereignty over Indians and their land, as the circumstance of the people [of the United States] would allow them to exercise.[13]

Most Native people believe the Doctrine of Discovery is mainly a bunch of legalese allowing sanctioned property theft. Indeed, the phrase "as the circumstance of the people would allow them to exercise" really means "we won't interfere with what you do, unless we want to."

If our lone human being, sovereign over himself and making all the rules, decides to break them—who is there to hold him accountable? And of our two, if one should covet the other's resources and "interfere" with the other's sovereign territory, does it leave but just one sovereign by the nature of interference in the other?

STORIES AND MEANING: LEGAL NARRATIVES

Pipe Mustache, like other tribal elders, refused in many cases to abide by government-initiated programs, failed to recognize or react to mandates, rules, and regulations or demands, and he was punished. Mustache believed that Native people had a right to "choose" the type of a future they wanted, a position that several other groups of people, tribes, and nations have maintained as well, most notably the Onondagas of the Iroquois Confederacy, who do not have a tribal government recognized by the 1934 Indian Reorganization Act,[14] as most other tribes in the United States have. They have issued their own passports and control a tiny plot of Aboriginal land near Syracuse, New York, that the federal government today is reluctant to interfere with. During the world wars members of the same confederacy refused to send men from their community into war until they themselves declared war on the enemy and allowed their men into military service as an ally of the United States.

In another example of tribal exercise of sovereignty, the highly reclusive Red Lake Chippewa of Northern Minnesota,[15] who historically managed to avoid allotment of their reservation into small family plots, still maintain an advisory council of chiefs for leadership decisions and exert a great deal of local control, including recent exclusion of the press from Red Lake reservation lands during a highly public mass shooting there in 2005.

And still another example is the reservation of the Pine Ridge Lakota Sioux,[16] where many people have chosen to abide in cultural richness and poverty in the country's poorest county and reservation over embracing many forced governmental education and economic development programs. It is never very polite to describe how the Lakota people are wired as thinkers, but they have fought both a historical and modern-day battle to remain Lakota. And while the U.S. government might not be able to force a lot of change and ideas upon the Pine Ridge community through an imposed order of enculturation, nevertheless education, economic development, and governmental influence at Pine Ridge play a greater role than previously in the lives of the Lakota people today, as long as the institutions are institutions that are created and embraced by the Lakota people themselves.

The late Vine Deloria, Jr., was called to the witness stand in U.S. Federal District Court in Washington State on Monday, December 16, 1974. Before him, several chiefs and witnesses had testified in court hearings that were meant to establish whether the United States had jurisdiction over individuals arrested in 1973 on the Pine Ridge reservation and in the village of Wounded Knee, a place highly symbolic of imposed U.S government policies and genocide. Deloria described the history of a series of treaties signed between the U.S. government and the various bands of the Great Sioux Nation, including Oglala, Sisseton, and Yankton, which led to a validation of tribal fishing rights.[17]

SOVEREIGNTY IN A SMALL-WORLD APPROACH

I return once again to my small-world approach. Sovereign human being Number 1, after invading the land of sovereign human being Number 2, says, "You will have education and learn all the things I know." This action enhances the sovereignty of Number 1, whether exercised in a powerful military fashion or more simply stated at the street level: "He who is the biggest bully gets what he wants."

Sovereign human being Number 2 rejects the idea, which might diminish the sovereignty of human being Number 1 if it somehow changes the balance of power and relationship between the two. Only a short time later, Number 1 also discovers that human being Number 2 has announced his own educational initiative, in which "all that needs to be learned will be learned on my own." The balance of sovereign power, or of just plain power, appears to be a fluid concept depending on force, willingness, and concessions of authority.

Are these futile attempts to exercise sovereignty, or are they sovereignty in its true form, involving attempts at forced action, rejection, and self-governance? Perhaps they just mirror some kind of human action of give and take that exists in the real world.

Over the course of history, the sovereignty vested in Native governments, which is alleged to derive from the consent of those it governed, was observed by other governments to be something inherent. Modern, democratic governments tended at least to espouse that theory when it served some vested relationship or moral basis.

Great Britain after its defeat in the War of 1812 insisted in a treaty of peace (the Treaty of Ghent, 1814)[18] that their Indian allies be given the recognition of their territorial boundaries and that the United States extend peace to "the Indian allies of Great Britain, and that the boundary of their territory be definitively marked out as a permanent barrier between the dominions of Great Britain and the United States."[19] The United States treaty delegation, led by John Quincy Adams, initially refused this provision but later in the proceedings responded by describing the policy of the United States in a much more restrained manner in regard to land claims.

Territory appears to have played a significant role in this discussion:

> Under that system the Indians residing within the United States are so far independent that they live under their own customs, and not under the laws of the United States; that their rights upon the lands where they inhabit or hunt, are secured to them by boundaries defined in amicable treaties between the United States and themselves; and that whenever those boundaries are varied, it is also by amicable and voluntary treaties, by which they receive from the United States ample compensation for every right they have to the lands ceded to them. They are so far dependent as not to have the right to dispose of their lands to any private persons, not to any Power other than the United States, and to be under their protection alone, and not under that of any other Power. Whether called subjects, or by whatever name designated, such is the relation between them and the United States.[20]

In other words, while the U.S. government was recognizing the sovereignty of tribes to live within their own rules and regulations within their own territories, they were also initiating a limited view of how that sovereignty could only be exercised and within the context of how the U.S. government would let them exercise it. We won't begin to discuss here the concept of fairness, nor the value of equity for transfer of vast tracts of land in treaties essentially forced upon the tribes, in warfare, political manipulation, or just plain deceit.

It is clear that sovereignty has to do with territory, and that it has to do with the exercise of power over some kind of defined constituent, or the power of interference within certain boundaries.

At the individual level, sovereignty at one time was vested in kings, queens, and monarchs and from ancient times was considered to be God-given to gifted individual leaders. Given the former situation in Iraq in which U.S. President George Bush said he prayed for guidance from God before invading the country,[21] we may have come a full circle.

CONCLUSION: SOVEREIGNTY, TERRITORY, AND POWER

The exercise of military power has historically been derived from the concepts both of sovereignty and power, the notion of extending one's sovereignty in order to protect the nation, expand the nation, acquire or control new resources, or subjugate new constituents for economic or other purposes, such as religious belief. The Vatican, while encompassing a very small geographical region, exercises a very well-known sovereignty in the exercise of certain powers, most of which appear to derive from boundaries defined by religious affiliation and not by geography.

Chief Oren Lyons elaborated that sovereignty had to do with "responsibility."[22] From his known point of view within the concepts of the Iroquois Confederacy, responsibility was mandated from the cultural expression of Native people who viewed their decisions as based on impact upon and responsibility to the whole environment of earth and universe—and, in particular, a responsibility to several generations of children "yet unborn."

Irresponsible exercise of sovereignty therefore may come at a price, and can no doubt be cited as the cause for the moral and political downfall of great leaders, and great and powerful governments.

The Cherokee Nation only recently became one of the first tribal nations to embrace freedom of the press constitutionally and to grant access to tribal government information as a right of its citizen members. Former Cherokee Nation chief Chad Smith championed the idea that other tribes, in an exercise of their sovereignty, have an obligation to assure that freedom of the press is ingrained in all actions of their public officials. But Smith also underscored the "responsibility" that journalists have to carry out that mandate.

Sovereignty is a pressing issue for our time. The late Cherokee Chief Wilma Mankiller admonished journalists one step further on journalistic responsibility in an address to members of the Native American Journalists Association in Tulsa, Oklahoma, in 2006, by reminding them that the "issue of sovereignty" and how non-Natives perceive it, is probably the foremost issue facing Indian Country today.[23]

That is, if non-Natives perceive it at all.

Within tribal governments, the issue of both free and restricted press is still in its infancy, as the first generation of Native American press and media law makes its way through newly established tribal courts in the process of establishing bodies of tribal media law in written form, an exercise in codifying the sovereign attributes that a tribe has retained, including power to restrict, allow, or demand transparency in the actions of tribal leadership.

What we know is that sovereignty plays an important role in the governance of individual and political entities whether it be in the individual choices of people like the late Pipe Mustache to withdraw from actions of other people or their governments, or whether governments or individuals seek to force their actions on others through sheer political or military might.

From the individual to township, county, state, tribal, and federal entities, the exercise of sovereignty appears to be shaped in many different forms and fashions, from the confiscation of a boat to regulating tribal and nontribal activities. Tribal governments have embraced the idea that sovereignty is an important basis for their continued existence as entities, and how sovereignty relates to self-governance and relationships is one of the most important ideas and tools developing today. To understand sovereignty is to understand the nature of continuing tribal existence.

And on the flip side, if you don't understand why sovereignty is the issue, you won't understand why tribes want to be more sovereign, or already are.

But about our two human beings exercising their sovereignty over their defined domain: whether they choose to rule collectively, or to interfere with each other, if they should meet their demise through some natural or God-bestowed calamity, the question might not be "What is sovereignty?" but ultimately "Who truly is sovereign?"

DISCUSSION QUESTIONS

1. What is the most basic definition of sovereignty that you understand?
2. List several sovereign rights that the United States government has given to tribal nations.
3. Is there a difference between individual and political sovereignty?
4. Give an example of how sovereignty might be achieved.
5. Describe how sovereignty and self-government work for, or against, each other.

NOTES

1. All items appeared in the August 7, 2006. *News from Indian Country,* an independent, Indian-owed newspaper, has been published twice a month since 1986. Offices can be found on the Lac Courte Oreilles Ojibwe Reservation located in

northern Wisconsin. Paul DeMain is the founder, CEO, and Managing Editor. http://www.indiancountrynews.com/ (accessed June 21, 2011).

2. Prior to 1871, treaties were used by the United States to purchase land from Indians. Provisions were usually included in the treaties, which recognized the Indians had the right to hunt, fish, and gather from the land sold to the United States.

3. Due to the ever-changing qualities of the Internet, there is no guarantee that the same result would occur at the top of the Google listings.

4. See *The Legal Conscience: Selected Papers of Felix S. Cohen,* edited by Lucy Kramer Cohen (New Haven: Yale University Press, 1960). Felix S. Cohen was a respected legal scholar, and this collection of his writings includes a section entitled "The Indian's Quest for Justice."

5. Quoted in Utter 1993, 266.

6. In a July 2007 *News from Indian Country* article, Thelma Nayquonabe explains that James "Pipe" Mustache was a ceremonial leader of the Ojibwe people of Wisconsin and Paul DeMain's namesake (*owiyowenh'enhyan*). Pipe became DeMain's mentor, delivering historical and ceremonial information to DeMain, eventually giving him the name Skabewis or Oshkaabewis, which means "ceremonial attendant" or "ceremonial messenger" in the Ojibwe language.

7. *Encyclopedia Britannica*'s online edition states in its article on the Kickapoo that a large group of them relocated to Texas in 1852. This group was one of many that relocated westward after ceding land in Illinois to the United States in 1809 and again in 1819. http://www.britannica.com/EBchecked/topic/317295/Kickapoo (accessed July 20, 2011).

8. *Lac Courte Oreilles Band of Lake Superior Chippewa Indians v. State of Wisconsin, United States of America,* 740 F.Supp., 1400 (W.D.Wis. 1990).

9. Michael Wendler, Bernd Tremml, and Bernard Buecker, in *Key Aspects of German Business Law: A Practical Manual,* 4th ed. (Berlin: Springer 2009), 5.2.1, explain, regarding German real property laws, that "real-estate property, as well as condominiums and heritable building rights, can be charged with a so-called usufruct ('Niessbrauch'). The usufruct grants the entitled party the right to take the property into his possession and make full use of it. In other words, the usufructuary is entitled to the personal use of the property as well as to any and all yields of the property such as renting and leasing rights."

10. Quoted in Cohen, *The Legal Conscience: Americanizing the White Man,* 1970, 321.

11. Quoted from Abraham Lincoln biography, http://whitehouse.gov/about/presidents/abrahamlincoln/ (accessed June 21, 2011). A full text of the Gettysburg Address, with background information, appears at http://en.wikisource.org/wiki/Gettysburg_Address (accessed June 21, 2011).

12. Quoted in Cohen 1970, 321.

13. Quoted in Wilkins and Lomawaima 2002. Also available as *Johnson v. McIntosh* (Supreme Court of the United States, 1823), 21 U.S. (8 Wheat.) 543, 5 L.Ed. 681., accessed July 21, 2011, http://thorpe.ou.edu/treatises/cases/johnsonhtml.

14. The Indian Reorganization Act (Wheeler-Howard Act), June 18, 1934, accessed July 21, 2011, http://www.cskt.org/documents/reorganizationact.pdf.

15. See http://en.wikipedia.org/wiki/Red_Lake_Indian_Reservation (last accessed July 21, 2011).

16. See http://en.wikipedia.org/wiki/Pine_Ridge_Indian_Reservation (accessed July 21, 2011).

17. Vine Deloria, Jr. (March 26, 1933–November 13, 2005) was an American Indian author, theologian, historian, and activist. See http://en.wikipedia.org/wiki/Vine_Deloria,_Jr., accessed June 21, 2011; this includes (under "Activism") a brief discussion of the 1974 Washington court case.

18. The Treaty of Ghent (8 Stat. 218), signed on December 24, 1814, in Ghent, currently in Belgium, was the peace treaty that ended the War of 1812 between the United States of America and the United Kingdom of Great Britain and Ireland; see http://en.wikipedia.org/wiki/Treaty_of_Ghent (accessed July 21, 2011).

19. Protocol of Conference, August 8, 1814 2d, in *American State Papers, Legislative and Executive Documents of the Congress of the United States, Class 1, Foreign Relations* (Washington, D.C.: Gales and Seaton, 1832), 3:708.

20. Indian Removal Debate 1830, 21 Congress, 1 Session Volume 6, Part 1, Columns 343–57.

21. At a summit held in Crawford, Texas, 2002.

22. Oren R. Lyons (b. 1930) is a Native American Faith keeper of the Turtle Clan of the Seneca Nation of the Iroquois Confederacy. Once a college lacrosse player, he is now a recognized advocate of indigenous rights; http://en.wikipedia.org/wiki/Oren_Lyons, accessed July 21, 2011.

23. Wilma Pearl Mankiller (born November 18, 1945 in Tahlequah, Oklahoma) was the first female chief of the Cherokee Nation. She served as the Principal Chief 1985–1995 and died on April 6, 2010; http://en.wikipedia.org/wiki/Wilma_Mankiller, accessed July 21, 2011. According to the April 10, 2010 issue of the *Tulsa World,* about 1,200 people attended the memorial service for Chief Mankiller in her home state of Oklahoma. For more information of the 2006 Tulsa conference of the Native American Journalists Association see chapter 12, "American Indians at Press: The Native American Journalists Association," by Mark Trahant.

11

A Shifting Wind?

Media Stereotyping of American Indians and the Law

andré douglas pond cummings

This chapter examines the intersection of stereotyping, the media, American Indians, and the law. In a targeted discussion of specific movies, offensive mascots, legal precedents, and U.S. history, the author navigates the interconnectedness of false perceptions and concrete realities—both historical and legal—that have contributed to media distortions of American Indians.

A modern sophisticated white businessman is sitting in a first-class train carriage, writing in a notebook, when suddenly, the train is "attacked" by a group of fierce American Indian warriors on horseback, whooping and shooting a barrage of arrows at the train. The "attack" on the train fails as the primitive and clumsy American Indian warriors are unable to breach the modern train car and fall awkwardly aside with each attempt. At the end of the advertisement, an American Indian is shown serving drinks on the train. Text at the conclusion of the commercial states, MAN WHO GO ON BIG TRAIN HAVE BIG IDEA.

Television advertisement, Virgin Rail Group, Ltd,
November 26, 2006

INTRODUCTION: WHEN LEGAL STEREOTYPES COLLIDE

An accurate historical narrative of the treatment imposed upon American Indians at the hands of the United States government reveals a sordid tale.[1] The portrayal and stereotyping of North America's Indigenous civilizations by the United States' popular media emulates this foul history.[2] The U.S. legal system's contemptuous judicial decrees and legal policies promulgated for more than two centuries testify to the government's and the popular media's hostility and historical abuse toward American Indians.[3] Unfortunately, both for historical (and modern) purveyors, each of these abhorrent deeds is memorialized for the world to read and see in countless broken treaties, motion pictures, literary works, and judicial records.[4]

In recent decades historians and scholars, both American Indian and non-Native alike, have skillfully documented the deceitful trail of broken promises and near annihilation.[5] In addition, the popular U.S. media and the U.S. legal system have intersected curiously over the years in a tag-team treatment of, and discrimination against, American Indians. The media—including print advertising, newspapers, literary works, television, online sources, and motion pictures—seem to have borrowed historical stereotypical characterizations from the judiciary and U.S. government policies, and vice versa, simultaneously portraying American Indians as ferocious and savage yet simple and helpless.[6] Proven instances of governmental abuse and discrimination, hostile portrayal and stereotyping by the media, and contemptible judicial decrees are innumerable.

In very recent years, there is some evidence that the discriminatory winds are shifting. Slowly and steadily, segments of the mass media seem to be trending toward a more honest account of U.S. history, and the portrayal of American Indians is becoming more reflective of reality and humanity.[7] Since the late 1990s, encouraging signs that the wind is shifting have signaled a potential sea change in the way that American Indians are presented to the U.S. public through the media and the law.[8]

That said, favorite American Indian stereotypes and comfortable discriminations die hard.[9] As the law and media stumble forward awkwardly, attempting to get it right, an assortment of U.S. contingencies, including professional sports franchises and American universities, cling desperately to timeworn typecasts and hostile imagery.[10]

While myriad options exist when attempting to describe the shameful historical treatment of American Indians, the following three brief snapshots are presented to convey the essence of that treatment and to invite contemplation of any further change in the curious intersection between the media and the law. The three snapshots include a glimpse of the historical treatment of American Indians by the U.S. government, followed by a look at the traditional stereotyping of American Indians by U.S. mass media, and finally a brief examination of a few of the historically offensive judicial decrees handed down by federal judges. Further examination of the connection between the modern media and the law will assess whether a sea change is truly upon us.

HISTORICAL SNAPSHOTS

U.S. Government Treatment of American Indians

The Wounded Knee Massacre, which occurred near Pine Ridge, South Dakota, on December 29, 1890, provides a violent snapshot of U.S. government attitudes toward American Indians during the period of "removal and relocation" policy that began in the early decades of the nineteenth century.[11] The

Lakota Sioux entered into numerous treaties with the United States government in the 1800s, only to see the treaties repeatedly violated in subsequent years.[12] This historical trail of breach and deceit culminated in the Wounded Knee Massacre in 1890 and the forced relocation of the remaining Lakota onto reservation wastelands.[13]

At midcentury the Sioux had reluctantly agreed to sign the Treaty of Fort Laramie (1851), which guaranteed them, among other things, a large reservation in South Dakota as a permanent home.[14] Thereafter, the government allowed hundreds upon hundreds of non–American Indians to settle on that same land, in violation of the treaty.[15] After numerous battles, in 1868 the Sioux were forced to sign a new Fort Laramie Treaty (1868) that radically diminished the size of their reservation.[16] While this new treaty usurped most of their land, it did leave the sacred Black Hills to the Sioux and promised that no additional land would be taken or removed from their ownership.[17] However, gold was discovered in the Black Hills in 1874, and soon after, Congress removed the Black Hills from the reservation, again in violation of treaty.[18] In 1889 the U.S. Congress removed a further 50 percent of what remained of Sioux land and carved what remained into six distinct reservations, dividing the Sioux among those new reservations.[19] Resistance to this last treacherous government action ended quickly with the massacre of hundreds of Lakota at Wounded Knee Creek in 1890.

The U.S. military (which suffered twenty-five casualties) killed nearly three hundred Sioux men, women, and children at Wounded Knee when the Lakota marched through the snow toward Pine Ridge, yet another new reservation home.[20] Wounded Knee is often viewed as the last of the armed conflicts between America's Indigenous people and the U.S. government. Still, the government was not finished with the Sioux in South Dakota. In 1904 and again in 1910, Congress removed additional lands from the six already stripped reservations. The Rosebud reservation, for example, was reduced to one-fourth of its pre–Wounded Knee area.

As one journalist wrote, "The United States has broken nearly every one of its Indian treaties. Most of them were broken to obtain Indian land."[21]

Stereotyping by U.S. Mass Media

It is irrefutable that the Hollywood motion picture industry and the corporate advertising mainstream in the United States historically has perpetuated hateful, disgraceful images of American Indians and stereotypes.[22] Rennard Strickland, in his important book *Tonto's Revenge: Reflections on American Indian Culture and Policy* (1997), carefully tracks Hollywood's strange fascination with and depictions of American Indians throughout the twentieth century. *Tonto's Revenge* details the insidious Hollywood stereotyping that depicted American Indians as savage, warlike, ferocious, primitive, simple, and fierce. Strickland, a law professor of Cherokee and Osage heritage, eloquently

MURDER OF MISS JANE MC CREA A.D.1777.

She was dressed to meet her bridegroom, and accompanied her Indian conductors... but by the way, the two chiefs disputed which of them should deliver her to her lover the dispute rose to a quarrel, and according to their usual mode of disposing of a disputed prisoner one of them cleft her head with his tomahawk.

Early U.S. lithographic art provided caricatures of American Indians. "Murder of Miss Jane McCrea, A.D. 1777" (New York: N. Currier, c. 1846). Courtesy of Library of Congress, Prints and Photographs Division, Washington, D.C.

describes Tinseltown's use of white actors to play famed American Indians, and points to the paradigm created in Hollywood of two Indian archetypes, the "savage sinner" and the "red-skinned redeemer."[23]

In an art exhibition and visual presentation he has created called *Marquee Massacres: Native Americans in One Hundred Years of Global Movie Graphics* Strickland forcefully illustrates, through movie posters and descriptions, the historical racism and stereotyping that fundamentally cemented current images of American Indians in the minds of young Americans. Strickland opines: "Hollywood didn't actually create the American Indian, but it some ways it might as well have."[24] Most of these images portray American Indians as "savage," "primitive," "helpless," "tragic," "dangerous," and "vicious."[25] This media stereotyping is pervasive because genuine exposure to real, living American Indians by U.S. citizens has been severely restricted due to governmental policies that placed Indians on reservations in remote deserts and frigid wastelands. Strickland and many others have put forth powerfully strident commentary and critique of this insidious stereotyping.[26]

Hollywood and television have not been and are not alone in perpetuating hostile American Indian stereotypes. Corporate America and U.S. print media, including newspapers and magazines, have run advertising campaigns, political cartoons, and commentary that perpetuated terrible myths and negative representations.[27] Cartoons in the colonial era often depicted the American Indian as a dangerous threat to white female settlers and pioneer daughters.[28] Mainstream newspapers and magazines, generally on hearsay, perpetuated the "savage" and "uneducated" stereotype in immeasurably harmful ways.[29]

In addition, since the 1800s, athletic teams in the United States have adopted American Indian words and symbols as their nicknames, mascots, and monikers. In the 1900s, professional sports franchises and National Collegiate Athletic Association (NCAA) member institutions adopted American Indian mascots, logos, and imagery that have served to deepen and strengthen the debilitating stereotypes described above. Still today, several professional sports franchises and NCAA institutions continue to promote and support mascots, imagery, "war chants," dances, "tomahawk chops," and imitations of traditional dress that maintain and teach anew age-old stereotypes and racism.[30]

Offensive Judicial Decrees

For all of the outrageous acts by the U.S. government against American Indians and for all of the denigrating stereotypes and typecasting by the U.S. popular media, there was support, on occasion encouragement, in these endeavors by judicial decree. Judicial decisions perpetuated and validated the American Indian as "savage" and without recognizable rights, as noncitizens.[31] In keeping with their notorious findings and language, U.S. Supreme Court justices stamped the American Indian as inferior, feeble, and brutal.[32]

In the 1831 U.S. Supreme Court case of *The Cherokee Nation v. The State of Georgia,* the majority justices wrote:

> The Indians are acknowledged to have an unquestionable, and heretofore an unquestioned right to the lands they occupy, until that right shall

be extinguished by a voluntary cession to our government. It may well be doubted whether those tribes which reside within the acknowledged boundaries of the United States can with strict accuracy be denominated foreign nations. They may more correctly perhaps be denominated domestic dependent nations. They occupy a territory to which we assert a title independent of their will, which must take effect in point of possession when their right of possession ceases—meanwhile they are in a state of pupilage. Their relations to the United States resemble that of a ward to his guardian. They look to our government for protection; rely upon its kindness and its power; appeal to it for relief to their wants; and address the President as their great father.[33]

As early as 1830, then, the United States Supreme Court was referring to America's original inhabitants as existing in a "state of pupilage" much like "wards" to their guardian and indicated that the American Indians considered the United States president as their "great father." Thomas Jefferson, by his own hand, bestowed the title of "great father" upon himself as president of the United States when referencing the American Indians in letters, documents, and executive communication.[34] By judicial decree, American Indian individuals were denigrated, devalued, and discriminated against.

The words of Chief Judge John S. Watts of the New Mexico Territory Supreme Court, recorded in 1869 in the case of *United State of America v. Jose Juan Lucero,* are particularly astonishing:

The idea that a handful of wild, half-naked, thieving, plundering, murdering savages should be dignified with the sovereign attributes of nations, enter into solemn treaties, and claim a country five hundred miles wide by one thousand miles long as theirs in fee simple, because they hunted buffalo and antelope over it, might do for beautiful reading in Cooper's novels or Longfellow's *Hiawatha,* but is unsuited to the intelligence and justice of this age, or the natural rights of mankind. The government of the United States, while thus dignifying these savages with the title of quasi nations, with whom the United States has, from time to time, and quite often, entered into stipulations to purchase their lands, have generally purchased at an average of about two cents an acre, and then sold it out to the people at from one dollar and a quarter to ten dollars and fifty cents per acre, thus making a speculation off of the Indian lands of over fifty millions of dollars, if their title is anything but an ingenious and benevolent fiction.[35]

As one legal scholar notes, the United States judiciary "has never voided a single congressional act that diminished or abrogated any inherent or aboriginal tribal right."[36]

LAW AND MEDIA: THE STRANGE INTERSECTION

The motion picture and television industries have released literally thousands of works depicting American Indians as weak, helpless, and incapable, yet simultaneously fierce, savage, and deceitful. In doing so, the industries were merely reflecting and refracting what was being delivered to them by the judiciary and the legislature of the United States, as captured in snapshot above. Strickland carefully recognized this strange intersection of law and media stereotyping in the late 1990s. Both in his book *Tonto's Revenge* and during his Hollywood movie poster presentation, *Marquee Massacres,* Strickland was careful to describe the role of Hollywood and the media in perpetuating negative stereotypes of American Indians. Bob Keefer's interview with Strickland as part of coverage of the exhibit in the *Eugene* (Ore.) *Register-Guardian* covers several main points of his message:

> In the past century, [Strickland] argues, Hollywood's Indians have had a profound influence on the lives of real Indians. That's because the movie version has been the main source of information, he says, for the non-Indian lawmakers who have decided the fate of real indigenous people. . . . "Most people's image of the Indian is related to what one sees on the screen, whether in TV or movies. And most decisions (about Indians' lives) are made, under the trust relationship, not by Indians themselves but by non-Indians."[37]

In actuality, what most of modern society perceives about American Indians, their culture and their historical relationship with the United States, has by and large come from ignorant and bigoted white male legislators, judges, producers, and writers. How much time did Chief Justice John Marshall spend with the Cherokee before he penned his infamous "ward of the state" language in *Cherokee Nation*? How many federal judges had ever known or interacted with any American Indians before stripping them of their rights, culture, and lands? How many legislators met and communed with American Indians before passing the Indian Removal Act in 1830, which uprooted and disenfranchised hundreds of thousands of American Indians, eventually leading to the Trail of Tears?[38] The likeliest scenario is that most legislators, judges, and Hollywood producers learned all that they knew from books, newspapers, and novels of equally ignorant and bigoted writers.[39] President Andrew Jackson, the primary architect of the brutal removal policies, did in fact have significant interaction with American Indians before assuming the presidency and instigating "removal." However, his experience came singularly as an "Indian fighter," where his duty was simply to force Native people to comply with U.S. government and legislative policies of hate, or face extermination.

Thus the relationship between the mass media and the law has worked in tandem to keep all parties badly misinformed and to perpetuate devastating stereotypes and bigoted policies. Early newspaper accounts of the savagery and ferocity of the American Indians misinformed the men who would later become judges.[40] The judges, by judicial proclamation, described American Indians to the world as helpless, weak, in need of paternal and parental oversight in order to survive, yet simultaneously primitive in their savagery.[41] In turn, developing screenwriters, movie producers, television writers, and magazine reporters took the legal and legislative decrees to heart and wrote stories and movies about a downtrodden and devastated people, including stirring portrayals of ferocious, yet primitive, savage, yet infantile American Indians.[42] These images, thanks to judges, legislators, moviemakers, and television producers, have been cemented in the psyche of U.S. citizens, and such imagery still pervades American culture.

A SHIFTING WIND: CAN THE MASS MEDIA GET IT RIGHT?

With this backdrop of ignorant reporting, paternalistic judicial decision-making, greedy legislative land grabbing, and ridiculous motion picture stereotyping, are things changing? Have the mass media begun to affect a sea change in attitude toward and portrayal of the American Indian? Has the legal community begun to coalesce around a much different approach to and view of American Indian rights? For the time being, it appears that Tonto may very well have his revenge.

Two very encouraging signs have emerged since the 1990s that indicate that the wind might be shifting. First, there has been an emergence and embrace of American Indian filmmakers and screenwriters in Hollywood. These emerging talents have been critically accepted and lauded and most importantly have struck nationwide and worldwide distribution deals for their new brand of motion pictures. Second, non-Native motion picture and television program producers and directors are taking seriously the importance of historical accuracy and honest portrayal of American Indians in their works. These producers and directors are conducting tireless research and have scoured historical records in order to present a more authentic representation and to provide a fresh insight as described below.

Emerging American Indian Filmmakers

Chris Eyre and Sherman Alexie are foremost among the emerging class of talented American Indian filmmakers and screenwriters. In 1998, Eyre and Alexie wrote, produced, and directed *Smoke Signals*. Released and distributed by the Weinstein brothers for Miramax Films, this major motion picture presented a view of Native American life that had previously rarely ever been seen. Rather than cowboys and Indians, rather than a colonial or western period piece, *Smoke Signals* presented a heartwarming and wry coming of age tale that transpired in the 1990s and was set on an American Indian reservation.[43] *Smoke Signals* premiered at Robert Redford's Sundance Film Festival, where it won several awards that resulted in a bidding frenzy for purchase and distribution that was eventually secured by Miramax.[44] *Smoke Signals* was released nationally, and millions of Americans received their first glimpse into the life of a modern American Indian on a contemporary reservation. The magnitude and success of *Smoke Signals* cannot be overstated.[45]

Building on the critical and commercial success of *Smoke Signals*, emerging American Indian filmmakers and writers are seizing opportunities to write, direct, and produce additional major motion pictures, most of which are set in modern reservation communities and many of which tell "normal" stories of real American Indians in the twenty-first century. Films such as *Skins* (2002), *The Fast Runner* (2002), *Edge of America* (2003), *The Business of Fancydancing* (2002), *Four Sheets to the Wind* (2007), and *Imprint* (2007) have been released nationally and/or been screened at Sundance or Cannes.[46] Every individual who views this new brand of American Indian filmmaking receives a message and an education that is starkly different from the misinformation, stereotyping, and typecasting delivered by two centuries of prejudiced popular media.[47]

The emergence of a new brand of American Indian filmmaker can also significantly impact the entire industry. Films that portray American Indian narratives will consistently cast American Indian actors for the roles. Motion picture companies operating on the Navajo Reservation in Arizona or New Mexico, or on a Sioux reservation in South Dakota, will hire local American Indians to work on the film. These new employees can then be mentored by the emerging group.[48] Much like Spike Lee's ascendance as a critically important African American filmmaker who specifically employs African American cinematographers, composers, actors, assistant directors, and consultants, among many others,[49] the emerging American Indian filmmakers have also taken their role seriously to groom young American Indian filmmakers, writers, and actors.[50]

In addition, the very act of an American Indian child or teenager sitting in a movie theater or watching a DVD and seeing a story told of an actual American Indian character who is not a warrior from the 1800s or a caricature from the 1900s, but is heroic in his or her own right, and is modern, current, and relevant, is incredibly important, both practically and psychologically.[51] The psychology and empowerment of such a simple act is overwhelming.

Non-Native Filmmakers Striving for Authenticity

Beyond the breakthrough represented by this emergence of gifted American Indian filmmakers and screenwriters, a small cadre of respected non-Native

American producers and moviemakers has begun seriously to challenge the stereotyping and racism that has permeated the media since before the founding of the United States. In the past few years, four or five period pieces have depicted, in richly textured detail, a historical authenticity rarely before seen on television or the big screen. These writers, producers, and directors have taken it upon themselves to research carefully, authenticate vigilantly, and present honestly the candid and malicious historical trampling of the rights of American Indians.

In 2007 HBO Films released *Bury My Heart at Wounded Knee*. The film turned an unapologetic eye on the tragic Wounded Knee Massacre and carefully chronicled the events that led up to that "last" battle between the U.S. government and the American Indians resisting removal from their homelands to barren reservations. The life of Sitting Bull was chronicled, including his attempt, with faithful supporters, to escape the government's removal policies by settling in Canada and nearly freezing to death. Actors, directors, and producers attempted to re-create the themes in Dee Brown's book *Bury My Heart at Wounded Knee* (1970) and took care to emulate reality as truthfully as possible, from the Pine Ridge Reservation village in South Dakota, to the authentic Sioux regalia and language.[52] Portraying the U.S. Congress as duplicitous, the film records how the government repeatedly and unapologetically breached its treaties. A verbal exchange in the motion picture, between a U.S. senator (Henry L. Dawes of Massachusetts) and a Dartmouth-educated Sioux doctor (Charles Eastman), captures the essence of this rare and authentic glimpse into U.S. History:

> Dawes: The Indian must own his own piece of Earth, Charles.
> Eastman: Did you know that there is no word in the Sioux language for that, sir?
> Dawes: For what?
> Eastman: "To own the earth." Not in any native language.[53]

Previously, in 2004 David Milch and HBO produced the series *Deadwood*.[54] Set in the Black Hills of South Dakota, *Deadwood* ruthlessly and graphically portrays the lives of the mostly white prospectors who broke treaty to settle on Sioux lands in an effort to mine the gold long rumored to be in the sacred Black Hills. While *Deadwood*'s treatment of the relationships with the Sioux is minimal, what Milch has done is to capture the filthy, racist, crude, and murderous lives led by white settlers who ignored both treaty and President Ulysses S. Grant's pleas to abandon the Black Hills. Based on painstaking research and replication, with admitted artistic liberty, *Deadwood* provides authentic insight into the lives, insensibilities, and greed of those who would steal land from the Sioux and ultimately become their neighbors.[55] Whatever "noble" construct Hollywood had attached to the nineteenth-century pioneers, settlers, and prospectors seeking to find their fortune in The West, *Deadwood* destroyed it. And it did so with accuracy and historical honesty.

Two additional series, among others, that have rejected the Hollywood stereotypes and false narratives from the nineteenth and twentieth centuries include Steven Spielberg and Turner Network Television's 2005 release of the series *Into the West* and the Ken Burns's 1996 PBS release *The West*.[56] Both of these historical extrapolations of the United States' expansion into the western territories seek to provide true and faithful accounts of the nation's narrative.

Each of these releases demonstrates a remarkable divergence from almost every single other period piece that previously had been foisted upon the American viewing public.[57]

CAN THE LAW GET IT RIGHT?

Once again, the worlds of Hollywood and the law collided at the conclusion of HBO Film's *Bury My Heart at Wounded Knee*. During the last scene of the motion picture, as the final language scrolled across the screen, the U.S. Supreme Court was referenced and quoted by the filmmakers:

> In 1980, the U.S. Supreme Court ruled that the 1876 seizure of the Black Hills violated treaties signed with the Sioux.
>
> In the majority opinion, Justice Blackmun wrote, "A more ripe and rank case of dishonorable dealings will never, in all probability, be found in our history."
>
> But the Court refused to restore the land to the Sioux, and ordered that compensation be paid instead.
>
> That award, now worth more than $600 million, remains unclaimed.
>
> To date, the Sioux will not agree to surrender their claim to the Black Hills, a place they feel is sacred.

Of course, this reference was to the U.S. Supreme Court case of *United States v. Sioux Nation of Indians* handed down in 1980.[58] Therein, as synopsized in the closing scene of *Bury My Heart at Wounded Knee,* the Supreme Court recognized the treacherous actions of the United States government and ordered damages as restitution in the amount of hundreds of millions of dollars.[59] True to the pride displayed by these Sioux tribes throughout the removal period, the specific request for land returned is the objective, and the damages award remains unclaimed.[60]

The curious connection between the law and the U.S. mass media's portrayal of American Indians has also developed in heartening ways during the past decade. In several important instances, American Indian plaintiffs have sued in the U.S. courts of law, and have tied the breathtakingly negative stereotyping of them, by the media, into victories in the courts. Several of these successes have arisen in the context of challenging American Indians mascots used by professional and collegiate athletic teams. These legal victories are heartening because the media have been exposed as perpetuating hateful stereotypes, and courts of law have recognized the disparagement aimed at American Indians throughout American history. Further, these glimpses of success in the courts have provided a series of examples that American Indian activists can use in challenging the continued use of hostile imagery.

Harjo v. Pro-Football, Inc.

In *Harjo v. Pro-Football, Inc.*,[61] a group of American Indian petitioners led by Suzan Shown Harjo sought cancellation of the trademarks held by the Washington Redskins, a participating club in the National Football League, claiming that the trademarks registered by the Washington professional football club were disparaging and in violation of federal trademark law. Federal trademark law prevents the registration of trademarks depicting "immoral, deceptive, or scandalous matter; or which may disparage or falsely suggest a connection with persons . . . beliefs . . . or bring them into contempt or disrepute."[62] The *Harjo* petitioners asserted that the word "redskin(s)," or a form of that word, appeared in each of the trademarks of which they sought cancellation.[63] *Harjo* argued that the word "redskin(s)" "was and is a pejorative, derogatory, denigrating, offensive, scandalous, contemptuous, disreputable, disparaging, and racist designation for a Native American person" and that the "registrant's use of the trademarks in the identified registrations 'offends' petitioners and other Native Americans."[64]

Principally, Harjo and her fellow petitioners entered dozens of U.S. mass media portrayals and stereotypes into evidence as confirmation of the disparagement and disrepute necessary to prove improper registration of a trademark. Harjo made clear that one derivation of the term "redskin" derived from the practice of the English crown offering a bounty for killing American Indians in the 1700s.[65] Bounty-collecting assassins were required to bring the red and bloody skin or scalp of the murdered American Indian to a specified location in order to receive payment and as proof of the kill.[66]

Next, Harjo and the petitioners showcased literally dozens of examples of mass media prejudice. Harjo insisted that the Trademark Board consider the historical setting and scenario in which the term "redskin(s)" has been used. Harjo provided evidence showing the frequency with which the word "redskin(s)" appears in mass media outlets in the context of savagery, violence, and oppression and arguing that repeated appearances of the term and imagery reinforce their derogatory character.[67] The *Harjo* petitioners entered into evidence newspaper articles, motion picture excerpts, dictionary definitions, encyclopedia references, and novels.[68] More than fifty motion picture clips had been evaluated by a film "expert" who had created for the plaintiffs a montage of the twenty or so most egregious examples of the use of the term "redskin" in major releases, which was also entered into evidence.[69] This expert testified that in almost every instance in which the term "redskin" was used in major motion pictures, it was accompanied by the terms "filthy" and "lying."[70] Such media evidence proved convincing to the Trademark Board.

In a stunning 1999 victory, the Trademark Board ruled for Harjo, finding that the term "redskin" through widespread media abuse had become a term of great disparagement and offense and that the trademark given to the Washington NFL football club should never have been registered.[71] Much attention and fanfare accompanied this unexpected victory.[72] Clearly, one reason that such significant attention was paid to this trademark victory was because Harjo and the American Indian petitioners were able to provide the Trademark Board with evidence that the portrayals of American Indians in the mass media, particularly in the context of the term "redskin," were debilitating and abusive.

The success *Harjo* achieved, however, was short-lived. In 2003 the U.S. District Court for the District of Columbia reversed the Trademark Board's decision.[73] The district court ruled that parties seeking to have a trademark registration canceled on the grounds that it may disparage or debase them had waited too long to bring their claim and thus were time-barred. In addition, American Indian petitioners have the burden of demonstrating disparagement by a preponderance of the evidence.[74] The district court held that the Trademark Board's factual findings were not supported by substantial evidence.[75] In 2004, Harjo and her co-petitioners appealed the reversal of the cancellation, but the decision has been subsequently affirmed[76] and reaffirmed.

National Collegiate Athletic Association Policy

Recognizing a shift in the wind, the NCAA in 2005 adopted a policy that prohibits a member institution from participating in NCAA-sanctioned postseason events if that institution maintains a mascot, moniker, nickname, or logo that is offensive, hostile, or derogatory to American Indian citizens.[77] In the policy announcement, the NCAA described its purpose: "The presidents and chancellors who serve on the NCAA Executive Committee have adopted a new policy to prohibit NCAA colleges and universities from displaying hostile and abusive racial/ethnic/national origin mascots, nicknames or imagery at any of the [eighty-eight annual] NCAA championships."[78] The NCAA, a powerful voluntary organization that regulates and supervises the athletic activities of the hundreds of member colleges and universities in the United States, declared unequivocally that the adoption, continued use of, and display of American Indian mascots, logos, and imagery was hostile, abusive, and unacceptable in modern higher education and competitive athletics.

Member institutions that were designated as being in violation of the new policy would be prohibited from displaying their offensive logos on the field of play or court or on a uniform, or from having a student dress up as an offensive mascot during postseason play or tournaments.[79] This bold move by the NCAA was heralded as forward-looking and progressive, but the organization diluted the effectiveness of the policy by creating an appeals process that allows specific universities to continue, under specific circumstances, to use hostile, demeaning, and abusive mascots that continue to perpetuate timeworn stereotypes.[80]

To date, several leading institutions have eliminated racist mascots and logos, choosing to adhere to the NCAA policy by adopting race-neutral monikers and nicknames.[81] However, on the basis of the ill-advised appeals process, other universities have garnered support from local tribes, and on that basis alone the NCAA has granted individual appeals and allowed a handful of institutions to continue to use mascots and rituals that mock and demean American Indian culture. These institutions include the Florida State University Seminoles and the University of Utah Runnin' Utes.[82]

The University of North Dakota has mightily resisted changing its moniker and logo since its appearance on the NCAA hostile and abusive list. Sentiment in North Dakota runs deep for the school's Fighting Sioux.[83] Although at least one local Sioux tribe, on many occasions, had affirmatively and undeniably acknowledged the offensive nature of the UND mascot and moniker,[84] the university administration continued in its discriminating tradition.[85] Rather than comply with the NCAA policy and change its mascot, North Dakota appealed. Absent the support of a local Sioux tribe, the NCAA rejected the appeal. Still determined to continue as the Fighting Sioux, UND sued the NCAA in federal court seeking an injunction against the NCAA's action.[86] Rather than face protracted litigation, the NCAA and UND settled the lawsuit before trial, and the Fighting Sioux saga continued through 2011.

McBride v. Motor Vehicle Div. of Utah State Tax Commission

In *McBride v. Motor Vehicle Div. of Utah State Tax Commission* three residents of the state of Utah who were Washington Redskins fans applied for and received vanity license plates that read REDSKIN, REDSKNS, and RDSKIN, which they proudly displayed on their automobiles.[87] The petitioners were American Indians who felt that the vanity plates were offensive and derogatory toward American Indians. They claimed that these particular vanity plates were in violation of a state statute that prohibited vanity license plates that are "offensive and derogatory, and expresses contempt and ridicule toward their heritage, ethnicity, and race in violation of Utah Code Ann. § 41-1a-411" and also in violation of Utah Administrative Code R873-22M-34, an administrative rule that forbade plates including terms that were "vulgar, derogatory, profane or obscene."[88]

The Utah Supreme Court reversed the Tax Commission's original holding that the term "redskin" was not an offensive term and ordered the Tax Commission to apply a "reasonable person" standard to determine if any of the phrases on the challenged license plates had any negative connotation.[89] Following this Utah Supreme Court reversal, the case was remanded to the Tax Commission to reevaluate using the appropriate standard. The Tax Commission then returned a unanimous decision that found that the term "redskin" did have at least one connotation that was offensive or derogatory.[90] Therefore, the vanity license plates were in violation of an administrative rule and the statutory law of the state of Utah, and the vanity plates were revoked.

Thus, through a bold, albeit late, NCAA policy, and by virtue of several recent victories in U.S. courts, it appears that groundwork is being laid upon which American Indian lawyers and activists can continue to turn the tide against a troubling history of discrimination, abuse, and mistreatment.

CONCLUSION: CHANGES AND AUTHENTICITY

Despite the now well-chronicled "shameful"[91] history of Government treatment of American Indians in the United States and despite the offensive stereotyping of American Indians by the U.S. popular media, it appears that a dose of optimism may be in order. In the past decade, the NCAA has recognized the deep-seated racism among its member institutions and has mandated an elimination of hostile imagery and discriminatory American Indian stereotypes in its universities and colleges. American Indian activists have learned that marshaling the readily available evidence of bigotry and typecasting in the mass media, particularly in motion pictures and newspapers, can be used to successfully challenge demeaning and derogatory mascots, nicknames, and monikers of professional and collegiate athletic teams. The U.S. judiciary is recognizing its own past discrimination and racism and has ruled in recent decades on behalf of aggrieved American Indian plaintiffs. Non-Native filmmakers, producers, and writers are beginning to find and actuate authentic representations of American Indians and are producing exciting new programs and films that reject the past and paint a truthful picture of the original Americans and their oppressors.

Ultimately, great hope, support, and brightness should be directed toward the emerging generation of talented, bold, visionary, and genuine American Indian filmmakers, screenwriters, and directors. This small but growing group is seizing upon opportunities to tell authentic and modern stories that resituate and redefine the modern American Indian.

Rather than relying upon or hoping that non-Native judges, administrators, legislators, and media leaders will halt the years of bigoted stereotyping and aching discrimination that has for so long plagued them, current American Indian lawyers, filmmakers, and writers are presenting their own visions of the truth. Authentic narratives and genuine storytelling can confront the

U.S. public conscience with a much different American Indian presence and characterization. Though challenges remain, this opportunity has never been so ripe.

DISCUSSION QUESTIONS

1. In what ways have historical media depictions of American Indians cemented stereotyped caricatures in the minds of many in the U.S. general public? In the global community?
2. Are American Indian filmmakers, writers, and screenwriters truly emerging in the film industry? Has this emergence been overstated?
3. Why is it important that American Indian writers, directors, and screenwriters tell their stories on television and in motion pictures, even if the message is not one that depicts past historical injustices or celebrates a historical American Indian hero?
4. How have the U.S. courts begun to recognize media stereotyping in their judicial decrees? Who is responsible for bringing instances of bias in the media to the attention of judges and courts?
5. What lessons can be taken from the recent decisions and policies by U.S. courts and the NCAA that will allow successful challenges to racist, stereotyped, or biased treatment or depictions of American Indians?

NOTES

Epigraph: Virgin Rail Group Ltd, t/a Virgin Trains, Advertising Standards agency, ASA Adjudications, http://www.asa.org.uk/asa/adjudications/Public/TF_ADJ_41 971.htm (accessed July 14, 2011).

1. Brown 1970.

2. Strickland 1997.

3. See generally *Cherokee Nation v. Georgia,* 30 U.S. (5 Pet.) 1 (1831); *United States v. Kagama,* 118 U.S. 375 (1886); *Choctaw Nation v. United States,* 119 U.S. 1 (1886).

4. Brown 1970; Strickland 1997; DeShane 2003; *Cherokee Nation v. Georgia,* 30 U.S. (5 Pet.) 1 (1831); *United States v. Kagama,* 118 U.S. 375 (1886); *Choctaw Nation v. United States,* 119 U.S. 1 (1886). Additional references include James Fennimore Cooper's description of the American Indian characters in his *Last of the Mohicans* (1826) as "savages" and detailing the "'wild,' 'fierce,' 'fiery' Indians" from a place of no experience and scant research.

5. Native: Strickland 1997; Yazzie 1996; Cohen 1982. Non-Native: Hyde 1956; Prucha 1984.

6. Strickland 1997.

7. Eyre 1998; Simoneau 2007; Milch 2004; Dornhelm and Mimica-Gezzan 2005; Linn 2007; Eyre 2003; Eyre 2002.

8. Simoneau 2007; Milch 2004; Dornhelm and Mimica-Gezzan 2005.

9. Crazy Horse, a nineteenth-century leader of the Oglala Sioux, never posed for a picture. Sitting for a portrait was a practice of the white invaders. He wanted no part of their ways. Crazy Horse also disdained the whites' custom of drinking alcohol and spoke out against the damage he saw it doing to his people. So the descendants of Tasunko Witko—his name in Lakota—found it a perversion when a Brooklyn company came out with Crazy Horse Malt Liquor in 1992, with a label sketch of an American Indian in full headdress. Dirk Johnson, "Complaints by Indians Lead to Bans on a Beer," *New York Times,* December 6, 1995, http://query .nytimes.com/gst/fullpage.html?res=950DE3DB1139F935A35751C1A963958260 (accessed July 29, 2011).

10. cummings 2000, 11; cummings 2008, 309; cummings and Harper 2009.

11. Pevar 1992, 4.

12. Wiessner 1995.

13. Brown 1970.

14. Canku Lúta, "Treaty of Fort Laramie," 1851, Red Road, Inc., http://www .canku-luta.org/PineRidge/laramie_treaty.html (accessed June 20, 2009).

15. Pevar 1992, 41.

16. "Fort Laramie Treaty of 1868," Department of Sociology and Anthropology, Creighton University, http://puffin.creighton.edu/lakota/1868_la.html (accessed July 5, 2008).

17. Pevar 1992.

18. Hyde 1956; Prucha 1984.

19. Simoneau 2007.

20. Lorie Liggett, "The Wounded Knee Massacre: An Introduction" (1998), in *1890s America: A Chronology,* by Dr. William Grant and Ken Kvorak, http://www .bgsu.edu/departments/acs/1890s/woundedknee/WKIntro.html (accessed July 5, 2008).

21. Pevar 1992.

22. Robert Schmidt, "A Brief History of Native Stereotyping," *Blue Corn Comics,* 2007, http://www.bluecorncomics.com/sthist.htm (accessed July 12, 2008).

23. Michael Hill, "Just in Time: A New View of the American Indian," *Baltimore Sun,* August 29, 204, http://hnn.us/roundup/comments/7151.html (accessed June 28, 2008).

24. Quoted in Bob Keefer, "The Hollywood Indian: An Exhibit of Movie Posters Shows How Filmmakers Molded Images of American Indians that Linger to This Day," *Register-Guard* (Eugene, Ore.), January 26, 2006, http://rgweb.register guard.com/news/2006/01/26/ar.marqueemassacres.0126.p2.php?section=arts (accessed July 7, 2008).

25. Keefer, "Hollywood Indian"; Schmidt, "Brief History of Native Stereotyping."

26. Merskin 1998, 333; Chandler and Johnson 1996, 65; Pewewardy 1999, 342.

27. "Whether depicted as a filthy, besotted idler or a maniacal savage wreaking havoc on helpless settlers, the cartoon Indian mirrored the thrust of Gilded Age popular prejudice more nakedly than any minority stereotype, save maybe those of the Mormon or the Roman Catholic hierarchy" (Fischer 1996, 103). See, e.g.,

Grant E. Hamilton, "The Nation's Ward," 1885: cartoon showing a snake portrayed as an American Indian coiled around a pioneer family, squeezing the life out of them; around a tree, Uncle Sam is feeding the snake from a bowl of "Government Gruel"; in the background, to the right, are government-sponsored educational facilities for Native Americans, to the left is a homestead scene under attack by Native Americans (http://lcweb2.loc.gov/cgi-bin/query/r?pp/PPALL:@field%28 DOCID+@lit%2897511827%29%29 [accessed July 9, 2008]).

28. Schmidt, "Brief History of Native Stereotyping"; Schmidt, "Savage Indians," *Blue Corn Comics,* 2007, http://www.bluecorncomics.com/savagena.htm (accessed July 14, 2011). Schmidt posts images from the 1860s depicting American Indians accosting white women and children, with headlines screaming "Women and Children Falling Victim to the Indian's Tomahawk," and other images showing American Indians terrorizing white settlers. He also depicts American Indian warriors preparing to kill white women and children.

29. Some examples: "General Hazen in the Spring of 1868 was acting superintendent of Indian affairs in Indian Territory, and was very successful in keeping the savage in a peaceful condition" (Captain E. A. ["Jack"] Hart, "How Fort Cobb Was Saved," *New York Tribune,* July 18, 1909, http://www.loc.gov/chronicling america/ndnp:2028744/display.html?n=0&scope=fulltext&pageNum=1&current Sort=&mode=list [accessed July 10, 2008]). "Many a young reader has tried to imagine what would be his feelings should he suddenly find himself bound and helpless in the hands of hostile Indians, bent upon putting him to the most cruel tortures which their savage ingenuity could devise" (James Elverson, "Peggy and the Indians," *Los Angeles Herald,* November 11, 1906, http://www.loc.gov/chroni clingamerica/ndnp:1886727/display.html?n=2&scope=fulltext&pageNum=1& currentSort=&mode=list [accessed July 10, 2008]). Elverson, "A Race for Life," *Los Angeles Herald,* January 27, 1907, http://www.loc.gov/chroniclingamerica/nd np:1891111/display.html?n=1&scope=fulltext&pageNum=1&currentSort=&mode =list (accessed July 10, 2008). Col. William Thompson, "Captain Applegate the White Chief and His Story of the Modoc War," *San Francisco Call,* July 19, 1908, http://chroniclingamerica.loc.gov/ndnp-repository/ndnp:1385059/raw/ndnp: 1385058/N75914 pdfFile.pdf (accessed July 10, 2008).

30. cummings 2000; cummings and Harper 2009; cummings 2008.

31. See generally *Cherokee Nation v. Georgia,* 30 U.S. (5 Pet.) 1 (1831); *United States v. Kagama,* 118 U.S. 375 1886); *Choctaw Nation v. United States,* 119 U.S. 1 (1886); *Sunderland v. United States,* 266 U.S. 226, 233 (1924); *United States v. Ex Parte Gon-Shay-Ee,* 130 U.S. 343, 350 (1889); *United State v. Ex Parte Mayfield,* 141 U.S. 107, 115–116 (1891); *Johnson v. McIntosh,* 21 US 543, 573, 587, 590 (1823); *United States v. Lucero,* 1 N.M. 422, 426 (1869). Note especially the following excerpts:

We do not doubt the power of the United States to impose such a restraint upon the sale of the lands of its Indian wards, whether acquired by private purchase and generally subject to state control or not. Such power rests upon the dependent character of the Indians, their recognized inability to safely conduct business affairs, and the peculiar duty of the federal government to safeguard their interests and protect them against the greed of others and their own improvidence. *(Sunderland v. U.S.)*

"The policy of congress has evidently been to vest in the inhabitants of the Indian country such power of self-government as was thought to be consistent with the safety of the white population with which they may have come in contact, and to encourage them as far as possible in raising themselves to our standard of civilization. (*U.S. v. Gon-Shay-Ee*)

[D]iscovery gave an exclusive right to extinguish the Indian title of occupancy, either by purchase or by conquest . . . the Indians were fierce savages . . . whose subsistence was drawn chiefly from the forest. To leave them in possession of their country, was to leave the country a wilderness. *(Johnson v. McIntosh)*

32. Wilkins 1997; Deloria and Wilkins 2000; Prucha 1984; Deloria and Lytle 1983; Wilkins and Lomawaima 2002.

33. *Cherokee Nation v. Georgia,* 30 U.S. at 17. Chief Justice Marshall continues:

If courts were permitted to indulge their sympathies, a case better calculated to excite them can scarcely be imagined. A people once numerous, powerful, and truly independent, found by our ancestors in the quiet and uncontrolled possession of an ample domain, gradually sinking beneath our superior policy, our arts and our arms, have yielded their lands by successive treaties, each of which contains a solemn guarantee of the residue, until they retain no more of their formerly extensive territory than is deemed necessary to their comfortable subsistence. (at 15, 20)

34. Ives 1996.
35. *United States v. Lucero,* 1 N.M. at 426.
36. Wilkins 1997, 10.
37. Keefer, "Hollywood Indian."
38. Prucha 1984; Carter 1976; Ehle 1988; Jahoda 1995; Foreman 1932; Rozema 2003; Wallace 1991; Anderson 1991. Note especially:

The bitter tale of the sad events that led inexorably to the final massacre at Wounded Knee began with the Trail of Tears. In 1830, the U.S. Congress passed a bill permitting the removal of all Native Americans living east of the Mississippi. Over the next twenty years more than fifty tribes were uprooted from their homelands and marched into the alien lands of the west—the first step in the destruction of an entire people. (Jahoda 1995, jacket)

During the first half of the nineteenth century as many as 100,000 Native Americans were relocated west of the Mississippi River from their homelands in the East. The best known of these forced emigrations was the Cherokee Removal of 1938. Christened Nu-No-Du-Na-Tlo-Hi-Lu—literally "the Trail Where They Cried"—by the Cherokees, it is remembered today as the Trail of Tears. (Rozema 2003, overview)

39. Taylor 2000, 371, 379. See also Brian W. Dippie, "American Indians: The Image of the Indian":

> Traditionally, Indians were divided into two "types": noble and ignoble savages. The Indian woman was either a princess or a drudge, the Indian man an admirable brave or a fiendish warrior. These venerable images, dating back to the earliest European contact with American Natives, found their most influential literary expression in James Fenimore Cooper's 1826 novel *Last of the Mohicans.*

(n.d., National Humanities Center, accessed July 13, 2008, http://nationalhuman itiescenter.org/tserve/nattrans/ntecoindian/essays/indimage.htm)

40. Fischer 1996; Schmidt, "Brief History of Native Stereotyping"; Schmidt, "Savage Indians." See also Hamilton, "The Nation's Ward,"; Hart, "Fort Cobb"; Elverson, "Race for Life"; Elverson, "Peggy and the Indians"; Thompson, "Captain Appelgate."

41. Wilkins 1997.

42. Strickland 1997.

43. See chapter 6, "*Smoke Signals:* Equipment for Living," for an extensive analysis of the Indigenous themes in this groundbreaking film.

44. Jeffrey Ressner, "They've Gotta Have It," *Time,* June 29, 1998, accessed July 14, 2011, http://www.time.com/time/magazine/ article/0,9171,988633,00.html.

45. In discussing the impact of *Smoke Signals,* controversial and beleaguered author Ward Churchill notes what most acknowledge:

> This is why the debut of *Smoke Signals* in 1998, the first release of a major motion picture directed by an Indian since Will Rogers, was such a vitally important event. Not only that, but the screenplay was also written by an Indian, adapted from a book of his short stories, and virtually the entire cast is composed of Indians, To top things off, the director, Chris Eyre, an Arapaho, teamed up with the scriptwriter, Spokane author Sherman Alexie, to co-produce the venture. Smoke Signals was thus, from top to bottom, an American Indian production, and that made it historically unprecedented. (1998)

46. Kunuk 2002, Eyre 2002, Alexie 2002, Harjo 2007, Linn 2007.

47. Clark 2005. Purportedly, *Smoke Signals* has been wildly popular on all of the American Indian reservations in the United States. Imagine the impact that authentic and genuine motion pictures will have on the actual American Indian youth who have been pilloried by negative media images from the moment they could watch a television program or movie or view an athletic contest. Witnessing

true characterizations rather than demeaning stereotypes and authentic heroes rather than Hollywood typecasting can literally have a positive psychological impact. Clark reports that

> Negative stereotypes about youths are profoundly detrimental to the health and well-being of adolescents. Images that distort reality can trigger fears or misperception about causality of and appropriate strategies for resolving problems. . . . The promotion of positive images can help dismantle the stereotypes...and eliminate the problems that it causes. (2005)

48. Matthew Fleischer, "Gone with the Wind: A Decade after *Smoke Signals,* Success Remains Elusive for Native American Filmmakers," 2007, *Nativevue,* accessed July 13, 2008, http://www.nativevue.org/blog/?p=513. While optimism is warranted, recent reports have indicated that the emerging cadre of American Indian filmmakers are now finding it difficult to get their movies made and their visions realized, ten years after *Smoke Signals* burst onto the scene. Fleischer, "Gone with the Wind." In addition, while audiences for these authentic American Indian films remain enthusiastic but modest, breathtaking stereotyping is still widespread on much larger scales, as evidenced by the hip hop group OutKast's roundly criticized portrayal of American Indians in its 2004 Grammy award show performance. See "CBS Apologizes for OutKast Performance: Some Saw Indian-Themed Number as Racist," CNN.com, February 16, 2004 (accessed March 26, 2009, http://www.cnn.com/2004/SHOWBIZ/Music/02/16/cbs.outkast.reut/index .html.

49. Lynn Hirschberg, "Spike Lee's 30 Seconds," *New York Times,* April 20, 1997, http://query.nytimes.com/gst/fullpage.html?res=9800E0D9153FF933A15757C0A 961958260&sec=&spon=&pagewanted=all (accessed June 19, 2009).

50. Ressner ("They've Gotta Have It") notes that Sherman Alexie recognized the impact that he and Chris Eyre might have on American Indian filmmakers as similar to Spike Lee's impact on African American filmmakers:

> Chatting in a plush Beverly Hills, Calif., hotel lobby a week before [*Smoke Signals'*] release, [Alexie is] clearly stoked at the prospect that it might crack open doors for other budding Native auteurs. "Right away, we've given the whole idea of Indian filmmakers credibility," he says, beaming at the notion that *Smoke Signals* could do for his people what Spike Lee's *She's Gotta Have It* did for African Americans. "Spike didn't necessarily get films made as much as he inspired filmmakers to believe in themselves. That's what's going to happen here. These 13-year-old Indian kids who've been going crazy with their camcorders will finally see the possibilities."

51. Robert Schmidt, "VIEWPOINT: UND Ignores Groups, Rulings, Studies That Oppose Nickname," *Native News Online,* February 12, 2006, http://groups .yahoo.com/group/NatNews/message/41546 (accessed June 20, 2009).

52. Simoneau 2007.

53. The DVD summarizes the sentiment delivered above by including the following quotation on its cover: "To own the Earth. There is no word for this in the Sioux language" Simoneau 2007.

54. Milch 2004.

55. See "Ann Oldenburg, "Cussing on 'Deadwood' Sets Tongues a-Wagging," *USA Today,* May 2, 2004, http://www.usatoday.com/life/television/news/2004-05 -02-deadwood-cursing_x.htm (accessed July 24, 2011). See also "On 'Deadwood' Set History Comes Alive," Associated Press/MSNBC, March 3, 2005:

> "[The] story is told," says Milch, "by bringing alive the process of evolution of a society," and, most importantly, by making the characters and their surroundings authentic. . . . The world of "Deadwood" is filled with the history of South Dakota's Deadwood in 1876, which Milch and his production team researched over a two-year period.

(http://www.msnbc.msn.com/id/7081175/ [accessed July 24, 2011]).

56. Dornhelm and Mimica-Gezzan 2005; Ives 1996.

57. Despite the authenticity, it should be noted that non-Native filmmakers tend to portray only the Plains tribes, particularly the Sioux, in their movies and teleplays. This represents its own bias, as authenticity in portrayal of the Sioux tribes singularly does not accurately reflect the diversity of the American Indian experience in the United States.

58. 448 U.S. 371 (1980).

59. *U.S. v. Sioux Nation of Indians,* 448 U.S. at 424. The Supreme Court majority held in Sioux Nation of Indians:

> [The Court of Claims] held that the Sioux were entitled to an award of interest, at the annual rate of 5%, on the principal sum of $17.1 million, dating from 1877. . . . In sum, we conclude that the legal analysis and factual findings of the Court of Claims fully support its conclusion that the terms of the 1877 Act did not effect "a mere change in the form of investment of Indian tribal property." Rather, the 1877 Act effected a taking of tribal property, property which had been set aside for the exclusive occupation of the Sioux by the Fort Laramie Treaty of 1868. That taking implied an obligation on the part of the Government to make just compensation to the Sioux Nation, and that obligation, including an award of interest, must now, at last, be paid.

60. Dirk Johnson, "To Some Sioux, Costner Now Dances with Devil," *New York Times,* February 24, 1995:

> The Supreme Court ruled in 1980 on behalf of the tribes, ordering the Federal Government to compensate the Indians for the property loss. But the tribes have refused to accept the money, insisting that they be given National Forest lands in the Black Hills, which they consider sacred. The

monetary compensation has been held in escrow . . . and is now about $380 million.

(http://query.nytimes.com/gst/fullpage.html?res=990CE7DD123CF937A15751 C0A963958260 [accessed June 21, 2009]). See also Linda Greenhouse, "Sioux Lose Fight for Land in Dakota," *New York Times,* January 19, 1982:

> The Oglala said they would not be bound by any monetary settlement and would be satisfied only by restoration of the land, which the Indians regard as sacred. . . . Their lawsuit asked for the land plus $10 billion in compensation for the removal of nonrenewable resources and $1 billion additional in damages for 'hunger, malnutrition, disease and death.

(http://query.nytimes.com/gst/fullpage.html?res=9405E2D81138F93AA25752 C0A964948260 [accessed July 25, 2011]).

61. 1999 WL 375907 (Trademark Tr. & App. Bd. 1999).

62. 15 U.S.C. § 1052(a) (2000).

63. *Harjo,* 1999 WL 375907 at *2.

64. *Harjo,* 1999 WL 375907 at *2.

65. *Harjo,* 1999 WL 375907 at *2; cummings 2000; cummings and Harper 2009.

66. *Harjo* at *2; Ives 1996.

67. *Harjo,* 1999 WL 375907 at *2.

68. *Harjo,* 1999 WL 375907 at *2.

69. *Harjo v. Pro-Football, Inc.* 50 U.S.P.Q.2d 1705 (1999).

70. *Harjo v. Pro-Football, Inc.* 50 U.S.P.Q.2d 1705 (1999).

71. *Harjo,* 1999 WL 375907, at *37.

72. The *New York Times* reported:

> In its ruling, the three board members said the derogatory connotation of the word "redskins" extends to the football team's name, such that it "may be disparaging of Native Americans to a substantial composition of this group of people." The board's decision strips the club and the National Football League's NFL Properties Inc. of Federally protected exclusive rights for using and licensing the "redskins" name and logos for merchandising.

"Court Finds Name May Be Disparaging," April 3, 1999 (http://query.nytimes .com/gst/fullpage.html?res=9C0CE6D71339F930A35757C0A96F958260 [accessed July 1,2008]). See also Karlyn Barker, "Redskins Name Can Be Challenged: Appeals Court Ruling Keeps Trademark Battle Alive," *Washington Post,* July 16, 2005, B1.

73. *Pro Football Inc. v. Harjo,* 284 F.Supp. 2d 96 (D.D.C. 2003).

74. *Pro Football Inc. v. Harjo,* 284 F.Supp. 2d 96 (D.D.C. 2003) at 117.

75. *Pro Football Inc. v. Harjo,* 284 F.Supp. 2d 96 (D.D.C. 2003) at 117.

76. See *Pro-Football, Inc. v. Harjo* (*Harjo* IV), 415 F.3d 44 (D.C. Cir. 2005).

77. cummings 2008. See also Myles Brand, "NCAA Takes High Road with Ban of Offensive Mascots," *USA Today,* August 11, 2005, 11A; NCAA press release,

"NCAA Executive Committee Issues Guidelines for Use of Native American Mascots at Championship Events," August 5, 2005, http://www2.ncaa.org/portal/media_and_events/press_room/2005/august/20050805_exec_comm_rls.html (accessed July 13, 2008); Greg Couch, "NCAA Knows All about Being Offensive," *Chicago Sun-Times,* August 7, 2005, A103; Mike Knobler and Tony Barnhard, "NCAA Refuses to Hail to Chiefs—or Braves," *Atlanta Journal-Constitution,* August 6, 2005, A1; Sean Smith, "NCAA: Mascot Ruling," *Boston Globe,* August 8, 2005, D1.

78. NCAA Press Release, August 5, 2005; cummings 2008.

79. NCAA Press Release, August 2005; cummings 2008; Ted Hutton, "Seminoles Get the Chop: NCAA Bans Indian Names during Postseason Play. *South Florida Sun-Sentinel,* August 6, 2005, 1A; Sharita Forrest, "NCAA Announces New Policy That May Affect UI Postseason Play," UIUC EDU, August 1, 2005, http://www.news.uiuc.edu/II/05/0818/ncaa.html (accessed June 19, 2009).

80. cummings and Harper 2009.

81. cummings 2008; cummings and Harper 2009.

82. cummings 2008; cummings and Harper 2009.

83. cummings 2008; David Dodds, "NCAA Waits for Tribal Input on UND Mascot: School Appealing 'Hostile' Judgment," *St. Paul Pioneer Press,* September 23, 2008, 5B; Steve Wieberg, "N. Dakota Needs Tribes' OK for Nickname." *USA Today,* October 29, 2007, 13C.

84. Standing Rock Sioux, "Resolution in Opposition to the University of North Dakota's Use of the Fighting Sioux," 2007, http://aistm.org/20071109.standing.rock.UND.resolution.htm (accessed July 25, 2011); Chris Lerch chronicles the debate over the "Fighting Sioux" nickname at UND, indicating that a multi-million dollar contribution hinges on continued use of the name, as well as documenting all of the American Indian students that discuss their experiences at UND being cheapened based on the mascot ("Fighting the Fighting Sioux," *Blue Corn Comics,* September 4, 2005, http://www.bluecorncomics.com/und.htm [accessed June 22, 2009]).

85. cummings 2008; "North Dakota Suing NCAA over 'Fighting Sioux' Ban." *Chicago Sun Times,* June 16, 2006, 39; Dean Spiros, "Sioux Nickname, Logo Ban Upheld by NCAA," *Minneapolis Star Tribune,* September 29, 2005, 1C.

86. cummings 2008; cummings and Harper 2009. See also *CHN* Staff Report, "Fighting Sioux' Lawsuit Delayed," *College Hockey News,* December 16, 2006: "The North Dakota administration has been defiant in its opposition to the NCAA's ruling, more so than any other university," http://www.collegehockeynews.com/news/2006/12/16_fighting.php (accessed July 29, 2011).

87. *McBride v. Motor Vehicle Div. of Utah State Tax Comm'n,* 977 P.2d 467 (Utah 1999) at 468.

88. *McBride v. Motor Vehicle Div. of Utah State Tax Comm'n,* 977 P.2d 467 (Utah 1999) at 468.

89. *McBride v. Motor Vehicle Div. of Utah State Tax Comm'n*, 977 P.2d 467 (Utah 1999) at 471.

90. Ray Rivera, "Panel Revokes 'Redskins' Plates Deemed as Slur," *Salt Lake Tribune*, March 4, 1999, A1: "The four-person commission, which included three new panel members, voted unanimously to reverse its 1996 decision allowing the personalized plates, which said 'REDSKIN,' 'REDSKNS,' and 'RDSKIN.' The change of heart came a month after the Utah Supreme Court ruled the Commission should have considered what an 'objective, reasonable' person would find offensive."

91. Ives 1996.

Part IV

Interior Views
and Authentic Voices

12

American Indians at Press

The Native American Journalists Association

MARK TRAHANT

One of the most influential groups in American Indian media is the Native American Journalists Association. Headquartered in Oklahoma, NAJA began its history through the efforts of a committed few. This chapter gives an intimate view of NAJA's origins.

The history of the Native American Journalists Association starts long before there was a NAJA. The story arc begins in a generation of challenge, at a moment when federal policy was written to terminate tribal governments and pretend that Indian people did not exist. Then, as the narrative shifted to one of self-determination, where Indian people had more control over their own affairs, so did the stories that were told by Native journalists.

Nearly a dozen Native American journalists met in Spokane, Washington, in 1969 to discuss their common problems and consider ways they might share news. Charles Trimble, who was then editor of the Denver-based *Indian Times,* had organized the retreat because of what he perceived as the "loneliness" of running a tribal publication.

> I called several editors I thought represented a good geographic cross section of Indian Country, and we decided to get together. The editors were Jim Jefferson of the *Southern Ute Drum,* Mary Baca of the *Jicarilla Chieftain,* Rupert Cost of the *Indian Historian,* Marie Potts of the *Smoke Signal* in California, Gwen Owle of the *Cherokee One Feather* in North Carolina, Carole Wright of the *Native Nevadan,* and Tom Connolly of the *Northwest Indian News.* It was the first time any of us had ever met in person, and it was a pretty exciting time.[1]

This exciting time started as a routine conference: editors sharing problems and looking for solutions. But the consensus that emerged was the founding of the American Indian Press Association (AIPA).

Two main purposes of the new organization were to improve training and professional standards for American Indian newspapers and to create a network for the sharing of ideas. But the most ambitious idea was to start a news service that reported stories about Indian Country for the tribal press. "Strangely unmentioned in our purposes was that of assuring protection of our collective First Amendment rights. Perhaps this was because we didn't want to appear to be challenging [tribal] governments when their existence was threatened by the federal policy of termination. It was an era of siege mentality, fear of outside terminators," Trimble said.[2]

The federal Indian termination policy, introduced in the mid-twentieth century, was an odd promise. If members of a reservation agreed to end their sovereign status and resign their control of reservation land, participating individuals would gain full U.S. citizenship, and the proceeds of the land transfer to federal authorities would be divided among tribal members. Essentially this exchange promised riches to those who voted in its favor, because each stood to gain a share of the distributed assets. The tribes that were targeted for termination were all resource-rich, and in the Colville Reservation case in Washington State that wealth came from vast stands of timber. It is important to remember that the Colville Tribe's governing body, the Colville Business Council, supported termination. The tribal chairman, Narcisse Nicholson, Jr., said that termination would work because with only a few exceptions, Colville tribal members were self-supporting. He added that "lack of employment, to the degree that it exists, is largely due to character faults which cannot be cured by paternalism."[3]

The nature of that termination threat, and others like it, meant that the new journalism organization would need to see its role differently than would a press association geared to a mainstream, "objective" news media. Journalists who met to form the first Native American press association soon became involved in advocacy against termination and support for those who opposed it.

"FREE THE INDIANS"

The motivation for termination was the idea that the federal government could "free the Indians" and end federal financial support and other government programs that exclusively served Native Americans and their reservations. "The Colville Tribe was in a death struggle in its final phases of being terminated," Trimble recalled, "and their great leader, Lucy Covington, asked us to put together a newspaper and a propaganda campaign to help us defeat the forces of termination."[4]

The main vehicle created for pursuing this goal was *Our Heritage,* a newspaper that reminded members of the Colville Reservation what was a stake. The newspaper profiled candidates opposed to termination and reported on recent lobbying efforts to stop termination bills. Trimble also cartooned. One of his most pointed efforts framed the money-versus-land issue: a panel shows a welfare agent telling a Colville mother, "I'm sorry we can't do anything for you. Why don't you go back to your reservation?" She responds: "We don't have anyplace to go. Our grandfathers sold our reservation."[5]

Trimble recalled years later that the new press association was so young that there were no funds for travel, or indeed for anything else. "So I went at my own expense," he wrote.

> When I arrived in Spokane where [Covington] met me, she sat me down in a room at the Indian Center there and told me what she expected of me. She wanted a newspaper that would tell what a tribe means to its people, and its true worth to them in terms of land, natural resources, and most of all their cultural heritage. She wanted the newspaper to be called *Our Heritage,* and she even described the logo she wanted for the masthead. It would be a pair of hands holding together the shape of the Colville Reservation. The logo would signify that the future of their reservation, indeed their nation, was in the hands of the people, not in the U.S. Government or the State of Washington, or anyone else.[6]

Covington's allies won. On May 8, 1971, Nicholson was defeated and was replaced by a candidate who was opposed to termination. A new business council called for more federal support, closed a reservation lake to outsiders, voted to take back law enforcement powers that had been ceded to the state of Washington, and declared its powers of inherent sovereignty. "We are a sovereignty within a sovereignty, and we must be allowed to rule ourselves," new Chairman Mel Tonasket said.[7]

On the larger stage, the Colville election ended the national policy of termination. A few months later Congress (and with it, the country) moved forward with a policy supporting tribal sovereignty.

BIRTH OF THE AMERICAN INDIAN PRESS ASSOCIATION

A few months before the Colville Tribe rejected termination, the American Indian Press Association formally set up its operations to report on the new era of resistance to termination. Trimble was named the first executive director of AIPA and the *Southern Ute*'s Jefferson was elected president. Representation on the board of directors ranged from Rose Robinson, a Hopi who worked at the federal Bureau of Indian Affairs (BIA), to Russell Means, a Lakota, who was then working at the Cleveland Indian Center. AIPA's first news release was issued on January 4, 1971, bylined "Indian Press Association," and it covered a news conference in Denver with BIA Commissioner Louis Bruce.

Two years later AIPA was operating a full-fledged news service in Washington, D.C. Richard LaCourse, a Yakama journalist, was named the news director. LaCourse had worked as an editor at the *Seattle Post-Intelligencer* and brought an air of professionalism to the organization. He created innovative news beats, such as following Indian organizations as they lobbied before the White House or the Bureau of Indian Affairs. "AIPA brought new life to Indian affairs in Washington," Trimble noted. "Would-be whistle blowers in federal offices, including the White House, were eager to give LaCourse information leaks about policy and silly foibles of the bureaucracy, and these stories and anecdotes spiced up the tribal papers." But AIPA soon encountered a logistical barrier: the Internal Revenue Service considered it to be a professional association and thus not eligible for not-for-profit status. This meant that it was impossible for AIPA to secure outside funding from foundations. "Our inability to raise funds eventually doomed the organization," Trimble wrote. AIPA died quietly in 1975.

Nevertheless, editors of tribal newspapers continued to publish—and still pushed for an organization to support those efforts.

LaCourse sent out a memorandum on March 25, 1977 to all Northwest Indian media ventures outlining his idea for a regional service based on the AIPA model.[8] "These matters may be pondered, ignored, discussed or rejected, as you will," he wrote. He described an operation similar to AIPA with an office in Portland or in Seattle that would cover regional Indian affairs with a weekly news packet to subscribers.

After several exchanges of letters from various tribal editors, more meetings were held over that year trying to get the Northwest Indian News Association off the ground.

One experimental goal was to fashion a cheap news service, but one that was faster than the old AIPA had been. I was then editor of the *Sho-Ban News* for the Shoshone-Bannock Tribe (Idaho), and we leapt to the challenge and bought a telex machine. It was one of those loud electronic keyboards and printers that were linked to Western Union's telegraph line. From that telex we could also send mailgrams for next-day delivery. The idea was to send out "instant"—that is, next day—news to every tribal newspaper. The telex machines were cheap, about $100, and a telex-to-telex message cost very little. But Mailgrams were expensive—about $10 each—and as no other tribal newspaper bought a telex, the idea faded away.

REGIONAL INDIAN NEWS

The Northwest Indian News Association (NINA) was formed on July 21, 1978. Sid Miller, editor of *Spilyay Tymoo* the publication of the Confederated Tribes of the Warm Springs Reservation of Oregon, was elected president. In addition to the news service, NINA proposed two additional and equally ambitious operations. Robert Johnson, editor of the *Indian Voice* in Sumner, Washington, planned a consortium of tribal newspapers (a publishers' association) to sell advertising jointly. And NINA floated the idea of an American Indian News Council. This would be a group of tribal leaders and editors who would look at coverage of Indian affairs as a whole and offer critiques of coverage. Tribal leaders supported the proposal, provided that outside money could be found. There was none. The advertising consortium produced a nice rate card and raised hopes, but few tribal newspapers saw any advertising. And the telex news service did not fare any better. The May 1979 newsletter was succinct: "As of May 31, NINA's news bureau service, entered into with *Sho-Ban News,* will be ended. We are short last month's payment of contract fee—about $400. Please hit up your accounting offices for payment of your dues."

NINA went the way of AIPA in 1980.

Three years later, Tim Giago, owner and editor of *Lakota Times,* sent letters to tribal newspapers encouraging delegates to gather on the campus of Penn State University to see if a new native journalism organization could be started. More than two dozen showed up. After securing seed money from the Gannett Foundation, Giago organized a second meeting in August 1983 in Tuskahoma, Oklahoma. The plan was to write a constitution and elect a board of directors.

Giago wrote: "We named the group the Native American Press Association."

> Thirteen Indian journalists showed up for that first official meeting. They were Adrian Louis of the *Lakota Times,* Mary Polanco of the *Jicarilla Chieftain,* Mike Burgess of the *Talking Leaf,* Sid Miller of the *Spilyay Tymoo,* Patty Bowen of the *Bishinik,* Minnie Two Shoes of the *Wotanin Wowapi,* Jose Barreiro of Cornell University, Anita Austin of the *NARF* (Native American Rights Fund) *Legal Review,* Lenore Keeshig-Tobias of *Sweetgrass Magazine,* Loren Tapahe of the *Navajo Times Today,* Verna Friday of *Sweetgrass Magazine,* George Gorospe of the *Pueblo News,* Richard LaCourse of the *Indian Finance Digest,* Professor Bill Dulaney of Penn State, and I of the *Lakota Times.*

The first convention was held in Warm Springs, Oregon, in the summer of 1984. Giago was determined not to repeat the mistakes of AIPA and other organizations. From its very beginning the new Native American Press Association (NAPA) was a not-for-profit organization with fundraising an important component. By the second convention, for example, NAPA was already successfully securing corporate sponsors from the Gannett and Cox newspaper companies.

NAPA's growth was steady. By the third convention (1987) more than two dozen tribal newspapers were members, as were many more individuals.

However, at the Albuquerque convention there emerged a philosophical difference of opinion. Giago saw NAPA as a publisher's organization that supported reservation-based newspapers, whereas Susan Arkeketa, editor of *NARF Legal Review,* and Paul DeMain, editor of *News From Indian Country,* saw the organization as a broader umbrella with a number of journalistic initiatives, including recruitment and sponsorship of individual journalists who would work in the mainstream media. Giago resigned as president, choosing not to run again.

A NEW DIRECTION FOR NAJA

Mike Burgess, editor of *Talking Leaf,* was elected president and Susan Arkeketa was named executive director. The new board outlined a three-year plan that set priorities such as providing scholarships, developing a job bank, and making the convention more focused on journalism education and training. The board also created a limited news service, hiring Nancy Butterfield (Ojibwe), as a freelancer to write a weekly package of stories.

I was elected president of the association a year later at the convention in Denver. My message at that convention was that there were too few American Indians and Alaska Natives in the media—at any level—and we should not limit participation. I suggested we drop the name "press association" because it did not reflect that diversity.

In 1990, at the fifth convention, in Fife, Washington, we did just that and members approved the name The Native American Journalists Association.

The focus of the organization shifted to the broader mission of encouraging Native journalists. When no funding surfaced for a news service, for example, the idea was dropped. But even by the early 1980s there had emerged an extensive network of high school and college support for Native American students. Early in the 1980s, Project Phoenix received a $200,000 grant—the largest in the organization's history—to reach young people with a competition and an annual training career conference before each convention.

NAJA also started to attract broadcasters. Patty Tahlahongva, a Hopi broadcaster, started NAJA News 4 as an intensive student internship. "What I try to stress to them is that it's a great career, but you have to be competitive. You have to be a good writer, fast and up on the news," she wrote. So NAJA News 4 produced two newscasts during the convention week working closely with professional mentors. "The students are really amazed. They say, 'Wow we didn't know that there were so many of you working in the business!' That's my passion. I have three students who are working in newsrooms, and some who are looking for jobs. To me, that's exciting. That's what it is all about."[9]

Similar programs were created for public radio, digital news, as well as a newspaper that is printed during the conventions.

NAJA also began to engage in research and public information. In May 1988, it published "From the Front Lines," a collection of essays from tribal journalists about the challenges of a free press in Indian Country. "It's not easy being a journalist covering your own community. And it's even more complex when you're a Native journalist covering your reservation," wrote *Sho-Ban News* editor Lori Edmo-Suppah. "All I can say is that you owe it to your people to keep your tribal people informed even though tribal leaders claim they're keeping information from the people because 'it's in the best interest of the tribe.' . . . Tribal people have a right to know what their tribal leaders are doing."

She was not alone in adopting a determined stance. "The sheer complexity of Indian issues, combined with the lack of knowledge that most Americans have on Indian issues, is usually seen as an overall deterrent when covering Indian stories," wrote D. Bambi Kraus in *The American Indian and the Media* (jointly published in 2000 with NAJA and the National Conference for Community and Justice).[10] "Many times, even when the decision to do an Indian story is made, the space and time granted to lay the foundation to understand the issue is inadequate to the task. Thus, the end result is an incomplete news story."

100 QUESTIONS

Other NAJA research projects have looked at the perception of American Indians through the media lens or offered a basic primer. One example, *100 Questions, 500 Nations: A Reporter's Guide to Native America* (2003), a popular compilation that had developed through several sources, had been added to the 2000 edition of *American Indians in the Media* and went on to circulate widely.[11]

NAJA also joined with the National Association of Black Journalists, National Association of Hispanic Journalists, and the Asian American Journalist Association to sponsor the first joint convention, UNITY '94. That was followed up with the creation of UNITY: Journalists of Color, with joint conventions that run in five-year cycles.

NAJA also became more willing to speak out on issues that concerned Native Americans. In 2002 the organization called on news organizations to no longer use sports mascots and nicknames based on American Indian stereotypes.

The American Indian Press Association had surfaced when American Indians and Alaska Natives were threatened with termination. NAJA, on the other hand, came of age during the era of self-determination, the federal policy of supporting (and funding) tribal governments to make their own decisions. NAJA was the ideal vehicle for promoting a journalistic version of that policy. Members ranged from those who worked for tribal newspapers, radio stations, and television enterprises to individuals who worked for The Associated Press or the *New York Times*.

CONCLUSION: PASSING THE TORCH

At the twenty-fifth anniversary of NAJA, celebrated at its 2008 convention in Albuquerque, Minnie Two Shoes, one of the founders at the Penn State meeting, looked back on her work and addressed the young people now at NAJA. "It makes me realize, that as part of what years ago we said we wanted, was to create journalists to come and take our place," she said on a student video. "Well, it's only going to take about half of you guys. Half of you persons are taking my place. Oh! Sad! And I've got some really tiny shoes to fill."

Sad, how? Yes, in retrospect, because Two Shoes died in 2010. But she was both joking and reflecting on the optimism of the number of young people who now attend NAJA conventions. The organization that once numbered in the tens, or a couple of dozen, was now counting its membership in the hundreds. Now, Native American journalists are working everywhere, including for their tribal radio stations and newspapers, or for a television station in large-market media areas like Phoenix or Oklahoma City. Native journalists have found new roles as storytellers for tribal and community enterprises as well as in mainstream media.

DISCUSSION QUESTIONS

1. What does the author mean when he speaks about the federal Indian termination policy? Do you think this policy would have been good or bad for American Indians?
2. What is the Bureau of Indian Affairs? Is this agency a positive or a negative force in contemporary American Indian affairs? Why, or why not?
3. Explain the significance of the Native American Journalists Association, the Asian American Journalists Association,, and the National Association of Black Journalists and describe how the UNITY conference came to be formed. Why is this important to journalists of color?

NOTES

1. Charles Trimble, "The American Indian Press Association . . . a Look Back," *Iktomi's Web,* April 2003, http://www.iktomisweb.com/Amer_Ind_Press_Assoc .pdf (accessed February 11, 2011). Now most easily available on Trimble's website at http://www.iktomisweb.com/Amer_Ind_Press_Assoc.pdf. See also Trahant 1998. Unless otherwise noted, most information in this chapter comes from these

two sources. See Charles Trimble, "Unsung Heroes: Lucy Covington, Termination Dragon Slayer . . . ," *Lakota Country Times,* October 10, http://www.lakotacountry times.com/news/2010-10-06/Voices/Unsung_Heroes_Lucy_Covington_ Termination_dragon_sl.html (accessed February 21, 2011).

2. Trimble 2003.

3. Trahant 1998.

4. Trimble 2003.

5. Trahant 2010, 24.

6. Trimble 2003.

7. Trahant 1998.

8. Material is quoted from a copy in my files, Fort Hall, Ida.

9. "News Watch: Q&A with Patty Talahongva." *News Watch*, San Francisco State University, May 8, 2002, http://newswatch.sfsu.edu/journal/su2002/050602 talahongva.html (accessed February 2011).

10. National Conference for Community and Justice 2000. *The American Indian and the Media,* 2d ed., edited by Mark Anthony Rolo (New York: National Conference for Community and Justice. The publication includes six articles and the "!oo Questions" mentioned below, note 11.

11. The NCCJ edition is now out of print. For readily available online editions see "Indian Country Resource Guide: 100 Questions for 500 Nations," http://www .sheriwhitefeather.com/theamericanindianandthemedia.pdf (accessed 8 August 2011); and "100 Questions: Who Is a Native American?" as developed by Reginald Stuart and Linda Fullerton (with numerous credits), http://www.leg.state.or.us/ cis/100_question.pdf (accessed 8 August 2011).

13

Cherokeespace.com

Native Social Networking

ROY BONEY, JR.

One of the greatest advances in mass media has been online social networking, which has opened the Internet to adoption in everyday life. With this recent advance in technology, American Indians with access to even the most basic computer set-up can now tell their own stories and immediately make those stories available to literally millions of people. This will be an effective tool to combat American Indian stereotyping. This essay is a personal reflection on one Cherokee user's experience with online social networking.

As I recall from my undergraduate days studying graphic design, the term "stereotype" denoted a printing process that involved making impressions on paper from a molded metal plate. Copies made from the plate were never exactly identical, as each had small imperfections, but the basic elements remained in each printing. This technique has since been replaced by modern electronic printing, but the idea of mass production is what drove its invention. It seems only fitting that our current understanding of the word "stereotype" comes at least in part from an influence in the history of mass media.

The image of the American Indian has been one of the greatest casualties of this influence. One only need to take a glimpse at films, television shows, video games, novels, toys, and various other elements from mainstream American culture to understand how the general population has seen, and still sees, Indigenous people. After hundreds of years, we are still defined largely by stereotypical images: noble savages, ignorant heathens, drunken drains on society, relics of history. And that's only a small handful of misconceptions.

The advent of new media technology has begun an equalizing trend. Technologies that were once the domain of money-laden media studios are now widely available to anyone who can afford a consumer-level computer, video camera, or mobile phone. The Cherokee Nation has become actively engaged in the digital world, having worked with Apple, Inc. to make the Cherokee syllabary available on the operating system of the iPhone and iPod Touch beginning in September 2010. This has enabled hundreds of millions of devices globally to support an American Indian language.[1] Cherokee language support was added to the iPad as well in a later software update.[2] Our community has adopted these devices and we are sending Cherokee text messages and emails and engaging the online world in our language. This serves as a complement to Apple's computer operating system Mac OS X, which has included the Cherokee syllabary and keyboard input methods in its standard language pack since 2003.[3] Third-party Cherokee fonts and keyboard input methods are also readily available for PCs running Microsoft Windows software.[4]

All this has helped create a digital ecosystem that allows the Cherokee community to use our language in digital media outlets. It honors a direct cultural inheritance from the Cherokee Nation printing press, established in the 1820s, which produced the bilingual newspaper the *Cherokee Phoenix*.[5] The Cherokee Nation used the modern communication technology of that era, the printing press, and adapted it for our own purposes. We are now utilizing the Internet as the new printing press, albeit one that is much, much more robust in scope. The *Cherokee Phoenix* itself survives today as a bilingual website.[6]

The social networking site Facebook has also been translated into the Cherokee language.[7] Cherokee users have flocked to the site. There are groups devoted to Cherokee politics, culture, language, and community events. The online encyclopedia Wikipedia appears in a Cherokee language version that is being added to and edited by fluent Cherokee language speakers.[8]

YouTube, which allows users to upload their own videos immediately to the site for free, has resulted in a video forum that can reach literally millions of viewers within a very short time. A culture has developed around YouTube, spawning digital celebrities with their own "channels," which can become popularized rapidly in a viral fashion. In the same fashion Cherokee have begun utilizing the power of YouTube to tell the world our point of view. The Cherokee Nation[9] and United Keetoowah Band of Cherokee Indians[10] each have a YouTube channel. The Eastern Band of Cherokee Indians utilizes videos placed on YouTube to promote cultural tourism.[11] Videos on Cherokee politics, history, and language are being created and uploaded by individual Cherokee users as well.

Despite these advantages to utilizing social networking, the medium presents challenges to the digital American Indian community that require much dialogue. Not only must we deal with the socioeconomic "digital divide" that separates Native communities from the mainstream, we must also deal with generational conflict within tribal communities. This conflict manifests in older generations' wariness of innovations. Dealing with culturally sensitive ideas—should these, or should they not, be adapted into modern technologies?—is a major part of the conflict.

To utilize sites such as Facebook and YouTube successfully, with a tribally accurate, culturally authentic, and respectful point of view, tribal communities need to be involved with content creation at all levels. This can range from the personal, such as digitally capturing an elder's birthday celebration for web consumption, to the governmental, such as webcasting a chief's speech to a tribal council. I have seen many of these developments as an active member in the digital Cherokee community, including the narrowing of the generational gap of technology usage. Many elders in our community have begun using social networking and text messaging to connect with the younger generation. When popular items like the iPhone and iPad and laptops support our language, our community has embraced them as Cherokee devices. It is no longer "their" technology. It is "ours."

Despite the best efforts and intentions of the digital Cherokee community, we are still in the infancy of becoming digital citizens. When one searches for "Cherokee" on YouTube, the results contain, for the most part, grossly inaccurate history lessons and misinformed cultural descriptions. Cherokee did not wear headdresses of the Plains Indian style, did not live in tipis, and did not become extinct on the Trail of Tears Indian Removal, as some of the videos would have you believe. One amusing commonality among many of the videos is the gratuitous use of the song "Indian Reservation" (written by John Loudermilk, most famously rendered by Paul Revere and the Raiders in 1971), featuring the refrain "Cherokee People! Cherokee tribe! So proud to live! So proud to die!"[12] It seems, jokingly, to have become the anthem of Cherokee everywhere, at least according to the mainstream culture. Yet the song was foisted upon us in another play at forced identity stereotyping. Even on Facebook our on-site translation project was targeted by a vandal who managed to alter the interface terms from the Cherokee syllabary into racially insensitive terminology. Fortunately, we were able to remedy the situation swiftly, but incidents such as this show that we are still battling the stereotypers of the world.

Many members of our Cherokee community have become intimately familiar with the culture of social networking media as active participants. I have many friends, colleagues, and family of all ages who utilize digital social media. Even some of the poorest in my community are active on these sites through web-enabled mobile devices like cell phones and digital media players. For those without these types of devices and services at home, web access can be gained at public libraries and schools. It is a new bond that we share as contemporary people, not only among our tribal communities, but also with the citizens of the world. As technology advances, many of these sites will evolve and some will even disappear altogether, but with an intimate knowledge of digital content creation, we can continue to stay in the game both as tribal people and as citizens in a globalized community. Perhaps one day a search for "Cherokee" on YouTube, or whatever new venue will replace it, will yield a majority of material that is not cringeworthy. Already a search on Google using the Cherokee syllabary term **ᏣᎳᎩ** instead of the English term "Cherokee" results in thousands upon thousands of results written in the

Cherokee language. Some of these are blogs and wikis created by Cherokee users, many of whom are friends and colleagues. This is a huge step forward on the road to smashing the stereotype mold.

DISCUSSION QUESTIONS

1. How do portrayals of American Indians differ in different media—for example, from film to the Internet?
2. How much of an influence does mass media portrayal of minorities have on the self-image of the people portrayed?
3. Does the globalizing of socialization make cultural identities stronger, or does it cause cultures to become more alike?
4. To what extent are American Indians utilizing social networking and other digital media?
5. Do you think a development such as online social networking really will make an impact in the fight against American Indian stereotypes? 1.

NOTES

1. "Cherokee Language Added to New iPhone and iPod Software," Cherokee Nation, http://www.cherokee.org/NewsRoom/FullStory/3341/Page/Default.aspx (accessed February 21, 2011).

2. "Apple—iPad—View the Technical Specifications for iPad," Apple, Inc., http://www.apple.com/ipad/specs/ (accessed February 21, 2011).

3. Apple employee (request to be unnamed), e-mail message to author, August 17, 2009.

4. "Iroquoian Keyboard Layouts, Downloads, and Keymaps," Chris Harvey, http://www.languagegeek.com/rotinonhsonni/keyboards/iro_keyboards.html (accessed February 21, 2011).

5. Robert J. Conley, *The Cherokee Nation: A History* (Albuquerque: University of New Mexico Press, 2005), 105.

6. "*Cherokee Phoenix* Language Homepage," *Cherokee Phoenix,* http://www.cherokeephoenix.org/culture/language/default.aspx (accessed February 21, 2011).

7. "Cherokee Language Now on Facebook," Christina Good Voice, *Cherokee Phoenix,* December 28, 2009, http://www.cherokeephoenix.org/20982/Article.aspx (accessed February 21, 2011).

8. "ᏉᏆᏆᏬᏗ," Wikipedia, http://chr.wikipedia.org (accessed February 21, 2011).

9. Utubecherokee, "YouTube—Utubecherokee's Channel," http://www.youtube.com/user/utubecherokee (accessed February 21, 2010).

10. "YouTube—UnitedKeetoowahBand's Channel," United Keetoowah Band of Cherokee Indians in Oklahoma, http://www.youtube.com/user/UnitedKeetoowah Band (accessed February 21 2011).

11. "Cherokee NC TV Spots," http://www.cherokee-nc.com/index.php?page=306 (accessed February 22, 2011).

12. "'Indian Reservation (The Lament of the Cherokee People),'" Wikipedia, http://en.wikipedia.org/wiki/Indian_Reservation_%28The_Lament_of_the_ Cherokee_Reservation_Indian%29 (accessed May 7, 2011).

14

Native Americans in the Twenty-First-Century Newsroom

Breaking through Barriers in New Media

JUAN A. AVILA HERNANDEZ

Native students who have completed specialized training programs in journalism are in high demand. This chapter gives an insider's view of how colleges and university programs that teach American Indian students are preparing them for careers in the new media of the information age. Students appreciate this type of quick responsiveness to the job market, and they receive encouragement that prepares them for the challenges and opportunities they will encounter as Native journalists in the mainstream arena.

During 2008 and 2009, U.S. newspapers experienced bankruptcies of their parent companies, widespread newsroom staff layoffs, the flight of operations from print to all-online formats, and a mass exodus of advertisers. While this economic tsunami rocked the professional stability and future of working and student journalists across the country, American Indian journalists remained somewhat isolated from the threats to their chosen profession. By early 2009, only one American Indian journalist working at a major daily newspaper, Mark Trahant (Shoshone-Bannock), had lost his job, when the *Seattle Post-Intelligencer* laid off newsroom staff and converted to a completely online format, according to a story posted on the online news source reznet.com.

The main reason that the downturn did not seem to affect American Indian journalists is academic: there are simply not enough American Indian journalists working at mainstream dailies to feel the impact.

According to Jeff Harjo (Muskogee), executive director of the Native American Journalists Association (NAJA), the national organization for indigenous reporters and editors, American Indian journalists make up 1 to 2 percent of U.S. newsroom staff. "The majority of our members are students, tribal members, people working for tribal media. Mainstream newspaper people are not a big part of our organization," he explains. Harjo is a former editor of tribal newspapers of the Absentee Shawnee Nation, Kickapoo Nation, and Seminole Nation—all in Oklahoma. NAJA membership attests to this fact. Of NAJA's 663 members in 2008, 242 were working radio, print, online, and television journalists, 154 were college journalism students, and 124 were high school journalism students.[1]

One way NAJA was impacted by the economic shortfalls at newspapers became evident at the association's national conference held in Albuquerque, New Mexico, in July 2009. The *New York Times* and *Chicago Tribune* foundations—consistent supporters of NAJA conferences—had both decided not to contribute to the 2009 conference. Journalism and media professors at mainstream universities as well as tribal colleges and universities (TCUs) ran a complementary—if loosely affiliated—campaign to promote journalism among American Indian students.

According to Denny McAuliffe (Osage), director of reznet.com—a journalism program at the University of Montana geared to recruiting American Indians for jobs in mainstream journalism—the economic crisis threatened the job pipeline for future journalists more than it limited current jobs for indigenous reporters and editors. "Where I see the turmoil in the newspaper business is not the closing," he said. "It's that the smaller newspapers are tightening. Remember, it's the smaller papers that tend to take our Native journalists." He added that only one reznet alumnus had been laid off in 2009. "Yes, it is affecting us but not drastically," he concluded.

The drive, dedication, and talent necessary to attain a career in journalism in its many traditional and unique forms in Indian Country has always come from American Indian students themselves. One prime example is journalist Luella Brien (Crow), a reporter at the *Billings Gazette* (Montana). When she speaks to students at the local high school and elementary schools about her work as a daily reporter, she shows her excitement about her job. "I like to talk to classes about my job and how much fun it is," says Brien, who spent two years at Little Big Horn College (Crow Agency, Montana) before she transferred to the Journalism School at the University of Montana at Missoula, graduating in 2006. "A lot of students, especially Indian students, don't even think that journalism is an option," she says.

Growing up on the Crow Indian Reservation in Montana, Brien caught the "journalism bug" in high school after the school paper printed a first-person account of her survival of a serious car wreck. Along with her talent, curiosity, and extraordinary work ethic, she capitalized on mentoring from a supportive high school English teacher and on national journalism programs geared to American Indian students.

Like most tribal colleges, Little Big Horn College does not offer courses in journalism as a separate subject. But in its regular writing curriculum, Brien discovered that writing came naturally to her. In 2002 she attended an intensive, three-week boot camp, the American Indian Journalism Institute, sponsored by Freedom Forum (a national press foundation) and the University of South Dakota. She also participated in the American Indian Journalism Career Conference at the Crazy Horse Memorial in the Black Hills of South Dakota. Through the institute she was awarded a seven-week internship at the *Seattle Times*. Since graduating from the university in Missoula, she has worked at several Montana dailies, most recently at the *Billings Gazette*. A single mother who grew up reading the gazette, Brien always dreamed of working there. "That's where I want to be," she says.

Because of her talent and her training, Brien has been able to find positions despite a downward trend in the size of daily newspaper editorial staffs. According to the 2008 newsroom census by the American Society of Newspaper Editors (ASNE), the total number of full-time journalists at daily newspapers shrank by 4.4% that year—about 2,400 journalists left daily reporting jobs because of buyouts or layoffs. Despite this trend, the percentage of minority journalists increased slightly in the same interval. Even more promising news was that the number of American Indians in newsroom positions was increasing, including supervisors, online producers, reporters, artists, and videographers. ASNE's census showed that in 1999 a total of 241 American Indians had worked in newsrooms in the United States; by 2007 the total had risen to 284.

Native students like Brien who have gone through specialized training programs are actually "hot property in high demand," according to McAuliffe of reznet, formerly a reporter and foreign desk assistant editor at the *Washington Post*. He has been involved in recruiting and training American Indian college students for journalism careers since the late 1990s. "Our students who we train through the American Indian Journalism Institute program have all found jobs, and some of them have actually gotten multiple offers," he says. Founded in 2001, the institute has sent graduates to internships with the Associated Press, the *New York Times, Arizona Republic,* and other major-market newspapers. McAuliffe founded and now directs reznet at the University of Montana in Missoula. He mentors and instructs Native students from around the United States, whose material is published on the program's online outlet, www.reznetnews.org. Several other organizations offer training opportunities for Native journalism students, including NAJA, South Dakota State University, and the University of South Dakota.

With some remarkable exceptions tribal colleges and universities (TCUs) have played a limited role in training journalists. Only a small percentage of TCUs offer journalism or media classes. A telephone survey of 32 TCUs conducted by *Tribal College Journal* in early 2008 showed that 9 colleges offered some sort of journalism and media courses or curriculum; 21 did not offer any journalism or media courses; and 2 offered one-year certificates in digital media or desktop publishing. Primarily two-year institutions providing a basic general education, TCUs emphasize instruction in science, math, business, nursing, and English. Electronic media programs can be expensive to run, and colleges must concentrate on programs with the greatest potential for employment, according to Dr. Frank Tyro at Salish Kootenai College (Montana). Thus, under current conditions TCUs are unlikely to offer extensive training in journalism.

· · ·

A former member of the NAJA Board of Directors, McAuliffe is disappointed that so many TCUs do not offer training in journalism and that very few TCU students participate in the Freedom Forum's annual three-week journalism summer boot camp. He hopes this pattern will change in the future. His mission is to find and nurture young American Indian students with a passion for journalism wherever they may be. Some of the most promising opportunities lie in new forms of digital media and the Internet. Since 2009, ASNE researchers have begun to include in their census accounts full-time journalists who work online. In 2010 a total of 1,700 newsroom staffers produced news that appeared on the web. Of this number, almost 18 percent were minority journalists.

A glance at the 2010 ASNE News Census reveals one alarming statistic. The number of Native Americans working at newsrooms across the United States in all positions (supervisors, editors, reporters, photographers) plunged from 293 in 2009 to 199 in 2010, downturn of 32 percent. The numbers of African American, Hispanic, and Asian newsroom employees also declined during the same period, although the drop was not nearly as severe for Native American journalists.

Meanwhile students have embraced the new technologies to tell their stories. At Oglala Lakota College in South Dakota, for example, students are learning how to create digital television programs. Four students from the program took part in the American Indian Journalism Career Fair at the Crazy Horse Memorial in April 2008. Their instructor, Kathleen Aplan (Cheyenne River Sioux), shares McAuliffe's and Brien's enthusiasm. "The opportunities for diversity in the media field are greater than ever," she says. "It's how far each student wants to take it."

The Oglala Lakota College program is relatively new compared with the television production programs at Haskell Indian Nations University (Kansas) and at Salish Kootenai College, which have been in place for decades. Back at the *Billings Gazette,* Brien ponders her advice for young journalism students. "No matter what they do, they shouldn't be afraid to be the only Indian in the room. We're kind of in a transition right now where more Indians are actually leaving [their home communities] and going to mainstream jobs. You can't be afraid to break new ground."

DISCUSSION QUESTIONS

1. What reasons does the author offer regarding why the economic downturn has not had an impact on American Indian journalists as much as on others?
2. Where would students find the study of journalism at TCUs? Why?
3. Does the chapter suggest that changes in journalism and media technologies will be good, bad, or neutral for American Indian journalists and journalism students? Cite specific evidence from the chapter to support your position.
4. Choose a TCU that interests you and view its website. Does the description of courses and co-curricular activities confirm or refute, in your opinion, some of the new directions for journalism described in this chapter?

ACKNOWLEDGMENTS

My thanks to the *Tribal College Journal of American Indian Higher Education,* where an earlier version of this chapter appeared in its Fall 2008 issue; and to Jeff Harjo, NAJA Executive Director, for his comments.

NOTE

1. Personal interview, June 15, 2008.

15

Joining the Circle

A Yakima Story

RAY CHAVEZ

Most of this chapter was originally published online as part of the "Diversity Diaries" series in 2004, sponsored by the Poynter Institute. Discussion here illustrates how journalism protocols can enhance, rather than undermine, accuracy and authenticity in reporting.

It was the spring of 1980, and I had been working in the Yakima Valley of east-central Washington State for only a few months. But in that time I had opened up news coverage of the Yakima Indian Nation,[1] which to my surprise had not been a regular beat at my newspaper, the *Yakima Herald-Republic*. The newspaper had previously covered only breaking news stories of the Yakima Nation and had not explored other stories about tribal life and customs. Reporters had tended to come around only when bad news occurred.

Armed with my newly minted master's degree from the University of Washington, I had returned to journalism by taking a general-assignment reporting position in the *Herald-Republic*'s East Valley bureau. I had begun coverage of Yakima Tribal Council meetings, at times greeted by skeptical eyes from council and tribal members. *He could be Indian,* they seemed to wonder, *but he is definitely not Yakima.* But I persisted. Armed with a working knowledge of indigenous life that I had gained from my grandmother—a woman of mixed tribal heritage, likely part Tarahumara from Old Mexico and part Mescalero Apache from the U.S. side of the border—I tried to explain tribal life to a largely white readership.

My meeting with an elderly Yakima woman was a much lighter occasion. It was the time of year for the annual Yakima Pow Wow, and I was assigned to do a feature color piece on the event. I was sensitive to the criticisms that the only time the newspaper had covered Indian news was during the Pow Wow and that the color pieces had tended toward patronizing the "quaintness" of tribal customs. For example, stories referred to and described the "costumes" the Yakima wore at such events. But these were not costumes; they were traditional native dress. (Do business executives wear costumes to their board meetings? No, they wear business attire.) Other stories in the *Herald-Republic* had referred to the various dances and songs at the Pow Wow as if they had singular meaning. The stories did not provide any background on the differences among the songs and dances and on their cultural and spiritual significance. I wanted my story to go deeper and to avoid such ethnocentric reporting tendencies. I wanted to get away from a white viewpoint and explain the meaning behind tribal observations.

I arrived during preparations for the Pow Wow, to search out different story angles. As I wandered through the dirt field that had been converted to a parking lot for the occasion, I couldn't help but admire the artwork on the cars, some of which had arrived from hundreds of miles away. These vehicles had become, as one tribal member explained, the new Indian ponies, brightly painted with Native designs and pastoral scenes, each with its own heraldic identity. The wonderful aroma of smoked salmon filled the air, and I followed this lure to a nearby tent and canopy. There she was.

The elderly Yakima woman greeted me with a toothless and endearing smile and asked me in. I explained who I was and asked if she would mind responding to a few of my questions. She didn't say no, and simply proceeded to speak in a steady, drumbeat manner, explaining what she was doing and why.

She said the salmon was sacred to the people of the Northwest and of the Yakima River, and that the Creator had given the fish to the people as a gift. She explained that all of Mother Earth's creatures had a spirit and that we must bless them for the giving of their flesh to nourish us. She spoke about the alder wood she had soaked the night before in river water, which was now smoldering, bathing in white smoke the salmon she had gently placed above the fire. The wood had to come from a tree that had given up its spirit and no longer grew—not from a tree that had been felled by human hands—thereby fulfilling its life circle on Mother Earth. She spoke eloquently not only of the other food she was preparing but of the spirit even of the rocks that had formed the rim of her fire pit—they too were gifts from the Creator that we must never take for granted. Other elder women of the tribe then chimed in with descriptions of their own food preparations.

There was gentle conversation, sometimes lapsing into the Yakima tongue, welcoming the new, young friend in their midst. The old woman then looked at me as I took more notes and smiled and said, "This is *tin now wit.*"

"*Tin now wit?*" I asked.

"Yes," she said, "*Tin now wit,* the Indian Way." I wrote my story, and that's the headline it carried.

Weeks later, I covered the opening of the Yakima Nation's Cultural Center. Toward the end of the ceremony, tribal elders announced that an honor song was about to be sung. We were told that during a dance in which tribal members had formed a circle on the Cultural Center floor, young women from the tribe would come forward to invite those who had made a significant contribution to the tribe to join the circle.

The drumbeat and honor song began, and much to my surprise, I found myself face to face with a teenaged Yakima girl. She stretched forth her hand, took mine, and ushered me to the circle.

Later I was told that the invitation had been in appreciation of "the storyteller"—I was the one who had told the true stories of the people. I was the one who had not taken a patronizing and condescending tone toward tribal customs. I was also told that the tribe appreciated the stories about positive things that happen in Indian country.

I have journalism awards to my credit. Some hang on my office wall or on my office shelves; some are in boxes, stored away. But of all my awards and plaques, it was the honor of an invitation to dance with the Yakima that stands tallest in my heart.

Coverage of a community should be complete. It should not be one-sided, focusing exclusively on the negative, but should be balanced, negative with positive. When a community, any community, sees a reporter come around on a regular basis and not just during times of crisis, its members begin to appreciate the effort to write with fairness and balance, the attempt to avoid stereotypes and to explain the community to the larger surrounding community. This courteous interest leads to a better mutual understanding and dispels fears spawned by ignorance and unfamiliarity.

DISCUSSION QUESTIONS

1. Why do you believe the author thought it was important to "open up" coverage of the Yakima Indian Nation when he became a reporter in the Yakima Valley?
2. What does the author believe to be the basis for Yakima tribal members' reluctance to be interviewed by the newspaper?
3. How do you think the story about the elderly Yakima woman could have been told differently, either for better or for worse?
4. Diversity coverage is often characterized as being focused on the "festivals and spectacles" of communities of color. Do you think this is a fair criticism? Why or why not?
5. Can you identify American Indian communities in your city, county, or state? What do you know about them from the media in your area?

NOTE

1. The nation recently adopted "Yakama" as the preferred spelling of its name.

Bibliography

Abound, E. Frances, and Anna Joong. 2008. "Intergroup Name-calling and Conditions for Creating Assertive Bystanders." In *Intergroup Attitudes and Relations in Childhood through Adulthood,* edited by Sheri R. Levy and Melanie Killen, 249–260. New York: Oxford University Press.

Aleiss, Angela. 2005. *Making the White Man's Indian.* Westport, Conn.: Praeger.

Alexie, Sherman. 2002. *The Business of Fancydancing.* Motion picture. Vashon Island, Wash.: Fallsapart Productions.

Allport, Gordon. W. 1954. *The Nature of Prejudice.* Reading, Mass.: Addison-Wesley.

Anderson, William L. 1991. *Cherokee Removal: Before and After.* Athens: University of Georgia Press.

Appadurai, Arjun. 1996. *Modernity at Large: Cultural Dimensions of Globalization.* Minneapolis: Public Worlds.

Aronson, Joshua. 2002. "Stereotype Threat: Contending and Coping with Unnerving Expectations." In *Improving Academic Achievement: Impact of Psychological Factors on Education,* edited by Joshua Aronson, 279–301. New York: Elsevier/Academic Press.

Banks, Dennis J. 1993. "Tribal Names and Mascots in Sports." *Journal of Sport and Social Issues* 17, no. 1:5–8.

Baughman, James L. 2001. "Who Read *Life?* The Circulation of America's Favorite Magazine." In *Looking at Life Magazine,* edited by Erika Doss, 41–51. Washington: Smithsonian Institution Press.

Bennett, W. Lance, and William Serrin. 2005. "The Watchdog Role." In *The Press,* edited by Geneva Overholser and Kathleen Hall Jamieson, 169–188. New York: Oxford University Press.

Berkhofer, Robert F., Jr. 1978. *The White Man's Indian: Images of the American Indian from Columbus to the Present.* New York: Alfred A. Knopf.

———. 1979. *The White Man's Indian: Images of the American Indian from Columbus to the Present.* New York: Vintage Books.

Bernstein, Alison R. 1991. *American Indians and World War II: Toward a New Era in Indian Affairs.* Norman: University of Oklahoma Press.

Bird, S. Elizabeth. 1999. "Gendered Construction of the American Indian in Popular Media." *Journal of Communication* 49, no. 3:61–83.

Bird, Elizabeth S. 2001a. "Indians Are Like That: Negotiating Identity in a Media World." In *Black Marks: Minority Ethnic Audiences and Media,* edited by Karen Ross and Peter Playdon, 105–122. Aldershot, England and Burlington, Vt.: Ashgate.

Bird, Elizabeth S. 2001b. "Savage Desires: The Gendered Construction of the American Indian in Popular Media." In *Selling the Indian: Commercializing and Appropriating American Indian Cultures*, edited by C. J. Meyer and D. Royer, 62–98. Tucson: University of Arizona Press.

Bowie, Jennifer. 1999. "Out of Their Hands: Framing and Its Impact on *New York Times* and Television Coverage of Indians and Indian Activism, 1968–79." Presented to the Association for Education in Journalism and Mass Communication, New Orleans, August 4–7.

Bowker, Ardy. 1993. *Sisters in the Blood: The Education of Women in Native America.* Newton, Mass.: WEEA Publishing Center.

Briggs, Kara, and Dan Lewerenz. 2003. "2003 Reading Red Report: A Call for the News Media to Recognize Racism in Sports Team Nicknames and Mascots." Native American Journalists Association. Accessed November 16, 2003. http://www.naja.com/red.html.

Brown, Bruce W. 1981. *Images of Family Life in Magazine Advertising: 1920–1978.* New York: Praeger.

Brown, Dee. 1970. *Bury My Heart at Wounded Knee: An Indian History of the American West.* New York: Holt, Rinehart & Winston.

Brummett, Barry. 1984. "Burke's Representative Anecdote as a Method in Media Criticism." *Critical Studies in Media Communication* 1, no. 2:161–178.

Burke, Kenneth. 1941. "Literature as Equipment for Living." In *The Philosophy of Literary Form: Studies in Symbolic Action,* 293–304. Baton Rouge: Louisiana State University Press.

Buscombe, Edward. 2006. *"Injuns!" Native Americans in the Movies.* London: Reaktion Books.Cajete, Gregory. 1994. *Look to the Mountain: An Ecology of Indigenous Education.* Durango, Colo.: Kivakí.

Carey, James. 1989. "Technology and Ideology: The Case of the Telegraph." In *Communication as Culture: Essays on Media and Society,* 155–177. New York: Routledge.

Carter, Samuel III. 1976. *Cherokee Sunset: A Nation Betrayed.* Garden City, N.Y.: Doubleday.

Chandler, Kim, and John Terrence Eck Johnson. 1996. "Eliminating Indian Stereotypes from American Society: Causes and Legal and Societal Solutions. *American Indian Law Review* 20:65–109.

Chronicles of American Indian Protest. 1971. Compiled and edited by the Council on Interracial Books for Children. Greenwich, Conn.: Fawcett Publications.

Churchill, Ward. 1998. "*Smoke Signals:* A History of Native Americans in Cinema." *Lip Magazine.* Accessed July 4, 2008. http://www.lipmagazine.org/articles/revichurchill_35_p.htm.

Clark, Sheila. 2005. "Dismantling Stereotypes about Adolescents: The Power of Positive Images." *Adolescent Health* 2, no. 5. Accessed June 20, 2009. http://www.socialworkers.org/practice/adolescent_health/ah0205.pdf.

Cobb, Amanda J. 2003. "This Is What It Means to Say *Smoke Signals:* Native American Cultural Sovereignty." In *Hollywood's Indian: The Portrayal of the*

Native American in Film, edited by Peter C. Rollins and John E. O'Connor, 206–288. Lexington: University of Kentucky Press.

Cohen, Felix S. 1960, 1970. "Americanizing the White Man." In *The Legal Conscience: Selected Papers of Felix Cohen,* edited by Lucy Kramer Cohen, 315–327. New Haven: Yale University Press. Reprinted Hamden, Conn.: Archon Books.

———. 1982. *Handbook of Federal Indian Law.* Charlottesville, Va.: Michie Bobbs-Merill.

Cohen, Geoffrey L., and Claude M. Steele. 2002. "A Barrier of Mistrust: How Negative Stereotypes Affect Cross-race Mentoring." In *Improving Academic Achievement: Impact of Psychological Factors on Education,* edited by Joshua Aronson , 303–327. New York: Elsevier/Academic Press.

Cole, Terrence M. 1992. "Jim Crow in Alaska: The Passage of the Alaska Equal Rights Act of 1945." *Western Historical Quarterly* 23, no. 4:429–449.

Coleman, Cynthia-Lou. 1992. "Native Americans Must Set Their Own Media Agenda," *Quill,* no. 8 (October).

Conley, Robert J. 2005. *The Cherokee Nation: A History.* Albuquerque: University of New Mexico Press.

Coombe, Rosemary J. 1997. *The Cultural Life of Intellectual Properties: Authorship, Appropriation, and the Law.* Durham, N.C.: Duke University Press.

Copeland, David A. 1993. "'The Sculking Indian Enemy: Colonial Newspapers' Portrayal of Native Americans." Presented to the Association for Education in Journalism and Mass Communication, Kansas City, Mo., July 30–August 2.

———. 1997, 2000. *Debating the Issues in Colonial Newspapers: Primary Documents on Events of the Period.* Newark: University of Delaware Press; Westport, Conn: Greenwood Press.

———. 1997. *Colonial American Newspapers: Character and Content.* Newark: University of Delaware Press.

Courey Toensing, Gale. 2007. "Maine Town Removes Offensive Name." *Indian Country Today,* October 29. . Accessed August 1, 2008). http://www.indian country.com/content.cfm?id=1096416003.

Coward, John M. 1999. *The Newspaper Indian: Native American Identity in the Press, 1820–90.* Urbana: University of Illinois Press.

cummings, andré douglas pond. 2000. "Lions and Tigers and Bears, Oh, My; Or, Redskins and Braves and Indians, Oh, Why": Ruminations on *McBride v. Utah State Tax Commission,* Political Correctness and the Reasonable Person." *California Western Law Review* 36:11–37.

———. 2008. *Progress Realized? The Continuing American Indian Mascot Quandary. Marquette Sports Law Review* 18:309–335.

———, and Seth E. Harper. 2009. "Wide Right: Why the NCAA's Policy on the American Indian Mascot Issue Misses the Mark." *Maryland Journal of Race, Religion, Gender and Class* 9:135–179.

Czitrom, Daniel J. 1982. *Media and the American Mind: From Morse to McLuhan.* Chapel Hill: University of North Carolina Press.

Davis, Laurel. 1993. "Protest against the Use of Native American Mascots: A Challenge to Traditional American Identity." *Journal of Sport and Social Issues* 17, no. 1:9–22.

Debo, Angie. 1940. *And Still the Waters Run: The Betrayal of the Five Civilized Tribes.* Princeton: Princeton University Press.

Delgado, Richard, and Jean Stefancic. 2001. *Critical Race Theory: An Introduction.* New York: NYU Press.

Deloria, Phillip J. 1998. *Playing Indian.* New Haven: Yale University Press.

———. 2004. *Indians in Unexpected Places.* Lawrence: University Press of Kansas.

Deloria, Vine, Jr. 1985. *American Indian Policy in the Twentieth Century.* Norman: University of Oklahoma Press.

———, and Clifford M. Lytle. 1983. *American Indians, American Justice.* Austin: University of Texas Press.

———, and David E. Wilkins. 2000. *Tribes, Treaties, and Constitutional Tribulations.* Austin: University of Texas Press.

DeShane, Brock. 2003. *Images of Indians: How Hollywood Stereotypes the Native American.* Film documentary. Starz Encore Entertainment.

Desjarlait, Robert. 2001. "Into the Crucible: Sexual and Physical Abuse in Indian Country." *The Circle: News from an American Indian Perspective,* September 30, 12. Accessed July 5, 2011. http://www.highbeam.com/doc/1P1-79148674 .html.

Dippie, Brian W. 1982, 1991. *The Vanishing American: White Attitudes and U.S. Indian Policy.* Middletown, Conn.: Wesleyan University Press. 2d ed. Lawrence: University Press of Kansas.

Disjksterhuis, Ap, and Ad van Knippenberg. 1996. "The Knife That Cuts Both Ways: Facilitated and Inhibited Access to Traits as a Result of Stereotype Activation." *Journal of Experimental Social Psychology* 32:271–288.

Dornhelm, Robert, and Sergio Mimica-Gezzan. 2005. *Into the West.* Television miniseries. Universal City, Calif.: Dreamworks.

Doss, Erika. ed. 2001. *Looking at Life Magazine.* Washington: Smithsonian Institution Press.

Dyer, Richard. 1993. *The Matter of Images: Essays on Representations.* London: Routledge.

Ehle, John. 1988. *Trail of Tears: The Rise and Fall of the Cherokee Nation.* New York: Doubleday.

Emert, Phyllis Raybin. 2003. "Native American Mascots: Racial Slur or Cherished Tradition?" *Respect* 2, no. 2:1, 4–6.

Ewen, Stuart. 1996. *PR! A Social History of Spin.* New York: Basic Books.

Eyre, Chris, director. 1998. *Smoke Signals.* Motion picture. Screenplay by Sherman Alexie. Plummer Ida.: Shadowcatcher Entertainment; Seattle: Welb Film Pursuits. Distributed by Miramax Films, New York and Los Angeles.

———. 2002. *Skins*. Motion picture. Pine Ridge Indian Reservation, S.D.: First Look International.

———. 2003. *Edge of America*. Motion picture. Salt Lake City: Showtime.

Feeny, Brian B. 1997. "Catching a Glimpse of Hegemony: The Covers of *Life* Magazine during the Gulf War." Presented at the Association for Education in Journalism and Mass Communication Annual Conference, Magazine Division, Chicago, Illinois.

Fighting' Whites. 2004. "Official Website of the Fightin' Whites Intramural Basketball Team of the University of Northern Colorado." 2004. Accessed December 8, 2004. http://www.fightingwhites.org/. *See now* http://www.cafe press.com/fightinwhite. Accessed August 25, 2011.

Fischer, Roger A. 1996. *Them Damned Pictures: Explorations in American Political Cartoon Art*. North Haven, Conn.: Archon Books.

Fiske, Susan T. 1998. "Stereotyping, Prejudice, and Discrimination." In *The Handbook of Social Psychology*, edited by Daniel T. Gilbert, Susan T. Fiske and Gardner Lindzey, 357–411. Boston: McGraw-Hill.

Foreman, Grant. 1932. *Indian Removal: The Emigration of the Five Civilized Tribes of Indians*. Norman: University of Oklahoma Press. 2d ed., 1953.

Foucault, Michel. 1972. *The Archaeology of Knowledge and the Discourse on Language*. Translated by A. M. Sheridan Smith. New York: Pantheon Books.

Francis, Daniel. 1992. *The Imaginary Indian: The Image of the Indian in Canadian Culture*. Vancouver, B.C.: Arsenal Pulp Press.

Freedman, Judy S. 2002. *Easing the Teasing: Helping Your Child Cope with Name-Calling, Ridicule, and Verbal Bullying*. New York: McGraw-Hill.

Freire, Paulo. 1970. *Pedagogy of the Oppressed*. Translated by M. Bergman Ramos. New York: Continuum.

Giago, Tim. 1991. "Overview on the American Indian." In *The American Indian and the Media*, edited by Tim Giago, Martha Crow, Tom Beaver, Pamela A. Kalar, and Paul O. Sand. N.p.: The National Conference of Christians and Jews, Minnesota-Dakotas Region.

Gordon, Lewis. 1995. *Bad Faith and Antiblack Racism*. Atlantic Highlands, N.J.: Humanities Press.

Gorman, Carl N. 1990. Preface. In *Warriors: Navajo Code Talkers*. Edited by Kenji Kawano. Flagstaff, Ariz.: Northland Publications.

Grassian, Daniel. 2005. *Understanding Sherman Alexie*. Columbia: University of South Carolina Press.

Green, Michael K. 1993. "Images of Native Americans in Advertising: Some Moral Issues." *Journal of Business Ethics* 12, no 4: 323–330.

Green, Rayna. 1975. "The Pocahontas Perplex: The Image of Indian Women in American Culture." *Massachusetts Review* 16, no. 4:698–714.

Grossberg, Lawrence, Ellen Wartella, D. Charles Whitney, and J. MacGregor Wise. 2006. *Media Making: Mass Media in a Popular Culture*. 2nd ed. Thousand Oaks: Sage Publications.

Gunn Allen, Paula. 1986. *The Sacred Hoop: Recovering the Feminine in American Indian Traditions.* Boston: Beacon.

Haines, Michael R., and Richard S. Steckel. 2000. *Population History of North America.* Cambridge: Cambridge University Press.

Hall, Stuart. 1997. "The Spectacle of the 'Other.'" In *Representations: Cultural Representations and Signifying Practices,* edited by Stuart Hall, 225–290. London: Sage.

Hamblin, Dora Jane. 1977. *That Was the "Life."* New York: W. W. Norton.

Harjo, Sterlin. 2007. *Four Sheets to the Wind.* Motion picture. Holdenville, Oklahoma: Kish Productions.

Harrell, Jules. P., Sadiki Hall, and James Taliaferro. 2003. "Physiological Responses to Racism and Discrimination: An Assessment of the Evidence." *American Journal of Public Health* 93, no. 2:243–248.

Harter, Eugene C. 1991. *Boilerplating America: The Hidden Newspaper.* Edited by Dorothy Harter. Lanham: University Press of America.

Hauptman, Laurence M. 1986. *The Iroquois Struggle for Survival: World War II to Red Power.* Syracuse: Syracuse University Press.

Hawes, Kay. 2001. "Fighting over the 'Chief' Splits Campus Community." *NCAA News,* April 23.

Heath, Robert L. 2000. "A Rhetorical Perspective on the Values of Public Relations: Crossroads and Pathways toward Concurrence." *Journal of Public Relations Research* 12, no. 1:69–91.

Henige, David. 1998. *Numbers from Nowhere: The American Indian Contact Population Debate.* Norman: University of Oklahoma Press.

Hilliard, William. 1992. "Stereotypes on the Sports Page." *ASNE Bulletin,* May/June, 20–21.

Hinsley, Curtis. 1981. *Savages and Scientists: The Smithsonian Institution and the Development of American Anthropology: 1846–1910.* Washington, D.C.: Smithsonian Institution Press.

Hon, Linda Childers. 1977. "Public Relations and the Civil Rights Movement." *Journal of Public Relations Research* 9, no. 3:182.

Honey, Maureen. 1984. *Creating Rosie the Riveter: Class, Gender, and Propaganda during World War II.* Amherst: University of Massachusetts Press.

Honneth, Axel. 1998. "Democracy as Reflexive Cooperation: John Dewey and the Theory of Democracy Today." Translated by John M. M. Farrell. *Political Theory* 26, no. 6:763–783.

Hoxie, Frederick E., and Peter Iverson. 1998. *Indians in American History: An Introduction.* 2nd ed. Wheeling, Ill.: Harlan Davidson.

Hyde, George E. 1956. *A Sioux Chronicle.* Norman: University of Oklahoma Press. *Indian Country Today.* 2003. "About Us." Accessed December 7, 2003. http://www.indiancountry.com/aboutus.

Ives, Stephen. 1996. *The West.* Motion picture. Brackettville, Tex.: Florentine Films.

Jackson, Gram, M.D. 1995. *Through Indian Eyes: The Untold Story of Native American Peoples.* Pleasantville N.Y.: Reader's Digest Association.

Jahoda, Gloria. 1995. *The Trail of Tears*. New York: Wings Books.

Jay, Robert. 1987. *The Trade Card in Nineteenth-Century America*. Columbia: University of Missouri Press.

Johnston, Carla B. 2000. *Screened Out: How the Media Control Us and What We Can Do about It*. New York: M. E. Sharpe.

Josephy, Alvin M., Jr. 1994. *500 Nations: An Illustrated History of North American Indians*. New York: Gramercy Books.

Kawano, Kenji. 1990. *Warriors: Navajo Code Talkers*. Flagstaff, Ariz.: Northland.

Keever, Beverly Ann, Carolyn Martindale, and Mary Ann Weston, eds. 1997. *U.S. Coverage of Racial Minorities: A Sourcebook, 1934–1996*. Westport, Conn.: Greenwood.

Kessler, Donna J. 1996. *The Making of Sacagawea: A Euro-American Legend*. Tuscaloosa: University of Alabama Press.

Keyssar, Alexander. 2000. *The Right to Vote: The Contested History of Democracy in the United States*. New York: Basic Books.

King, C. R. 2003. "De/scribing Squ*w: Indigenous Women and Imperial Idioms in the United States." *American Indian Culture and Research Journal* 27, no. 2:1–16.

King, Richard C., and Charles Fruehling Springwood. 2000. "Fighting Spirits: The Racial Politics of Sports Mascots." *Journal of Sport and Social Issues* 24, no. 3:282–304.

Kleg, Milton. 1993. *Hate, Prejudice, and Racism*. Albany, New York: SUNY.

Klein, Laura, and Lillian Ackerman. 1995. "Introduction." In *Women and Power in Native North America*, edited by Laura Klein and Lillian Ackerman, 3–16. Norman: University of Oklahoma Press.

Kunuk, Zacharias. 2001. *The Fast Runner (Atanarjuat)*. Motion picture. Ingloolik, Nunavut: Aboriginal Peoples Television Network.

Lamb, Diane. 1999. "A Critical Analysis of the Newspaper Coverage of Native Americans by the *Daily Oklahoman* Newspaper for 1998." Presented to the Association for Education in Journalism and Mass Communication, New Orleans, August 4–7.

Laws of the Cherokee Nation, Enacted by the General Council in 1826, 1827 & 1828. 1828. New Echota, C.N.: Printed by Isaac Helyn Harris.

Lewis, David. 1995. "Native Americans and the Environment: A Survey of Twentieth-Century Issues." *American Indian Quarterly* 19:423–450.

Linn, Michael. 2007. *Imprint*. Motion picture. Pine Ridge Indian Reservation, S.D.: Linn Productions.

Lippmann, Walter. 1921. *Public Opinion*. New York: The Free Press.

———. 1922. *Public Opinion*. New York: Harcourt Brace.

Littlefield, Daniel F., and James W. Parins. 1984. *American Indian and Alaska Native Newspapers and Periodicals, 1826–1924*. Vol. 1. Westport, Conn.: Greenwood Press.

Logan, Charles Russell. 1997. *The Promised Land: The Cherokees, Arkansas, and Removal, 1794–1839*. Little Rock: Department of Arkansas Heritage.

McGuire, Tim. 1991. "Racism in Sports," speech delivered during racism and sports conference in St. Paul, Minn., November 20. http://www.naja.com/pr-mcguire.html.

Marubbio, M. Elise. 2006. *Killing the Indian Maiden: Images of Native American Women in Film.* Lexington: University Press of Kentucky.

May, Philip A. 1994. "The Epidemiology of Alcohol Abuse among American Indians: The Mythical and Real Properties." *American Indian Culture and Research Journal* 18, no. 2:121–143.

Melkote, Srinivas, and H. Leslie Steeves. 2001. *Communication for Development in the Third World: Theory and Practice for Empowerment.* 2nd ed. New Delhi: Sage.

Merskin, Debra. 1998. Sending up Signals: A Survey of Native American Media Use and Representation in the Mass Media. *Howard Journal of Communications* 9:333–345.

Merskin, Debra. 2001. "Winnebagos, Cherokees, Apaches, and Dakotas: The Persistence of Stereotyping of American Indians in American Advertising Brands." *Howard Journal of Communication* 12:159–169.

Merton, Robert K. 1957. *Social Theory and Social Structure.* New York: Free Press.

Metz, Sharon. 1995. "Crazy Horse Malt Liquor Equals Racism." *Peace and Freedom* 55, no. 3.

Meyrowitz, Joshua. 1993. "Images of Media: Hidden Ferment—and Harmony—in the Field." *Journal of Communication* 43, no. 3:55–66.

Mihesuah, Devon A. 1996. *American Indians: Stereotypes and Realities.* Atlanta: Clarity.

———. 2003. *Indigenous American Women: Decolonization, Empowerment, Activism.* Lincoln: University of Nebraska Press.

Milch, David. 2004. *Deadwood.* Television series. Frazier Park, Calif.: HBO.

Mindich, David T. Z. 2000. *Just the Facts: How "Objectivity" Came to Define American Journalism.* New York: NYU Press.

Monmonier, Mark. 2006. *From Squaw Tit to Whorehouse Meadow: How Maps Name, Claim, and Inflame.* Chicago: University of Chicago Press.

Morgan, Hal. 1986. *Symbols of America.* New York: Viking Press.

Morris, Richard, and Mary Stuckey. 1998. "Destroying the Past to Save the Present: Pastoral Voice and Native Identity." In *Cultural Diversity and the U.S. Media,* edited by Yahya Kamalipour and Theresa Carilli, 137–148. Albany: SUNY Press.

Murphy, James E., and Donald Avery. 1983. "A Comparison of Alaskan Native and Non-native Newspaper Content." *Journalism Quarterly* 60:316–322.

Murphy, James E., and Sharon M. Murphy. 1981. *Let My People Know: American Indian Journalism, 1828–1978.* Norman: University of Oklahoma Press.

Murphy, Sharon M. 1979. "American Indians and the Media: Neglect and Stereotype." *Journalism History* 6, no. 2:39–43.

Nabokov, Peter. 1999. *Native American Testimony: A Chronicle of Indian–White Relations from Prophecy to the Present, 1492–2000.* New York: Viking.

Nagel, Joane. 2000. "Ethnicity and Sexuality." *Annual Review of Sociology* 26: 107–133.

National Collegiate Athletic Association. Minority Opportunities and Interests Committee. 2002. "Report on the Use of American Indian Mascots in Intercollegiate Athletics to the NCAA Executive Committee Subcommittee on Gender and Diversity Issues." October. Accessed July 18, 2011. http://www .ncaa.org/wps/wcm/connect/NCAA/Legislation%20and%20Governance/ Committees/Assoc-wide/Moic/2003/Mascot%20Report/mascotreport .htm.

National Collegiate Athletics Association (NCAA). "NCAA Executive Committee Issues Guidelines for Use of Native American Mascots at Championship Events." Press release, August 5, 2005. Accessed July 11, 2011. http://www .ncaa.org/wps/wcm/connect/NCAA/Media+and+Events/Press+Room/ News+Release+Archive/2005/Announcements/NCAA+Executive+Com mittee+Issues+Guidelines+for+Use+of+Native+American+Mascots+at+ Championship+Events.

National Conference for Community and Justice 2000. *The American Indian and the Media.* 2d ed. Edited by Mark Anthony Rolo (New York: National Conference for Community and Justice.

Native American Journalists Association (NAJA). "NAJA Calls upon News Media to Stop Using Mascots." 2002. Accessed December 8, 2004. http://www .naja.com/pr-stopmascot.html.

Neumann, Kurt. director. 1956. *Mohawk.* Motion Picture. Produced by Edward L. Alperson. Twentieth-Century Fox.

Newton, Julie-Ann. 2000. *The Burden of Visual Truth.* Newbury Park, Calif.: Sage.

Nye, Daniel. 2003. *America as Second Creation: Technology and Narratives of New Beginnings.* Cambridge: MIT Press.

100 Questions for 500 Nations. Various dates and sources. See National Conference for Community and Justice 2000, available online at http://www.sheri-whitefeather.com/theamericanindianandthemedia.pdf, accessed 8 August 2011. *See also* "100 Questions: Who Is a Native American?" as developed by Reginald Stuart and Linda Fullerton (with numerous credits), accessed 8 August 2011, http://www.leg.state.or.us/cis/100_question.pdf.

Oxford English Dictionary. 1989. "squaw, n.²" 2nd ed. Accessed August 1, 2008. http://o-dictionary.oed.com.janus.uoregon.edu/cgi/entry/50235256?single =1&query_type=word&queryword=squaw&first=1&max_to_show=10.

Papa, Michael, Arvind Singhal, and Wendy Papa. 1999. "Organizing for Social Change through Feminist Action: The Paradoxes and Contradictions of Communicative Empowerment." *Communication Theory* 10, no. 1:90–123.

Parins, James W. 2006. *Elias Cornelius Boudinot: A Life on the Cherokee Border.* Lincoln: University of Nebraska Press.

Parman, Donald L. 1994. "World War II: The Exodus." In *Indians and the American West in the Twentieth Century.* Bloomington: Indiana University Press.

Perdue, Theda. 1977. "Rising from the Ashes: The *Cherokee Phoenix* as an Ethno-histoical Source." *Ethnohistory* 24, no. 3:207–218.

Perry, Barbara. 2002. "From Ethnocide to Ethno Violence: Layers of Native American Victimization." *Contemporary Justice Review* 5, no. 3:231–247.

Pevar, Stephen L. 1992. *The Rights of Indians and Tribes: The Basic ACLU Guide to Indian and Tribal Rights.* Carbondale: Southern Illinois University Press.

Pewewardy, Cornel D. 1998. "Why Teachers Can't Afford to Ignore Indian Mascots." National Indian Education Association. Accessed September 19, 2002. http://earnestman.tripod.com/fr.education.htm.

———. 1999. "The Deculturalization of Indigenous Mascots in U.S. Sports Culture." *Educational Forum* 63:342.

Phillips, Ruth. 1998. *Trading Identities: The Souvenir in Native North American Art from the Northeast, 1700–1900.* Seattle: University of Washington Press.

Pinel, Elizabeth C. 1999. "Stigma Consciousness: the Psychological Legacy of Social Stereotypes." *Journal of Personality and Social Psychology* 76:114–128.

Prucha, Francis Paul. 1984. *The Great Father: The United States Government and the American Indians.* Lincoln: University of Nebraska Press.

Rahnema, Majid. 2010. "Participation." In *The Development Dictionary: A Guide to Knowledge As Power,* edited by Wolfgang Sachs, 116–131. New York: Zed Books.

Ramírez-Berg, Charles. 1990. *Latino Images in Film: Stereotypes, Subversion, Resistance.* Austin: University of Texas Press.

Riley, Sam G. 1976. "The *Cherokee Phoenix:* The Short Unhappy Life of the First American Indian Newspaper." *Journalism Quarterly* 53, no. 4:666–671.

Rosaldo, Renato. 1989. "Imperialist Nostalgia." In *Culture and Truth: The Remaking of Social Analysis,* 68–90. Boston: Beacon Press.

Rosenstein, Jay. 1997. *In Whose Honor? American Indian Mascots in Sports.* Documentary film. Produced, written, and edited by J. Rosenstein. New York: New Day Films.

Rosenstein, Jay. 2001. "*In Whose Honor?* Mascots and the Media." In *Team Spirits: The Native American Mascots Controversy,* edited by C. Richard King and Charles Frueling Springwood, 241–256. Lincoln: University of Nebraska Press.

Rozema, Vicki. 2003. *Voices from the Trail of Tears.* Winston-Salem, N.C.: John F. Blair.

Rutledge, Kathleen. 2003. "Respectfully, We'll Call That Team 'Washington.'" *Lincoln Journal Star,* January 26.Sanchez, John. 2003. "How American Public Schools Using Down-Linked News Media Shape American Indian Identity." *Howard Journal of Communications* 14, no. 1:39–48.

Sanchez, John. 2003. "How American Public Schools Using Down-Linked News Media Shape American Indian Identity." *Howard Journal of Communications* 14, no. 1:39–48.

Sanchez, John. 2009. "News Media Framing of American Indians: A Study of Ten Years of American Indian News Reports from the ABC, CBS, and NBC Broadcast Evening Network News Programs." Author's files.

Sanders, Thomas E., and Walter W. Peek. 1973. *Literature of the American Indian.* New York: Glencoe.

Sheffield, R. Scott. 2004. *Canada in "The Red Man's on the Warpath": The Image of the "Indian" and the Second World War.* Vancouver: University of British Columbia Press.

Schroeder, Jonathan E., and Janet L. Borgerson. 2005. "An Ethics of Representation for International Marketing Communication." *International Marketing Communication* 22, no. 5:578–600.

Schudson, Michael. 1978. *Discovering the News: A Social History of American Newspapers.* New York: Basic Books.

Secola, Keith. 1992. "NDN Kars" (1987). On *Circle.* Compact disc. Phoenix, Ariz.: AKINA.

Sentman, Mary Alice. 1983. "Black and White: Disparity in Coverage by *Life* Magazine from 1937 to 1972." *Journalism Quarterly* 60, no. 3:501–508.

Sheppard, Laverne. 1991. "Advice from the Inside." In *The American Indian and the Media,* edited by Tim Giago, Martha Crow, Tom Beaver, Pamela A. Kalar, and Paul O. Sand. N.p.: The National Conference of Christians and Jews, Minnesota-Dakotas Region.

Simoneau, Yves. 2007. *Bury My Heart at Wounded Knee.* Motion Picture. Calgary, Alta.: HBO Films.

Singer, Beverly. 2001. *Wiping the War Paint Off the Lens: Native American Film and Video.* Minneapolis: University of Minnesota Press.

Sloan, William David, and Julie Hedgepeth Williams. 1994. *The Early American Press, 1690–1783.* The History of American Journalism, 1. Westport, Conn.: Greenwood Press.

Smith, Andrea. 2001. "The Color of Violence against Women." *ColorLines* 3(4).

Smith, Andrew B. 2000. "Shooting Cowboys and Indians: Silent Western Films, American Culture, and the Birth of Hollywood." Ph.D. dissertation, University of California, Los Angeles.

Smits, David D. 2007. "The 'Squaw Drudge.'" In *Native Women's History in Eastern North America Before 1900: A Guide to Research and Writing,* edited by Rebecca Kugel and Lucy Eldersveld Murphy, 27–49. Lincoln: University of Nebraska Press.

Snyder, Mark. 1984. "When Belief Creates Reality." In *Advances in Experimental Social Psychology,* edited by Leonard Berkowitz 25:248–306. San Diego: Academic Press.

Spencer, Steven J., Claude M. Steele, and Diane M Quinn. 2002. "Stereotype Threat and Women's Math Performance." In *Readings in the Psychology of Gender: Exploring Our Differences and Commonalities,* edited by Anne E. Hunter and Carie Forden, 54–68. Needham Heights, Mass.: Allyn & Bacon.

Starr, Emmet. 1967. *Starr's History of the Cherokee Indians.* Edited by Jack Gregory and Rennard Strickland. Fayettesville, Ark.: Indian Heritage Association.

Staurowsky, Ellen J. 1999. "American Indian Imagery and the Miseducation of America." *Quest* 51, no. 4:382–392.

Stedman, Raymond William. 1982. *Shadows of the Indian: Stereotypes in American Culture.* Norman: University of Oklahoma Press.

Steele, Claude M. 1997. "A Threat in the Air: How Stereotypes Shape Intellectual Identity and Performance." *American Psychologist* 52, no. 6: 613–629.

———. 1998. "Stereotyping and Its Threat Are Real." *American Psychologist* 53, no.6:680–681.

———, and Joshua Aronson. 1995. "Stereotype Threat and the Intellectual Test Performance of African Americans." *Journal of Personality and Social Psychology* 69, no. 5:797–811.

Steele, Jeffrey. 1996. "Reduced to Images: American Indians in Nineteenth-Century Advertising." In *Dressing in Feathers: The Construction of the Indian in American Popular Culture,* edited by S. Elizabeth Bird, 45–64. New York: Westview.

Stole, Inger L. 2006. *Advertising on Trial: Consumer Activism and Corporate Public Relations in the 1930s.* Urbana: University of Illinois Press.

Strickland, Rennard. 1997. *Tonto's Revenge: Reflections on American Indian Culture and Policy.* Albuquerque: University of New Mexico Press.

———. 2005–2006. "Commentary: Sequoyah Statehood, the Oklahoma Centennial and Sovereignty Envy: A Narrative and a Public Proposal." *American Indian Law Review* 30, no. 2:365–371.

Strinati, Dominic. 1995. *An Introduction to Theories of Popular Culture.* London: Routledge.

Stubben, Jerry D., and Gary Sokolow. 2005. *Native Americans and Political Participation: A Reference Handbook.* Santa Barbara, Calif.: ABC-Clio.

Tafoya, Nadine. 2005. "Native American Women: Fostering Resiliency." In *Psychotherapy with Women: Exploring Diverse Contexts and Identities,* edited by Marsha Pravder Mirkin, Karen L. Suyemoto, and Barbara F. Okun, 297–312. New York: Guilford.

Tan, Alexis, Yuki Fujioka, and Nancy Lucht. 1997. "Native American Stereotypes, TV Portrayals and Personal Contact." *Journalism Quarterly* 74:265–284.

Taylor, Rhonda Harris. 2000. *"Indian in the Cupboard:* A Case Study in Perspective." *International Journal of Qualitative Studies in Education* 13, no. 4:371–384.

Tebbel, John, and Mary Ellen Zuckerman. 1991. *The Magazine in America: 1741–1990.* New York: Oxford University Press.

Tharp, Julie. 2000. "'Fine Ponies': Cars in American Indian Film and Literature." *American Indian Culture and Research Journal* 77–91.

Thornton, Russell. 1990. *American Indian Holocaust and Survival: A Population History since 1492.* Norman: University of Oklahoma Press.

Townsend, Kenneth William. 2000. *World War II and the American Indian.* Albuquerque: University of Mexico Press.

Trahant, Mark N. 1998. "The 1970s: New Leaders for Indian Country." In Hoxie and Iverson 1998, 235–252.

———. 2010. *The Last Great Battle of the Indian Wars: Henry M. Jackson, Forrest J. Gerard and the Campaign for the Self-determination of America's Indian Tribes.* Fort Hall, Ida,: Cedars Group.

United States Comission on Civil Rights. 2001. *Commission Statement on the Use of Native American Images and Nicknames as Sports Symbols.* Accessed June 27, 2011. http://www.usccr.gov/press/archives/2001/041601st.htm.

Utter, Jack. 1993. *American Indians: Answers to Today's Questions.* Lake Anne, Mich.: National Woodlands Publishing Co.

Van Dijk, Teun. 1993. *Elite Discourse and Racism.* Newbury Park, Calif.: Sage.

Vannoy Adams, Michael. 1985. "Deconstructive Philosophy and Imaginal Psychology: Comparative Perspectives on Jacques Derrida and James Hillman." *Journal of Literary Criticism* 2, no. 1:23–39.

Voloshinov, V. N. 1973. *Marxism and the Philosophy of Language.* Translated by L. Matejka and I. R. Titunik. Cambridge: Harvard University Press.

Wainwright, Loudon. 1986. *The Great American Magazine: An Inside History of "Life."* New York: Alfred A. Knopf.

Walker, Margaret U. 1997. *Moral Understandings: A Feminist Study in Ethics.* New York: Routledge.

Wallace, Anthony F. C. 1991. *The Long, Bitter Trail: Andrew Jackson and the Indians.* New York: Hill and Wang.

Washburn, Wilcomb E. 1973. *The American Indian and the United States: A Documentary History,* vol. 2. New York: Random House.

Watner, Carl, and Wendy McElroy. 2004. *National Identification Systems: Essays in Opposition.* Jefferson, N.C.: McFarland.

Watson, Elmo Scott. 1943. "The Last Indian War, 1890–91—A Study of Newspaper Jingoism." *Journalism Quarterly* 9:205–219.

Weber, Max. 1958. *The Protestant Work Ethic and the Spirit of Capitalism.* [Translated by Talcott Parsons.] New York: Scribner. 1958.

Weiser, Marjorie P. K. 1978. *Ethnic America.* New York: H. W. Wilson.

Welsch, Roger L. 1996. "Enter Laughing: But Beware the Es-ex Factor." *Natural History* 105 (July):64–65.

West, Dennis, and Joan M. West. 1998. "Sending Cinematic Smoke Signals: An Interview with Sherman Alexie." *Cineaste* 23, no. 4:28–32.

Weston, Mary Ann. 1996. *Native Americans in the News: Images of Indians in the Twentieth Century Press.* Westport, Conn.: Greenwood Press.

Wiessner, Siegfried. 1995. "American Treaties and Modern International Law." *St. Thomas Law Review* 7:567.

Wilcox, Dennis L., Phillip H. Ault, William K. Agee, and Glen T. Cameron. 2001 *Essentials of Public Relations.* New York: Addison-Wesley.

Wilkins, David E. 1997. *American Indian Sovereignty and the U.S. Supreme Court: The Masking of Justice.* Austin: University of Texas Press.

———, and K. Tsianina Lomawaima. 2002. *Uneven Ground: American Indian Sovereignty and Federal Law.* Norman: University of Oklahoma Press.

Williams, David R., Harold W. Neighbors, and James S. Jackson. 2003. "Racial/Ethnic Discrimination and Health: Findings from Community Studies." *American Journal of Public Health* 93, no. 2:200–208.

Williams, Mary Elizabeth. 1998. "Without Reservations." *Salon,* July 2. Accessed June 13, 2011. http://archive.salon.com/ent/movies/int/1998/07/02int.html.

Wilson, Clint C. II, and Felix Gutierrez. 1985. *Minorities and Media: Diversity and the End of Mass Communication.* Beverley Hills, Calif.: Sage.

———. 1995. *Race, Multiculturalism and the Media: From Mass to Class Communication.* Thousand Oaks, Calif.: Sage.

Winfield, B. H., and J. Hume. 2007. *The Continuous Past: Historical Referents in Nineteenth-Century American Journalism.* Journalism and Communication Monographs, vol. 9, no. 3 (Association for Education in Journalism and Mass Communication).

Winfrey, Oprah (Supervising Producer). 1992. "American Indians." Television broadcast. *The Oprah Winfrey Show: Racism in 1992.* Directed by P. Kimball, Executive Producer D. Di Maio. Chicago: Harpo Studios.

Wolverton, Brad. 2007. "After Years of Debate, U. of Illinois Drums Out Its Controversial Mascot." *Chronicle of Higher Education,* March 2, 00. Accessed July 13, 2011. http://chronicle.com/article/After-Years-of-Debate-U-of/21707/.

Yazzie, Robert. 1996. Hozho nahasdlii—We Are Now in Good Relations: Navajo Restorative Justice. *St. Thomas Law Review* 9:117–129.

Young, Stephen Dine. 2000. "Movies as Equipment for Living: A Developmental Analysis of the Importance of Film in Everyday Life." *Critical Studies in Media Communication* 17, no. 4:447–468.

Contributors

Meta G. Carstarphen, Ph.D., APR, is Graduate Director and Gaylord Family Professor for the Gaylord College of Journalism and Mass Communication at the University of Oklahoma. She served as Associate Dean for Academic Affairs from 2005 to 2007. Her research about Oklahoma's African American and Native American newspapers has been supported by a multiyear endowed professorship from the Gaylord Family Endowment. She teaches courses in public relations writing and campaigns, as well as in race, gender, and the media, research, and cultural studies within the media. Her course Race, Gender and the Media was chosen as one of the university's seven 2005–2006 Dream Courses. It was the first Dream Course awarded to the Gaylord College. She developed this interdisciplinary class for Gaylord College in 2002, as a vehicle for engaging students to probe discussions about contemporary media and socially constructed ethnic and gender portrayals. She has focused her academic research over topics of race, gender, rhetoric, and the media. Over the course of her academic career she has published twenty-eight refereed articles, book chapters, and conference proceedings, as well as feature articles, book reviews, poetry, and fiction. She has edited two books, *Sexual Rhetoric: Media Perspectives on Sexuality, Gender and Identity* (1999) and the collection in this volume. She co-authored *Writing PR: A Multimedia Approach* (2004) and *Race, Gender, Class, and the Media* (2011).

John Sanchez (Apache) was formerly with the American University in Washington, D.C., where he served as the Academic Director of the American Indian Leadership Program and taught American Indian Leadership and Politics. Under his leadership, that program was recognized by President Clinton's panel on race initiatives as one of the top five of its kind in the country. Sanchez also works in Washington, D.C., as a consultant to Indian Country in education, diversity, and mass communications initiatives. Now an associate professor at Penn State, he teaches in the College of Communications, where he specializes in news media ethics and serves as director of the American Indian Speaker Series and coordinator of Penn State's Traditional American Indian Powwow. His research interests lie primarily at the intersection of contemporary American Indian cultures and the American mass media. He publishes his research in American Indian journals, teacher education journals, and communication studies journals and is working on a book manuscript,

American Indian Identity in the 21st Century; The New Faces of an Ancient People.

Juan A. Avila Hernandez, Yoeme and Yoi (Yaqui and Mexican), is a journalist, historian, filmmaker, and multimedia producer. He is a former reporter for the Center for Investigative Reporting (San Francisco), where he worked as an Associate Producer on two Frontline/PBS documentaries. His work has appeared in the *National Catholic Reporter, Sacramento Magazine, SF Weekly, Indian Country Today, Tribal College Journal,* and *CNN,* among other publications and media outlets. He has presented his research on Yoeme history and the California Indian Education Association—the topic of his upcoming documentary—at numerous national and international conferences. He has taught courses for Native American Studies at the University of California–Davis and the Collegiate Seminar Program and History Department at St. Mary's College of California in the San Francisco Bay Area and is currently completing his dissertation on twentieth-century Yoeme History. He began his own media company, buttonboxmedia.com, in 2010.

Roy Boney is a full-blood citizen of the Cherokee Nation in Tahlequah, Oklahoma. He is an award-winning artist, filmmaker, and digital media specialist. He holds a B.F.A. in graphic design from Oklahoma State University and an M.A. in studio art from the University of Arkansas at Little Rock, where he was a fellow at the Sequoyah Research Center. He has been adjunct instructor of multimedia design at Northeastern State University and Cherokee language animation instructor for the American Indian Resource Center. He currently works in the Language Technology Program for Cherokee Nation Education Services Group.

Miranda J. Brady is an assistant professor in the School of Journalism and Communication at Carleton University in Ottawa, where she teaches courses on the intersections of communication and identity, race, discourse, and representation. Her research takes a critical/cultural approach and explores the construction of identity in the media and other highly mediated cultural institutions like museums. In particular, her focus is on race and ethnicity with an emphasis on Indigenous identity. She holds a Ph.D. in Mass Communication with a minor in Social Thought from Pennsylvania State University.

Ray Chavez was a city editor of his hometown newspaper, the *El Paso Herald-Post.* He previously worked as a reporter at the *Seattle Times* and the *Yakima Herald-Republic,* with other reporter/editor assignments at the *Albuquerque Tribune,* the *Miami Herald,* and the *Sioux Falls Argus Leader.* He is a two-time winner of teaching awards from the Poynter Institute for Media Studies and has taught at San José State University, the University of Texas at El Paso, the

University of Colorado, and the University of South Dakota, where he served as chairman of the journalism department. His teaching/research interests include writing, editing, ethics, history, the ethnic press, and multicultural communication.

andré douglas pond cummings, Professor of Law at the West Virginia University College of Law, teaches business organizations, securities regulation, civil procedure, sports law, and entertainment law. Prior to joining the faculty at West Virginia University, cummings worked at the Chicago-based law firm of Kirkland & Ellis LLP, focusing his practice on complex business transactions including mergers, acquisitions, divestitures, and securities offerings of publicly traded corporations. Simultaneously, he represented clients in the sports and entertainment industries, including athletes in the National Football League, record labels, and Hollywood screenwriters, novelists, and other authors. cummings has written extensively on issues regarding investor protection, racial justice, and affirmative action, and recently published a book, *Reversing Field: Examining Commercialization, Labor, Gender, and Race in 21st-Century Sports Law* (with Anne Marie Lofaso). cummings has been recognized as Professor of the Year on three occasions since 2005, including the University Distinguished Professor Award by the West Virginia University Foundation. He holds a J.D. from Howard University School of Law, where he graduated *cum laude* and with distinction.

Paul DeMain, of Ojibway, Mohawk, and Delaware descent and a citizen of the Oneida Nation of Wisconsin, is CEO of Indian Country Communications and editor of *News from Indian Country,* a position he has served since 1986. His professional experience includes writing business plans, publishing, editing, layout and design, audio and video production, investigative reporting, and management. He remains active in politics and traditional cultural activities and has served on several boards of directors, including that of the Native American Journalists Association (several terms and as president), of UNITY: Coalition of Journalists (1992–1994, 1998–1999), and of the Sequoyah Research Institute of the University of Arkansas at Little Rock (1996–present). He hosted WOJB's 88.9 FM *Morning Fire* program from 1996 through 2000.

Stacey J. T. Hust, Ph.D. (University of North Carolina at Chapel Hill, 2005), is assistant professor of communication at Washington State University. Her research explores whether the mass media can be used for health promotion through strategies such as entertainment education and media advocacy. Her research has also examined the media's effects on sexual and reproductive health, as well as gender identity construction. Her work has been published in a number of books and journals, such as *Mass Communication and Society, Journal of Health Communication, Health Communication, Journal of*

International Advertising, Women and Health Journal, and *Public Relations Review.*

Lynn Klyde-Silverstein is a former reporter and copy editor. She worked for four years as a sports and news copy editor at the *Connecticut Post* in Bridgeport. She also spent three years as a sports reporter for the *Herald-Sun* in Durham, N.C., where she covered professional softball and Division I college basketball and soccer, as well as high school and recreational sports. She is an assistant professor of journalism and mass communications at the University of Northern Colorado.

Patty Loew is an enrolled member of the Bad River Band of Lake Superior Ojibwe. She is also a professor in the Department of Life Science Communication at the University of Wisconsin–Madison. She is the author of two books: *Indian Nations of Wisconsin: Histories of Endurance and Renewal* (2001) and *Native People of Wisconsin* (2003), a social studies text for elementary school children. She has written dozens of scholarly and general-interest articles on Native topics and has produced several Native-themed documentaries, including *After the Storm* (2010), *Nation within a Nation* (1998), and *Spring of Discontent* (1990), which have appeared on commercial and public television stations throughout the United States. In 2007 her award-winning PBS documentary, *Way of the Warrior*, which examined the role and cultural meaning of Native American military service, aired nationally.

Jennifer Meness is Algonquian First Nation from Pikwàkanagán, Ontario, Canada. She holds a Master of Arts in Communication from Marquette University. She is a champion fancy shawl and jingle dress dancer in the powwow circuit and a traditional storyteller mentored in the art by the world-renowned Cherokee storyteller and author Gayle Ross. Meness tours professionally, sharing native culture with audiences around the world through performances, lectures, and workshops. Past venues include the Kennedy Center for the Arts and the Smithsonian Institution.

Debra Merskin, Ph.D. (Syracuse University), is associate professor and head of the Communication Studies sequence at the School of Journalism and Communication at the University of Oregon. Her research addresses issues of representational ethics in visual and verbal discourse in mass media texts. Her publications appear in journals such as the *Howard Journal of Communications, Sex Roles, American Behavioral Scientist,* and *Mass Communication and Society* and in books such as *Growing up Girls* (1999), *Commodity Racism, Mediated Women: Representations in Popular Culture* (1999), *Sexual Rhetoric: Media Perspectives on Sexuality, Gender, and Identity* (1999), and *Dressing in Feathers: The Construction of the Indian in American Popular Culture* (1996).

She is currently completing a book about the social, psychological, and cultural context for stereotyping in American mass media.

Selene G. Phillips (Wabigonikewikwe), Ph.D., Purdue University, is a member of the Lac du Flambeau Band of Lake Superior Ojibwe Nation and an assistant professor at the University of Louisville, where she teaches writing and media studies. Her doctorate is in American Studies with emphasis in Native American studies, communication law, and journalism. She researches Native American newspapers and images as well as Sacagawea and the Lewis and Clark expedition. Her articles, chapters, reviews, and poems have appeared in *Journal of Health Communication* (2011), *American Indian Culture and Research Journal* (2005, 2006, 2010), *Yukhika-latuhse?* (2007), *From Generation to Generation: Maintaining Cultural Identity Over Time* (2005), *Sociological Quarterly* (2000), *Papers of the Thirty-first Algonquian Conference* (2000), and *People to People: An Introduction to Communications* (1997). She is also a Chautauquan, performing first-person interpretations of Sacagawea and Mary Todd Lincoln. She has worked as a television and radio news anchor, reporter, and producer; a communications specialist, writer, and publicist for Purdue University; and a job developer/counselor for the American Indian Business Association. She served on the Indiana Governor's Native American Council and as president of the Native American Press Archives advisory board.

Victoria Sanchez is an Assistant Vice Provost for Educational Equity at Penn State, where she works with A Framework to Foster Diversity (the university's diversity strategic plan) and with Penn State's commissions for diversity and equity. She holds a Ph.D. from The Ohio State University, specializing in American Studies and American folklife, with specific emphasis on contemporary American Indian issues, intersections of identity, tradition, and popular culture, and American Indian literature. She has held teaching appointments at Penn State and several other universities and colleges, emphasizing issues of diversity and equity in courses such as American Studies, American Indian literatures, and American authors. Her publications have appeared in journals such as *Communication Studies, Western Journal of Communication,* and *Southern Folklore.*

Ruth Seymour, Ph.D., is an assistant professor of journalism at Oakland University in Rochester, Michigan. Since the 1990s she has taught news reporting, editing, professional grammar, feature writing, intergroup journalism, and intercultural communication. She previously reported for the *Detroit Free Press* (1978–1986) and the *Detroit News,* where her writing about an array of racial and cultural communities garnered journalistic and humanitarian awards. Her published research has focused on linguistic text analysis, cultural authenticity in mass media, and methods of experiential instruction. With the Poynter Institute for Media Studies in 2000–2001 she directed an off-site fellowship for journalists and community leaders aimed at improving multicultural coverage in metro Detroit. She has also co-led an annual workshop for U.S. journalism professors at Poynter called Diversity across the Curriculum. Seymour's most recent research documents discriminatory patterns of syntax and power attribution in elite U.S. newspaper coverage of racial minorities.

Mark Trahant is an independent journalist. He writes a weekly column and posts often on Twitter (including daily news poems). He was recently a Kaiser Media Fellow and is the former editor of the editorial page for the *Seattle Post-Intelligencer.* He is a member of Idaho's Shoshone-Bannock Tribe and a former president of the Native American Journalists Association. He is the author of *The Last Great Battle of the Indian Wars* (2010), about Henry Jackson, Forrest Gerard, and the campaign for American Indian self-determination. He lives in Fort Hall, Idaho.

Index

References to illustrations appear in italics.

Ackerman, Lillian, 138
Adams, John Quincy, 180
Adolescents and children, 138–39, 160, 204n47
Advertising: and African Americans, 154; in *American*, 38, 39; American Indian Mental Health Association of Minnesota on, 162; and American Indians, 38–39, 40–51, 97, 153–58, 161–62, 163–65; by Argo Corn Starch, *155*, 156; and "bad Indians," 153, 154; by Bosco, 49; by Cherokee Clothing, 50; by Chief Wenatchee Apples, 157; and civilizable savage, 153, 154; of Covarrubias, 44; by Crazy Horse Malt Liquor, *155*, 157, 163–64, 201n9; defined, 39; by Diamond Lawnmowers, 155–56; by Dole Pineapple, 44–45; and ethnostress, 154; Gray on, 158; Green on, 153; by Greyhound, 48; by Haig and Haig, 48; Harjo on, 158; Hawaiians in, 43, 44; by Heinrich, 46–48; Ingram in, 49–50; by Jeep Cherokees, 50; by Jeris, 49; by Kentucky Club, 49; by Land O' Lakes, 50, 156; in *Life*, 38–39, 40–51; by Lifebuoy, 49; male archetypes in, *155*, 156; in mass media, 38; Merskin on, 153; and minorities, 154–55; by Mohawk Carpets, 50, 156–57; by National Life Insurance Company, 46–48; for New Mexico, 43, 48; by Nicholson File Company, 49; and

"noble savages," 44–45, 46, 47, 50, 153, 154; and the "other," 155, 156; by Pacquins, 49; Pewewardy on, 153; and "playing Indian," 40–43, 48; and Pontiac, 42–43, 156; by Riggs, 44–45; by Ronson, 43; by Southern Pacific, 46, 47; "squaw" in, 49, 50; Staurowsky on, 153; Steele on, 153, 155–56; and stereotypes, 153, 154, 155, 156, 157–58, 161–62, 163–65, 187, 189, 201n9; and stereotype threat, 154; and tourism, 48, 50; by Vermont Maid Syrup, 46; by Wildroot, 49; by Winnebago, 156; and World War II, 39
African Americans, 52n14, 154, 160, 230. *See also* Minorities
AIPA, 213–14, 215, 216, 219
Alaska, 38
Albanians, 92n8
Albany, N.Y., 12, 17n5
Alcoa, 36
Alcohol abuse, 102, 222
Alexie, Sherman: background of, 99; on humor, 99; on Lee, 205n50; and *Smoke Signals*, 94, 95, 97, 99, 101, 105, 106, 192–93
Algonquians, 132. *See also* American Indians
Allen, J., 141
Allport, Gordon, 158–59, 164–65
American (magazine), 38, 39
American Ethnology, Bureau of, 32n32
American Indian and the Media, The (Kraus), 219
American Indian Journalism Career Conference and Fair, 229, 230

CPSIA information can be obtained at www.ICGtesting.com
Printed in the USA
LVOW102004270612

287680LV00002BB/1/P